FORMUI

UNSEEN A

FORMULA ONE

UNSEEN ARCHIVES

Tim Hill

Photographs by the
Daily Mail

p

This is a Parragon Book
This edition published in 2003

Parragon
Queen Street House
4 Queen Street
Bath, BA1 1HE, UK

Produced by Atlantic Publishing
Designed by John Dunne
Origination by Croxsons PrePress

A catalogue record for this book is available from the British Library.
ISBN 1 40540 295 4

Printed inChina

Contents

Introduction

Spectacular sporting theatre

Motor racing was born along with the internal combustion engine. In its infancy there were the Gordon Bennett races and the Indianapolis 500; its formative years spawned Le Mans and the Mille Miglia; but the sport came of age with the inception of the Formula One World Drivers' Championship in 1950.

The ingredients for an utterly compelling spectacle were already there: speed, excitement, dramatic confrontation; gladiatorial combat in which the victors took the laurels and the glory, while the losers all too often paid the ultimate price. What was missing was a pinnacle of achievement, a blue riband event. That final piece of the jigsaw was slotted into place at Silverstone, on 13 May, 1950.

Since that inaugural year, the world championship has grown exponentially. Today's F1 circus criss-crosses the globe; sponsorship and commercialism have made it a huge business enterprise; the stars of the modern era are multi-millionaires, feted like film stars.

But the essential appeal remains the same: man and machine operating on the limit in a competitive cauldron, with the imperfections of both making for spectacular sporting theatre. It applies as much to the present battle between Schumacher and Hakkinen as it did to the great rivalry between Fangio and Moss half a century ago.

Just 27 men have won the coveted title in its 51-year history. Who was the greatest? Fangio, the five-time champion whose four-wheel drifts verged on the balletic? Schumacher, the wunderkind who fulfilled all his early potential and sets the standard today? In between there has been Clark, Lauda and Prost. And, of course, the mercurial Ayrton Senna. Along with the giants that each era has produced, there have been many stars whose flame flickered all too briefly, such as Rindt and Villeneuve.

Using a wealth of archive photographs, many of which have never been published before, this book tells the story behind those 51 glorious successes. It also chronicles the many agonies, disappointments and tragedies that triumph has left in its wake.

Acknowledgements

The photographs from this book are from the archives of the Daily Mail. The pleasure this book will give to the many fans of Formula One is a tribute to the dedication of the staff, past and present, in the Picture Library at Associated Newspapers.

Particular thanks to Steve Torrington, Dave Sheppard, Brian Jackson, Alan Pinnock, Paul Rossiter and all the staff including:

John Bater	Derek Drew	Rachel Swanston	Philip Lambourne
David Stanley	Steve Murray	David Lavington	Chris Nelthorpe
Tom McElroy	Raymond Archer	Robert Sanders	Denise Hoy
Leslie Adler	Terry Aylward	Andrew Eva	Bob Dignum
Tony Fordham	Oscar Courtney	Bill Beasley	Mark Ellins
Steve Cooper	Andrew Young	Charles Whitbread	Katie Lee

Thanks also to

Christine Hoy, John Dunne, Cliff Salter, Richard Betts, Peter Wright, Trevor Bunting Simon Taylor and Frances Hill.

FORMULA ONE

UNSEEN ARCHIVES

1950
The first world championship

In February 1950 the Fédération Internationale de l'Automobile made the historic decision to link together six established Grands Prix in a single competition; the Formula One World Championship was born.

Alfa Romeo had been out of racing for a year, but news of a championship to contest enthused the famous marque to make a swift return to the sport. It proved to be a very sound decision.

Fagioli, Farina and Fangio

The inaugural year was dominated by Alfa's three star drivers, the legendary "three Fs": Luigi Fagioli, Giuseppe Farina and Juan Manuel Fangio. Fagioli was already a veteran of 53, and was recruited to the team when Consalvo Sanesi was injured in the Mille Miglia. Farina, aged 43, had been steeped in motor cars and motor sport since childhood; he was related to the famous Italian coachbuilder Pinin Farina, a name which survives to the present day and still evokes style and quality. Fangio, at 38, was the "baby" of the team. He was a product of Argentina's government-sponsored academy, an institution whose aim was to nurture the most talented drivers.

Of the other contenders, Alberto Ascari was the most prominent. He was just 31, and the son of Antonio Ascari, one of the most famous racing drivers of the 1920s. Ironically, Ascari senior had enjoyed some of his greatest successes after joining Alfa Romeo in 1920. Now, thirty years later, Ascari junior was taking on a formidable three-pronged Alfa strike force in his Ferrari. The Maranello team was desperately trying to get its new car up and running, a 4500cc V-12 that it was hoped would be a match for the Alfas. But that came too late for the championship season of 1950. Ascari and Ferrari would have their day, but the inaugural season belonged to Alfa.

Seven-race championship

It was technically a seven-race championship: six European rounds, plus the Indianapolis 500. In practice, however, the 500 tended to stand apart in the calendar. It continued to yield championship points until 1960, but in that time only one Formula One driver competed in the American classic.

The inaugural race was at Silverstone, on 13 May. The king and queen, plus a 150,000-strong crowd, witnessed a walk-over for Alfa. Farina won, with Fagioli in second place.

Fangio had retired eight laps from the end, but Alfa still took third, courtesy of their fourth-string works driver Reg Parnell.

Monte Carlo pile-up

At Monte Carlo a week later there was a multiple pile-up on the first lap. Farina, lying second to Fangio, spun and hit a wall, then bounced back onto the road. He was hit first by Jose Froilan Gonzalez's Maserati, and the blocked road put another eight cars out of the race. Fangio was unaware of the incident until he came round again. Some quick thinking and a deft touch saw him weave through the carnage, and he went on to win, a lap clear of Ascari.

Fangio suffered another retirement in the next race, the Swiss Grand Prix. Farina won, with Fagioli again coming second. All three Ferraris blew up, and Louis Rosier's Talbot came in third. In the Belgian Grand Prix, at Spa, it was Fangio who headed Fagioli home, with Rosier again in third. Transmission problems for Farina meant that he had to settle for 4th place. With two rounds to go, the table now stood thus: Farina 22 points, Fagioli 18, Fangio 17.

Fangio scored an easy win in the French Grand Prix, with Fagioli yet again in second. This time it was Farina who was unlucky: fuel pump problems meant that he could only trail in 7th, out of the points. Both Fangio, with 26 points, and Fagioli, on 24, had thus overhauled Farina as the circus headed for its final stop of the year: Monza.

For their "home" Grand Prix, Alfa had fielded two more cars, driven by Piero Taruffi and Consalvo Sanesi. When Fangio's gearbox failed on lap 24, he took over Taruffi's mount, but that car then dropped a valve. His chance of the title was gone. Ascari, now driving the full 4500cc Ferrari, was lying second, in the early part of the race, between Farina and Fangio. He was playing a waiting game, for he knew that the Alfas needed two refuelling stops, the Ferrari only one. He did take the lead, but then his car expired in a cloud of smoke. Like Fangio, he switched horses, taking over the Ferrari of Dorino Serafini. He clawed his way back to second, ahead of Fagioli, but at the end of the 313-mile race he was still a minute behind Giuseppe Farina. Farina's win put him on 30 points, three ahead of Fangio. The title was his.

Farina's championship

There were encouraging signs for Ferrari as the inaugural championship reached its climax, but it was clearly Alfa Romeo's year. Alfa had won all six European races, and its "big three" occupied the top places in the Drivers' Championship. Fagioli would not improve on his third position. Fangio would better his runner-up spot a number of times as the decade unfolded. But it was Giuseppe Farina who secured his place in the history books by becoming the sport's first World Champion.

Farina is first world champion

Left: The doctor and the graduate. Farina had a doctorate in political economy from Turin University; Fangio was the foremost graduate of Argentina's famous state-sponsored driving academy.

Below: Silverstone, 11 May, 1950. The Alfa Romeo team gears up for the inaugural world championship race.

Previous page: Team-mates and rivals. Farina (standing) and Fangio, pictured during a practice at Silverstone in August. At this point both Alfa Romeo stars had a chance of taking the world crown. With only the Monza Grand Prix to go Fangio had 26 points, Farina 22.

Alfa Romeo reign supreme

Right: Farina takes the chequered flag in the British Grand Prix, the first of the three wins that brought him the 1950 championship.
Below: Silverstone in 1950 was a rudimentary but very fast circuit. The former airfield track staged the British Grand Prix for the first six years of the championship.
Opposite: Alfa Romeo mechanics get to work on the legendary 158 model. This car, together with its successor the 159, reigned supreme between June 1946 and July 1951.

Farina drives like a 'madman'

Opposite below: Farina adds the International Trophy Race at Silverstone to his list of successes in 1950. Fangio said he learned a lot about Grand Prix driving from the Italian, but also criticised him for driving "like a madman".

Opposite top: First faltering steps for BRM. Mechanics struggled to overcome teething problems on the new V-16 car in time for the International Trophy Race. The car, driven by Raymond Sommer, limped out of the action early on, with the partisan crowd voicing its disapproval. It would be nine long years before BRM posted its first Grand Prix success.

Above: An estimated crowd of 150,000 packed into Silverstone for the British and European Grand Prix. King George VI, the Queen and Princess Margaret were present, the first time that members of the royal family had attended a major motor racing event.

1951
The Ferrari challenge

Alfa Romeo were not to have things all their own way in the 1951 championship. The challenge from the new, unsupercharged Ferraris made for a nailbiting series which went to the wire. Alberto Ascari had accumulated just 12 points in the inaugural year, finishing a distant fourth. However, in the last round at Monza there had been signs that the new 4.5-litre unsupercharged Ferrari would pose a threat to Alfa's dominance.

Fangio sets the pace

In the opening round, in Switzerland, Fangio scored a fine victory. Ascari was hampered by a badly burnt arm, an injury sustained in a Formula Two race, and finished 6th. Two places further back was an up-and-coming Englishman driving an HWM - Stirling Moss.

Reigning champion Giuseppe Farina took the honours in Belgium. Fangio, his team-mate, suffered a jammed wheel during a routine pit stop. It took nearly 15 minutes to fix, and the Argentinian finished 9th, although he did pick up a consolation point for setting the fastest lap. The Ferraris of Ascari and Villoresi filled the minor placings but well adrift of Farina, whose winning margin was 3 minutes.

The title race really began to hot up in the next round, run on the fast Rheims circuit. Ascari was chasing Fangio hard, when his gearbox failed. Ferrari's new boy, Jose Froilan Gonzalez, was called into the pits, and Ascari, the senior driver, returned to the fray in his car. Fangio, too, needed to switch horses, taking over Fagioli's Alfa when his own car experienced magneto trouble early in the race. Fangio crossed the line first, a minute ahead of Ascari, with Villoresi again third.

Italian rivals

The Ferraris were getting increasingly closer to defeating their great Italian rival, and they finally achieved it in the next race. It wasn't Ascari who ended Alfa's supremacy, though. He retired with gearbox trouble. When Gonzalez came in for a routine stop, Ascari recognised that his team-mate was in excellent form and this time he didn't pull rank. It proved to be sound judgement. Knowing that the Alfas required two refuelling stops to the Ferraris' one, Fangio had tried to establish a healthy lead. But he couldn't shake Gonzalez off, and when the latter swept into the lead, even Fangio's best efforts were to no avail. The "Pampas Bull" came home nearly a minute ahead of his fellow-countryman. Meanwhile, there was a degree of British success down the field, as the BRMs of Reg Parnell and Peter Walker both completed the 90-lap race, finishing 5th and 7th respectively.

Only a second place finish from Fangio prevented Ferrari from taking a clean sweep of the top six finishers at the German Grand Prix. The Alfa Romeo camp had been in turmoil during practice, rushing to make last-minute repairs and adjustments to the cars. They went into the race with no great hopes, having taken note of the times the Ferraris had set. The wily Fangio recognised his car's comparative shortcomings and drove at a fast, regular pace. He kept the car within its limits and, more importantly, he kept in contention with the leaders. He actually led for a time, but fell back to second after his extra stop for fuel. He maintained that position to the end. Ascari had won, but Fangio had got the better of the other Ferraris, Gonzalez, Villoresi and Taruffi, who finished in that order after him. Second place, together with the fastest lap, meant that Fangio left Germany with seven points to add to his championship tally.

Fangio by six points

Alfa Romeo introduced a new, faster version of the Alfetta at Monza, but Fangio was forced out with mechanical trouble. It was another good day for Ferrari, with Ascari and Gonzalez finishing first and second.

The final round was at Barcelona. Going into the race Fangio held a 3-point advantage over Ascari: 28 - 25. It proved to be a miserable day for the Italian. The Ferraris were running with enough fuel to carry the entire distance, but had changed to smaller-diameter rear wheels than usual. The rough Pedralbes circuit ripped into the Ferraris' tyres, which needed changing every few laps. Ascari's chance was gone, while Fangio won the race to give him the championship by 6 points. It was the beginning of a long period in which "El Chueco" - "the bandylegged one" - would dominate the sport.

At the end of the season Alfa Romeo knew that the ageing 158 model, which dated back to 1938, needed to be replaced if a serious challenge to Ferrari was to be mounted. Government money was needed, but was not forthcoming. Alfa had no alternative but to withdraw from Grand Prix racing. This was potentially a disastrous decision for the sport, as it left the way clear for total Ferrari dominance and an uncompetitive championship. The FIA responded by announcing that the 1952 Grand Prix series would be held to 2-litre, Formula Two rules.

BRM struggle

Above: Ferrari and Alfa Romeo share the first four places in the British Grand Prix. BRM continues to struggle against the crack Italian outfits, Reg Parnell and Peter Walker finishing 5th and 7th respectively. Parnell had been the 4th Alfa Romeo works driver behind the "3 Fs" in 1950, and had just joined BRM.

Left: Goggles up for Farina (standing) and Fangio as they take a breather from doing battle on the track. Farina again spearheaded the Alfa Romeo team in 1951, but his career went into steady decline after winning the inaugural championship.

Previous page: Stirling Moss and Josephine Lowry-Corry at a glittering social event in 1951. Moss was the rising star of British motor racing, but his big breakthrough was still three years away.

Farina, Fagioli and Fangio...

Right: Giuseppe Farina won just one championship race in 1951. His driving style involved him in many accidents during his career. He survived them all, only to be killed in a road accident while driving to the French Grand Prix in 1966.

Below: Farina, the team leader of Alfa Romeo's legendary "3 Fs". The others were the veteran 52-year-old Luigi Fagioli and Juan Manuel Fangio, the "baby" of the team at 39!

Opposite: A hirsute young Stirling Moss poses behind the wheel of his HWM. His early progress was hampered by his insistence on driving for uncompetitive British teams.

1952
Irresistible Ascari

Ferrari remained unfazed by the ruling body's decision to stage the 1952 championship under Formula Two rules. The 2-litre category had the desired effect in that it attracted a lot of entries, but it failed to halt a Ferrari landslide. The combination of the new car, the 4-cylinder Tipo 500, and the driving skills of Alberto Ascari proved irresistible. Ascari won six times, while his team-mate Piero Taruffi won the remaining European event to give the Scuderia a clean sweep.

Global appeal

The 8th round of the championship was the Indianapolis 500. This year it clashed with the opening European event, the Swiss Grand Prix. Ferrari and Ascari chose to compete in the United States, but it wasn't a happy experience. Ascari was running 12th when he was forced to retire. The 500 had been included in the World Championship to give it more global appeal, and to attract the interest of American motor sport fans. It would remain a championship event until 1960, but Ascari's failed attempt in 1952 was the only time that a driver competing in the European series tried his hand on the famous banked circuit.

In Ascari's absence, Taruffi scored a comfortable win in Berne. He came home almost three minutes ahead of his nearest rival, Rudi Fischer, who was driving a privately-entered Ferrari. The minor placings show how the number of marques competing proliferated this year. Jean Behra brought his Gordini home in third; 4th and 5th places went to Britons Ken Wharton and Alec Brown, driving a Frazer-Nash and Cooper-Bristol respectively. Connaught, HWM and ERA were other names that featured during the season. Stirling Moss had pinned his hopes on a new Bristol-engined ERA. When it finally made its debut, at Spa, he crashed out on the first lap. It would not be a year in which Moss would enhance his reputation as the rising star of British motor racing.

With the withdrawal of Alfa Romeo, Fangio had joined Officine Maserati. His former team-mate Giuseppe Farina had gone to Ferrari, but Fangio wanted to be the undisputed number one in any team he drove for. That was on offer at Maserati, but wouldn't have been the case at Ferrari. There was a new 6-cylinder car in the pipeline for Fangio, too, but as events transpired the reigning champion was sidelined for the entire season.

Fangio out for the season

Fangio had been competing in Ireland, when he received word from Maserati that they wanted him to put the new car through its paces in a non-championship race at Monza. After a frustrating journey hampered by bad connections, Fangio took to the wheel, exhausted. Unsurprisingly, he made a mistake at a corner, and was flung out of the car, his neck broken. He would not reappear until 1953.

In the six remaining European races Ascari proved unstoppable. He led Farina home in both Belgium and France. In Belgium, at least, British fans had a new name to cheer. Mike Hawthorn, driving a Cooper-Bristol, received many plaudits for the way he gave the much more powerful Ferraris a run for their money. He was lying third when his petrol tank sprang a leak, and finished a highly creditable 4th.

At Silverstone Ascari led from start to finish. Taruffi followed him home this time, but a full lap adrift. Hawthorn finished an excellent 3rd, proving that his performance in Belgium had been no fluke. The dapper, bow-tied Hawthorn, his appearance earning him the soubriquet "Le Papillon", was fast becoming the golden boy of British sport.

Ferrari clean sweep

Ferrari occupied the first four places at the German Grand Prix, Farina, Fischer and Taruffi filling the supporting roles behind the usual star performer. It was much the same story in the sand dunes of Zandvoort, a new championship venue. Farina and Villoresi took the minor placings in yet another Ferrari clean sweep.

It was only in the final race at Monza when Ascari was provided with some stern opposition, and that was after the world title was already in the bag. Jose Froilan Gonzalez finally had the new Maserati in which to take the fight to Ascari, and he did so in blistering style. The Argentinian roared into an early lead, but an overlong pit stop for refuelling cost him dear. Ascari needed no second invitation, and came through for his 6th victory in a row. Gonzalez was almost a minute behind in second, but at least he had the twin consolations of beating the Ferraris of Villoresi and Farina, and also of sharing the fastest lap with the new world champion.

Having seen a glimpse of what the new Maserati was capable of, everyone now keenly awaited the new season, when a fully-fit Fangio would be back to challenge Ferrari's supremacy. But 1952 was Ascari's moment of glory. His 36-point maximum haul was something that not even Fangio would quite match in any of his five title successes.

Hawthorn challenges Ferraris

Above: The Hawthorns at work at the family business in Farnham. Leslie Hawthorn bought the garage when Mike was two years old. Mike shows that he is handy under the bonnet, having trained as an engineer.

The Ferraris were invincible in 1952, but Hawthorn enjoyed considerable success in his Cooper, ending the season joint-fourth in the championship.

Left: Following Alfa Romeo's withdrawal from racing, Farina moved to Ferrari in 1952, where he finished runner-up to Ascari.

Previous page: Alberto Ascari.

Three steps to success...

Right: Following in father's wheeltracks. Leslie
Hawthorn comments: "You need three things
for success in motor sport: a good car,
meticulous preparation and a good driver. We
are lucky in having all three". 23-year-old
Mike Hawthorn became an overnight
sensation after winning two races at the Easter
Goodwood meeting. The fact that Fangio,
driving a similar car, trailed home behind him
in sixth place in one of the races prompts
much speculation that Britain has finally
unearthed a talent capable of challenging the
world's best.

Below: Moss had high hopes for 1952 in the
new ERA, but the car was dogged by
problems.

Opposite: Stirling Moss helps out with the
maintenance of his Bristol-engined ERA prior
to the British Grand Prix at Silverstone.

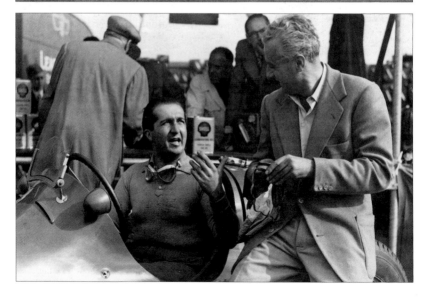

Moss continues his 'drive for British'

Opposite top: Mike Hawthorn in action at Goodwood.
Opposite below: Alberto Ascari chats before the start of a race.
Above: Fangio gives his BRM the thumbs-up after testing in April.
Left: Stirling Moss at the wheel of his ERA in 1952. His determination to "drive British" meant that Hawthorn supplanted him as the young star of British motor racing.

1953
Ferrari versus Maserati

The 1953 championship always looked likely to be a battle royal between Ferrari and Maserati, and so it proved, the two teams sharing the top six places in the title race that year. Fangio had made a full recovery by the time the season got under way. He spearheaded the Maserati team, supported by fellow-countrymen Jose Froilan Gonzalez, and the man he regarded as his protégé, Onofre Marimon. Meanwhile, the mighty Ferrari outfit had strengthened its line-up in the close season. Ascari, Farina and Villoresi were joined by Mike Hawthorn, who had impressed Enzo Ferrari so much the previous year. Hawthorn had been initially apprehensive about signing for a foreign team and committing himself to full-time professional status. But eventually he made the decision to join the Scuderia, and took his place as the circus moved to Buenos Aires for Argentina's first championship race.

As in the previous year, the series was run as a Formula Two competition. The Argentine Grand Prix made it a nine-event championship – effectively eight, if the Indianapolis 500 was discounted – with the best four finishes counting.

Ascari and Fangio battle it out

Ascari and Fangio set the tone for the season by battling it out in the opening round. There was a new Maserati in the pipeline, but it wasn't quite ready, and Fangio started the race in the 1952 model. He was chasing Ascari hard when his engine blew up. It left the reigning champion with an easy win, a lap clear of team-mate Villoresi. Hawthorn marked his debut with a solid 4th, and it was only the Maserati of Marimon in third place which prevented a clean sweep for the Maranello cars.

Tragedy

The race was marred by tragedy, after a boy ran onto the track in front of Farina's car. The former champion swerved in an attempt to avoid an accident, but in doing so careered into the spectators. Ten people lost their lives in the tragic incident.

Ascari also ran out a comfortable winner in the Dutch Grand Prix, while Fangio again failed to finish, this time because of an axle problem. Farina made it another one-two for Ferrari, but the highlight of the race was Gonzalez's third place. When his Maserati's rear axle broke, he took over team-mate Felice Bonetto's car and chased the Ferraris hard for a shared 3rd place.

For a time it looked as if Spa would see the breaking of the Ferrari stranglehold. Both

Gonzalez and Fangio, now in their new Maseratis, stormed away in the early part of the race. But both then hit trouble. Gonzalez's race ended when his accelerator pedal broke. Fangio's engine expired, but he carried on the race in the car of one of the junior Maserati drivers. He was still out of luck, though, for he skidded on a patch of oil and crashed out of the race. He was lucky to escape with only minor injuries. Ascari, who had been well off the pace in the early part of the race, came through for yet another success – his 9th Grand Prix win in a row.

Superb Hawthorn

Ascari found himself outpaced yet again at Rheims, and this time no ill fortune befell those ahead of him. The race turned into an epic duel between Fangio and Hawthorn, the pair racing wheel to wheel. Hawthorn squeaked home by a car's length after a clever late-braking manoeuvre on the very last corner.

Ascari had managed only 4th in France, but at Silverstone normal service was resumed. It was clear now that on fast circuits the extra power of the Maseratis came into its own; on slower tracks, such as Silverstone, the Ferraris' superior handling was the critical factor. Ascari led the race the whole way, while Fangio had to content himself with second.

Farina's last victory

Ascari was out of the points at the German Grand Prix, yet drove one of the finest races of his career. He got off to a blistering start, then lost a wheel and had to limp into the pits on three wheels and a brake drum. He took over Villoresi's car and gave furious chase, setting a Formula Two record for the Nürburgring circuit as he did so. With third-placed Hawthorn in his sights, Ascari's car expired in a pall of blue smoke. It was Farina who kept up Ferrari's 100% record in the championship, showing the kind of form that had brought him the world crown three years earlier. It was to be the last victory of his career.

Ascari clinched his second championship in the Swiss Grand Prix at Bremgarten. He and Fangio were yet again vying for the lead, when both were forced into the pits. Fangio's car was beyond help and he took over Bonetto's Maserati. He drove the car so hard in an effort to get back into contention that it expired in a cloud of dense smoke. Ascari, meanwhile, had needed only a change of plugs and rejoined the race in 4th place. With the mark of a true champion he battled his way back to the front to take the chequered flag from team-mates Farina and Hawthorn.

Champion Ascari in a spin

With the title race already settled, Fangio and Maserati finally got it right in the final race at Monza. The Argentinian ace battled for the lead with Ascari and Farina, the lead changing hands many times. Going into the last lap it was still anybody's race. Then, after 313 miles of close slipstreaming, Ascari finally made a rare mistake, spinning his Ferrari at the very last corner. Farina mounted the grass to avoid a collision, and Fangio coolly avoided trouble to win his only race of the season. He finished runner-up in the final table, on 28 points. But the crown went for the second year running to Alberto Ascari. His 34.5-point haul may not have quite matched his maximum of 1952, but it confirmed the blue-helmeted maestro's domination of the sport for the second year running.

Top: Alberto Ascari takes the plaudits after the inaugural French Grand Prix at Pau, where he beat Hawthorn (right) and Harry Schell. Hawthorn took his revenge in the championship race at Rheims, where he won and Ascari finished fourth.
Above: The master returns. After a year out through injury, Fangio was back for the 1953 season, still with Maserati.
Previous page: Alberto Ascari.

Unbeatable Alberto Ascari

Opposite top: Ascari had just celebrated his 35th birthday when he won at Silverstone. Fans make the most of the opportunity to get a close look at the champion and his Ferrari 500. Ascari followed up his six Grand Prix wins in 1952 with five more in 1953. It was an extra-ordinary 2-year period of domination for Ascari and Ferrari.

Opposite below: Ascari takes the flag at Silverstone, having covered the 263-mile distance at an average speed of 92.97mph.

Above: The start of the British Grand Prix which Ascari won comfortably on his way to his second world crown.

Ferrari's crack team

Right: 26 September, 1953. Mike Hawthorn wins the Goodwood Trophy in a Ferrari "Thin Wall" Special to round off a fine season.
Below: Ascari on his way to victory at Silverstone. He beat Fangio into second place that day, and in the championship overall.
Opposite top: Ferrari's crack team for 1953. Hawthorn, Ascari and Farina took three of the top four places in the championship that year.
Opposite below: Keen spectators above the pit lane try to catch sight of their favourite cars and drivers.

1954
Fangio's Crown

Even before the dust had settled on the 1953 season, it was widely known that Mercedes-Benz would be returning to the Grand Prix arena the following year. Alfred Neubauer, the Stuttgart team's famous manager during the pre-war era, was still in charge. And when the illustrious marque signed none other than Fangio to lead their 1954 campaign, it undoubtedly posed a serious threat to the supremacy the Italians had enjoyed in the competition's four-year history.

Reigning champion Alberto Ascari certainly took the threat seriously, for he decided that he needed a stronger team behind him in order to compete. This was in spite of the fact that he had spent five successful years with the mighty Ferrari stable. The reason was simple: Lancia was also developing a new car, designed by Vittorio Jano. Jano had been the man behind the classic Alfa Romeos of the 1930s, and Ascari put his faith in him to produce a car that would keep the reigning champion at the top of the tree.

Fangio's home soil victory

1954 also saw the end of the Formula Two era and the introduction of a 2.5-litre limit on engine size. Neither the Mercedes nor the Lancia was ready for the season opener, which was once again in Argentina. It was a race which was fascinating for the way in which fortunes fluctuated with the weather conditions. It was dry when the race started, and the Ferraris of Farina and Gonzalez were dominant. But when the rain began to fall, Fangio took control and went on to win. After the race, the Ferrari team which took 2nd and 3rd places lodged a protest, claiming that more than the permitted three mechanics had worked on Fangio's car during a pit stop. The protest was thrown out, and Fangio celebrated on home soil.

The Argentinian ace had been forced to borrow a Maserati to compete in Argentina, and he had to do likewise in Belgium, the new Mercedes still not quite ready to go. It proved to be an inspired decision, for he won there, too. This was a particularly fine victory, for Fangio had to drive the latter part of the race with a collapsed suspension. Ferrari again had to settle for second place, this time in the shape of Maurice Trintignant.

In third place at Belgium was Stirling Moss. Moss had gone into the new season with no competitive British car available for him to drive. He had seen Hawthorn's star rise by joining Ferrari, but the fiercely patriotic Moss had so far resisted any move to a non-British outfit. The situation became urgent, and Moss had bought a Maserati 250F in order to make a fist of it in 1954. It was to prove a watershed in the British star's career.

Mercedes are back

The Mercedes made its long-awaited appearance in the next race at Rheims. It was a dazzling debut for the streamlined W196, for both Fangio and his team-mate, Karl Kling, ran away with it. The pair finished a lap ahead of Ferrari's Robert Manzon. The third Mercedes driver was another unfamiliar name, Hans Herrmann, who completed a triumphant day for the team by returning the fastest lap. Kling and Herrmann were by no means top drawer drivers, but thanks to the superb Mercedes they enjoyed their share of success during the season.

The jubilant German camp came back to earth with a bump at Silverstone, however. For it was here that the Mercedes' weakness was revealed. On the difficult British circuit the flaws in the car's roadholding were exposed. The streamlined bodywork concealed the front wheels, and the drivers, Fangio included, found it difficult to position the car for cornering. The corners were marked out with oildrums, and Fangio's car hit them regularly. His Mercedes was a battered mess by the finish, but he did hold on to 4th place. Gonzalez and Hawthorn came home first and second, making it an enjoyable day for Ferrari at long last.

Tragedy at Nürburgring

The German team produced an unstreamlined version of the W196 for their home Grand Prix at the Nürburgring. Fangio dominated the race and won, despite being deeply upset by the death of Onofre Marimon in practice. Gonzalez, like Fangio a fellow-countryman and close friend of Marimon, was so distraught that he handed over his car to Hawthorn, who finished the race in second place.

Fangio was a convincing winner yet again in the Swiss Grand Prix at Bremgarten, but he reverted to the streamlined car at Monza, and he didn't have things all his own way. Even on the fast Italian track the W196's cornering proved suspect. Both Gonzalez and Ascari who was driving a Ferrari on the day vied with Fangio for the lead. But it was Moss who stole the show. He had been so impressive in the Maserati that he was given a works car to drive. He was leading the race with just nine laps to go, when his oil-tank ruptured. He restarted, but his engine gave out short of the line. In typically determined fashion, he pushed the car to the finish. It earned him only 10th place, but the crowd gave this magnificent effort its due. Fangio won the race, but he later declared it a moral victory for Moss.

The Lancia V-8 made its appearance at the final race of the season, in Barcelona. Both Villoresi and Ascari lasted only a few laps, although Ascari did have the consolation of recording the fastest lap. Fangio also hit trouble, the Mercedes' oil and water overheating after paper was sucked into the air intake. Hawthorn went on to notch his second Grand Prix victory, and in the process edge out his Ferrari team-mate Gonzalez for the runner-up spot in the Drivers' Championship.

Six victories clinch the title for Fangio

The crown was Fangio's, of course. The fact that he struggled home third in Barcelona hardly mattered. With six victories, and only the best five finishes counting, the Argentinian had already done more than enough to make him the most convincing winner of the coveted title thus far.

Top: Contrasting styles. The stunning Mercedes W196 had revolutionary looks as well as exceptional performance. Fangio's car looks a very different beast from the Connaught of Bill Whitehouse just behind.

Above: One-two for Ferrari. Gonzalez wins from team-mate Hawthorn. This was the second and last win of the Argentinian's career. The first had been in the same race three years earlier.

Previous page: Fangio chats with long-time partner Donna Andreina.

Testing time for Collins and Hawthorn

Above: Peter Collins at the wheel of a Ferrari driving through the rain.

Opposite top: Mike Hawthorn in the Vanwall Special at Aintree. On hand is Vanwall driver Peter Collins, who had put the car through its paces during its development.

Opposite left: Mike Hawthorn and the "Old Man", Tony Vandervell, look less than impressed with the new Vanwall. Hawthorn's move to Vanwall in 1955 was short-lived: the car wasn't up to scratch, and after a blazing row Hawthorn stormed out and finished the year back at Ferrari.

Opposite right: Fangio with Peter Collins.

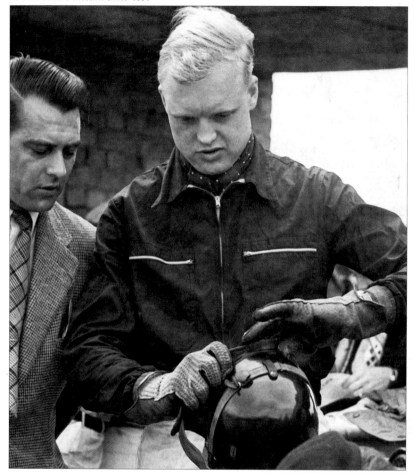

Unhappy year for Hawthorn

Above: Hawthorn drove brilliantly throughout the season to finish runner-up in the championship. It was an unhappy year for the Briton, however. He was badly burned in an early-season crash; his father was killed in a road accident; and Hawthorn himself was subjected to vitriolic attack after being excused from National Service.

Turning point for Moss

Above: The pit lane is a hive of activity during practice for the British Grand Prix. The Mercedes W196 was the star of the year, but Jose Froilan Gonzalez's Ferrari came out on top in this race.

Left: Moss wins the Daily Telegraph Trophy race at Aintree. His reward for a successful season is a berth alongside Fangio at Mercedes in 1955.

It was his efforts on the track that caught the eye in 1954. This was the turning point in Moss's career, for he finally gave up on British marques and bought himself a Maserati.

1955
Tragic year of change

By the start of the 1955 season, Mercedes had ironed out the roadholding and oil-leakage problems that had dogged the W196 the previous year. Moss also came on board to join Fangio. This was a remarkable turnaround, for just twelve months earlier, when Moss had been desperately trying to secure a competitive drive for the 1954 season, Mercedes had declined the offer of his services. Moss's great efforts during that campaign now convinced the German outfit that he was the man to provide support for Fangio. An improved car and a strengthened driver line-up made the Stuttgart outfit look the team everyone had to beat in 1955.

Only two go the distance

The opening race in Argentina turned into a nightmare, both for the drivers and for the race organisers. It was held in such enervating heat that only two drivers, Fangio and Roberto Mieres, completed the 233-mile race without having to hand over their cars to other drivers. Fangio won, and Mieres was fifth in his Maserati, but allocating the points beyond those two was a mathematical headache. The Ferrari which finished second had been driven by Gonzalez, Farina and Trintignant. Farina and Trintignant had also had a stint in the third-placed Ferrari, along with Umberto Maglioli. The 4th-placed Mercedes had been shared by Moss, Kling and Herrmann. And so it went on. Fangio's 9 points was clear: he had won and set the fastest lap. It was eventually decided that Farina and Trintignant should be awarded 3-and-one-third points; Gonzalez and Mieres 2; Maglioli 1-and-one-third; and Moss, Kling and Herrmann 1 point each.

Ascari killed in practice

Alberto Ascari, who had had such a miserable time of things with Lancia in 1954, failed to finish in Argentina, as did his team-mate Villoresi. In the next round, at Monaco, Ascari was leading, when his Lancia hit straw bales and plunged spectacularly into the harbour. Ascari emerged unscathed. A few days later, he was invited to give his team-mate Eugenio Castellotti's Ferrari a practice run at a deserted Monza. Unaccountably, the former champion took a bend flat-out and ploughed straight on. Ascari's death had eerie similarities to the death of his father, also a renowned racing driver. Both lost their lives at the age of 36, and both left behind a wife and two children.

Monaco was to be the only race of the series that Mercedes failed to win. Fangio had led for 50 laps, then retired. Moss took over in front, but he, too, failed to finish. Ferrari's Maurice Trintignant drove a steady race, moving through the ranks as others dropped out to score an unlikely victory.

The eternal shadow

Lancia withdrew from racing after Ascari's death, leaving the potential of the D 50 unfulfilled. Castellotti still entered one privately, though, in the next round in Belgium. He was going well until his engine gave out on the 16th lap. The race was a comfortable one-two for Fangio and Moss.

Moss was earning a name for himself as Fangio's "eternal shadow". He was invariably to be found in Fangio's wheel-tracks, and honing his already considerable skills behind the wheel. His fortunes contrasted markedly with those of Mike Hawthorn. Hawthorn's two years at Ferrari had seen him eclipse Moss as the most successful British driver. But for the 1955 season he had decided to join Vanwall. After a string of mechanical glitches, culminating in an early exit from the Belgian race with an oil leak, Hawthorn had a stormy encounter with Vanwall boss Tony Vandervell. It resulted in his return to Ferrari for the remainder of the season.

83 people die in Le Mans tragedy

Before the next race, at Zandvoort, many of the top drivers competed at Le Mans. It was here, on Saturday 11 June, that tragedy struck, on a scale never before seen in the history of motor sport, a tragedy that was to have significant ramifications for the World Championship.

Some two and a half hours into the race, the Mercedes of Pierre Levegh hit Lance Macklin's Austin Healey, somersaulted over the safety barrier, and exploded into a packed spectators' enclosure. Eighty-three people, including Levegh himself, lost their lives.

As a result of the disaster, the Grands Prix of France, Germany, Spain and Switzerland were cancelled, leaving just three more rounds to decide the championship. At Zandvoort Fangio and Moss led the rest home yet again. Hawthorn's return to Ferrari offered no immediate success; he suffered gearbox trouble, but at least managed a finish, albeit in 7th place.

Aintree Grand Prix

Aintree staged the British Grand Prix for the first time, and it was here that Mercedes gave its greatest show of strength. The pupil finally beat the master in this race, Moss edging out Fangio by a matter of inches. Many people, Moss included, were left wondering whether Fangio had allowed Moss a home victory. What is certain is that Moss drove superbly on the day, and he was learning all the time from the acknowledged maestro.

Mercedes had the top four finishers at Aintree, Kling and Taruffi occupying third and fourth places. Meanwhile, the race marked the quiet debut of an Australian, driving a Cooper - Jack Brabham.

The final race was again at Monza, but this time on the high-speed banked circuit. Moss failed to finish, but at least set the fastest lap of more than 134mph. It was Taruffi who was left to follow Fangio home in yet another one-two for Mercedes. Castellotti battled hard to give the Italian fans something to cheer about. He finished less than a minute behind Taruffi in third place, and that was also where he finished in the final championship table.

The fact that Castellotti's final tally was just 12 points shows the dominance of Mercedes and its two premier drivers. Moss had finished on 25, but Fangio was the star turn. He had reached the 40-point mark for the second successive season, and it had brought him his third world title. with every prospect of more to come.

Champions to quit

Mercedes announced at the end of the year that it was withdrawing from racing to concentrate on its production car operation. It meant that Fangio and Moss were both seeking a new team for the 1956 campaign. The Argentinian was looking for a car that would keep him at the top, the Briton for a car that would help him depose the undisputed champion.

Above: Moss in action on his way to finishing runner-up behind Fangio in the 1955 championship.
Previous page: Fangio at Aintree for the British Grand Prix, where he finished second behind Moss. This result prompted much speculation that the Argentinian allowed his young team-mate to have his first taste of Grand Prix success on home soil.

Fangio's third world crown

Opposite above: Moss's Silver Arrow sports the Union Jack on the bodywork. When Mercedes announced its withdrawal from racing, the intensely patriotic Moss's first thought was to try and find a competitive British drive for 1956.

Opposite below: Peter Collins from Kidderminster, England, driving a privately owned Maserati.

Above right: Four wins and a second place took Fangio to the 40-point mark for the second successive season in 1955. It was his third world title in five years.

Above left: Mike Hawthorn, pictured during practice for the British Grand Prix at Aintree in July. He had almost quit the sport a month earlier, having been deeply affected by the Le Mans tragedy, which occurred on 11 June. Hawthorn was exonerated from any blame for the crash which cost 83 lives, and was eventually coaxed back behind the wheel.

1956
Collins hands it to Fangio

On the surface of it the 1956 championship looked like a tame re-run of the year before. Fangio won again, and Moss was runner-up again. But the bald facts don't do justice to a season that was full of drama, both on and off the track.

For Fangio and Moss the first decision was to find new teams for whom to ply their trade. The former team-mates went their separate ways. Fangio joined Ferrari, although the cars fielded by the Maranello team in 1956 were actually modified Lancias. Superficially, it looked like an excellent decision; after all, it was to bring him his fourth world crown. But underneath there was seething discontent, and it was one of Fangio's unhappiest years. He was constantly suspicious about the standard of preparation that his cars received. He had no affection for the Maranello outfit and left as soon as the season was over.

Moss chooses Maserati

Moss was torn between patriotic fervour and the search for the most competitive car in which to challenge Fangio's supremacy. He had enjoyed some fine successes with Mercedes, but was now desperately keen to fight the new campaign in a British car. He tried out all three British contenders: Connaught, BRM and Vanwall. But he harboured nagging thoughts that Maserati offered his best chance of unseating Fangio. He anguished over the decision, but in the end it was Maserati who got his signature.

The battle lines were clearly drawn between the rival Italian camps, who would dominate the championship. Alongside Fangio, Ferrari had Luigi Musso, Eugenio Castellotti and the young Englishman Peter Collins. Jean Behra and Cesare Perdisa provided strong support to Moss at Maserati.

Fangio sets the pace

First blood went to Fangio and Ferrari in the opening round in Argentina. His own car failed him early on, and he took over the mount of team-mate Musso to win from Behra. Moss had had a spell in front, but his engine also gave out. There lay one of the critical factors of the entire season: when Moss hit trouble, he struggled for points; when Fangio had a problem, he invariably took over the cars of well-placed team-mates and added significantly to his championship tally.

Monaco was another case in point. Moss drove a textbook race to gain his second Grand Prix win, while Fangio took over Collins' car to finish second. Fangio had been totally out of sorts that day. First he spun his Lancia-Ferrari, then, in a desperate effort to claw back ground on Moss, he repeatedly hit barriers and kerbs. The car was a mess when Fangio finally came into the pits, but he still came away from Monte Carlo with three useful points for a shared second place. Behra brought his Maserati home third, while the unfortunate Castellotti drew the short straw by having to take over Fangio's battered machine. He finished fourth.

Peter Collins leads the pack

Collins emerged from the shadows of the sport's more illustrious names by gaining back-to-back wins in Belgium and France. Moss and Fangio both had spells in front at Spa, but both hit trouble. Fangio's transmission problem was terminal, but Moss on this occasion did reappear; he took over Perdisa's car to finish third. Collins had got home ahead of local favourite Paul Frere, driving a Ferrari.

The Ferraris of Fangio, Collins and Castellotti set the pace at Rheims. After Fangio was delayed by a lengthy pit stop, Collins was left to take the honours, inches ahead of Castellotti. Behra was third, Fangio fourth, and Moss, who once again had to take over Perdisa's car, had to settle for a shared fifth.

Collins was now leading the title race on 19 points, with Behra on 14, and Fangio on 13. But it was all change after the British Grand Prix at Silverstone. The works BRMs of Hawthorn and Tony Brooks made a dramatic impact early in the race. They led for the first ten laps, but both then had problems. Moss hit the front in his Maserati, but he succumbed to axle trouble. Fangio came through to score a somewhat fortuitous victory. Collins grabbed second, but only after he had taken over Alfonso de Portago's Ferrari.

Championship all to play for

The championship was now wide open. Collins still led, on 22 points, but Fangio was breathing down his neck on 21, and the consistent Behra was on 18.

There was no luck about the reigning champion's win in the German Grand Prix. This was one of the few glimpses of vintage Fangio in his unsettled year at Ferrari. He won emphatically, with Moss second. Behra was again in the points in third, but it was Collins who now ran out of luck. He was lying second, when his fuel tank fractured. Once again he took over de Portago's car, but this time he crashed out of the race. He wasn't hurt, but it meant he was now eight points adrift of his Argentinian team-mate going into the final round at Monza.

Collins' magnanimous gesture

Both Collins and Behra still had a chance of overhauling Fangio, though to do so they each needed to win in Italy and set the fastest lap in the process. Fangio was forced out of the race with steering trouble, and he faced an agonising wait, with the destiny of the title seemingly out of his hands. Then came one of the most magnanimous gestures in sporting history. Collins, lying second and with an excellent chance of taking the title himself, pulled into the pits and offered Fangio his car. Fangio gratefully accepted and tore after race leaders Moss and Musso. Musso is said to have refused to hand his car over to Fangio, and the Argentinian ace must have permitted himself a wry smile when Musso's steering went just before the end. Fangio couldn't catch Moss, whose victory meant that he overhauled both Behra and Collins to finish runner-up for the second year. A shared second place was enough to secure Fangio's fourth world crown, but it was a title that he always acknowledged owed a great deal to the magnanimity of Peter Collins.

Collins reputedly said that he made the gesture because he would have plenty of other opportunities to take the title. Sadly, that was not to be the case.

Above: Fangio (right) exchanges words with motor racing's Spanish aristocrat Alfonso de Portago.
Previous page: Maserati team-mates Stirling Moss and Jean Behra talk tactics.

Peter Collins - sporting hero

Below: Peter Collins at Stow corner during the RAC British Grand Prix at Silverstone. The race was over a distance of 303 miles.

The final race of the Grand Prix season at Monza saw one of the most magnanimous gestures in sporting history. Collins, lying second and with an excellent chance of taking the title himself, pulled into the pits and offered Fangio his car. Fangio gratefully accepted and eventually finished second which was enough to win the championship. Collins reputedly said that he made the gesture because he would have plenty of other opportunities to take the title. Sadly, that was not to be the case.

Right: Moss enjoys a cockpit smoke.

Brabham and Surtees - champions in the making

Above: Champion in the making. 1956 was the second year that Jack Brabham left his Australian home to race in Britain. He competed in a battered old Maserati 250F and, unsurprisingly, enjoyed little success. Here, wife Betty is required to push, while son Geoffrey rides with dad.

Left: John Surtees receives his latest motorcycling trophy after winning at Oulton Park, May 1955. Presenting the trophy is Mrs Geoff Duke, wife of another motorcycling great. Surtees would accumulate seven world titles before seeking a fresh challenge in motor racing.

1957
Third time unlucky for Moss

Fangio and Moss were both on the move before battle recommenced in 1957. Fangio put an end to his unhappy year at Ferrari by rejoining Maserati. That was the team Moss had agonised over joining in 1956, making the decision only when it was clear that there was no competitive British alternative. A year on, things were different. Moss had driven a Vanwall to victory in the Daily Express Trophy race in 1956. The car had impressed him then, and another season of development and refinement now made it a real prospect for the championship series. Vanwall boss Tony Vandervell was naturally delighted to have Moss on board, and Moss was equally delighted to have a crack at Fangio in a competitive British car.

Only Behra and Fangio finish

Fangio may have been approaching his 46th birthday as the campaign got under way, but he was out of the blocks quickest. In the customary curtain-raiser in Argentina Fangio's team-mate Jean Behra and the Ferraris of Eugenio Castellotti and Peter Collins all had spells in front. But Fangio then turned on the style. He crossed the line ahead of Behra, who was the only other driver to complete the 100-lap race. It was an excellent day for Maserati. Carlos "Charley" Menditeguy, the latest in Argentina's production line of top-flight drivers, finished third. Harry Schell, who had left Vanwall the previous year, was fourth.

Maserati even had the honour of taking the fastest lap, thanks to Moss, of all people. Vanwall hadn't made the trip to South America, so Moss had secured himself a drive in a borrowed Maserati. Gearbox trouble at the start put paid to his chances of winning, but he recovered to finish 8th, setting the quickest lap in the process.

Two Ferrari drivers killed

It was a terrible day for Ferrari. Collins, Hawthorn and Musso all retired, while Castellotti had a hairy moment when he lost a wheel. Castellotti had a lucky escape that day, but just a few weeks later he was killed while testing a Ferrari at Modena. Ferrari lost another driver before the second round of the championship at Monte Carlo. The popular Alfonso de Portago was killed while competing in the Mille Miglia.

Fangio won again at Monaco, though he was helped by the fact that a multiple pile-up took out some of his closest rivals. After taking an early lead, Moss hit the barricade at the chicane on the 4th lap. The track became littered with poles, and for the Ferraris of Collins and Hawthorn it was race over. Tony Brooks, driving the second Vanwall, was also caught up in the mêlée, but managed to extricate himself. He went on to finish 20 seconds behind Fangio.

Brabham pushes it for sixth place

The greatest ovation of the day was reserved for Jack Brabham. He drove superbly to take his 2-litre Cooper-Climax into third place. When his fuel pump failed five laps from the end, the gritty Australian pushed the car half a mile to come home in 6th place.

Financial problems meant there was no race in either Holland or Belgium, so the circus now moved to France. Moss missed the race at Rouen through illness, and with his biggest rival out of the picture, Fangio yet again made hay. It was the Argentinian's first appearance on the track, yet he gave a virtuoso display. His full-throttle drifts round the fast corners were spectacularly impressive, and he came home 50 seconds ahead of Luigi Musso's Ferrari.

In spite of the early-season setbacks, the star of Vanwall and Moss was undoubtedly in the ascendant. It all came right for the team in the home Grand Prix at Aintree, on 20 July. Moss was leading the race when he swapped his ailing car for Tony Brooks' mount. That put him back in 6th place, but Moss carved his way back to the front in magnificent style. His victory was the first by a British car in a major Grand Prix since 1923.

Lap record falls ten times

Fangio had been out of contention at Aintree, his car not running properly, but at the Nürburgring, on 4 August, he was back to his best. It was to be his final Grand Prix success, and many felt that he saved the best till last. He began the race with a half-full tank, the plan being to build up a sizeable lead which would more than compensate for the extra refuelling stop. In fact, Fangio was 28 seconds ahead when he came into the pits, but by the time he rejoined the race he was now more than 60 seconds down on Hawthorn and Collins. Undaunted, he set about catching them, breaking the lap record no less than ten times as he did so. He passed both Ferraris on the penultimate lap, and crossed the line 3.6 seconds ahead of the Farnham Flyer.

Suspension problems meant that the Vanwalls were never in the picture in Germany, but it was a different story in the last two rounds. Italy was the scene for both: Pescara and Monza.

Fangio's fifth world crown

Pescara was added to the series to compensate for the loss of Belgium and Holland. The 16-mile road circuit was a tricky combination of long straights and tortuous mountain stretches. Enzo Ferrari is said to have banned his cars from participating in Italian road races, and Hawthorn and Collins were left without a drive. Luigi Musso was unhappy with the decision, for he still entertained hopes of winning the title. He managed to borrow a car for the race, and in the early stages he headed both Moss and Ferrari. But Moss soon passed him, and when he retired on the 10th lap, it brought Fangio up to second. That was how they finished, a result which confirmed Fangio's fifth world crown.

Moss and Fangio fought an epic battle at Monza, and the Englishman again came out on top. That victory gave Moss a final tally of 25 points; for the third year running he had finished runner-up to Fangio in the Drivers' Championship.

Apart from the dazzling success of Mercedes in 1954-55, the 8-year history of the championship had been dominated by Italian marques. Now, with Ferrari struggling, and Maserati announcing its withdrawal from racing, it finally looked as if a British car could actually win the coveted title.

Above: Moss and his Vanwall team-mate Tony Brooks each have a hand on the trophy after their shared win in the British Grand Prix at Aintree. It was the first success for a British car in a major race for more than 30 years.
Previous page: Peter Collins and Mike Hawthorn.

Fangio at his peak

Below: Fangio celebrated his 46th birthday during the 1957 championship season, yet he was at the peak of his powers. Four wins in the superb Maserati 250F were enough to give him his fifth world crown.

Right: John Surtees at the Isle of Man TT. The motorcycle ace won 6 TT races, as well as 7 world titles before turning to Formula One.

Opposite: Compatriots and rivals. Vanwall's number two driver Tony Brooks (left) chats to Ferrari's Mike Hawthorn.

1958
Tragedy for champion Hawthorn

Fangio did make a few cameo appearances during 1958, but the previous year effectively marked the great man's retirement from the sport at the top, where he belonged. His decision was a fillip for all who harboured title aspirations, none more so than the man who had played second fiddle in the championship for three successive years: Stirling Moss.

Moss stayed with Vanwall for 1958. Indeed, the whole line-up remained unchanged, Tony Brooks and Stuart Lewis-Evans ably filling the supporting roles. It was a happy team, and a fiercely competitive one.

1958 saw the introduction of new regulations regarding the type of fuel the cars could use. Prior to then, teams could use any mix they pleased; now, 130-octane aviation fuel was mandatory. The Vanwall team was still hastily carrying out the necessary adjustments when the championship season kicked off in Argentina. Moss took the opportunity to enter the race in a Rob Walker 2-litre Cooper-Climax. Despite the best efforts of Ferrari's Luigi Musso to catch him, Moss scored the unlikeliest of victories.

Waiting game

The Vanwalls were ready in time for Monaco, but it was to be a race which had ominous import for the rest of the year. All three cars failed to finish. Reliability problems would stack up frustratingly as the season progressed, and cost Moss dear in the final reckoning.

Meanwhile, the little Cooper did it again in Monte Carlo. It was Maurice Trintignant who played the canny waiting game this time, driving steadily and biding his time. One by one the faster cars fell by the wayside, and Trintignant emerged the winner, a repeat performance of 1955. Ferrari had to be content with the minor placings, Musso and Collins following the Cooper home.

British cars dominated at Zandvoort. They occupied the first two rows on the grid, with the three Vanwalls taking the front-row berths. Brooks and Lewis-Evans failed to finish, but it was glory for Moss, and he led a British clean sweep. The BRMs of Harry Schell and Jean Behra followed Moss home, giving that marque its most successful outing to date. Roy Salvadori's Cooper-Climax came in fourth, and Cliff Allison sneaked into the points for the second race running by finishing sixth in the new Lotus. The only cheer for Italy on the day was Hawthorn's fifth place in his Ferrari.

Another setback for Moss

Moss suffered another setback at Spa, but this time he only had himself to blame. He missed a gear, the revs shot up beyond their critical point and the engine blew. It was still a great day for Vanwall, though, as Brooks and Lewis-Evans came first and third respectively. Further down the field history was being made as the Italian Maria-Teresa de Filippis became the first woman to compete in a world championship race. Driving a Maserati she finished 10th, two laps adrift of the winner.

At Rheims in 1953 Mike Hawthorn had squeezed home fractionally ahead of Fangio after a classic encounter. Five years on, the same race was notable for both men, but for very different reasons. Fangio finished the race in fourth place and made his final bow to the sport he had graced. For Hawthorn and Ferrari it was the turning point in the series. He won the race, and in doing so threw down the gauntlet to the British teams in general, and Moss who finished second in particular. Ferrari's delight was muted by the death of Luigi Musso, who crashed at Muizon while challenging Hawthorn for the lead.

Peter Collins killed at Nürburgring

Moss and Hawthorn were tied on 23 points as the circus moved to Silverstone. For Moss it was a case of another day, another engine going up in smoke. His race was over after 24 laps. Hawthorn took the upper hand in the championship by finishing second to team-mate Peter Collins. Having been without a win for two years, Ferrari had now scored back-to-back victories.

There was more misery for Moss at the Nürburgring a fortnight later, when magneto trouble put him out of the race after just four laps. The Ferraris of Collins and Hawthorn again looked likely to prevail, but Tony Brooks took up the challenge for Vanwall and passed both of them. Tragedy then struck. As he battled for the lead with Brooks on the 11th lap, Peter Collins' Ferrari went off the track at 100mph. He died in the resulting crash.

Hawthorn had seen what happened and retired almost immediately. He was devastated by the loss of a team-mate and close friend.

As the sport mourned the loss of one big name, another was making an early step on the ladder. New Zealander Bruce McLaren drove his Cooper superbly to finish first in the Formula 2 class, and fifth overall.

There were no gremlins for Moss at the first ever Portuguese Grand Prix, staged at Oporto. He ran out a comfortable winner, having been on pole. But Hawthorn finished second yet again to maintain the impetus in his challenge for the title. As things turned out, the misinterpretation of a pit signal proved immensely costly. The signal informed Moss that Hawthorn had set the fastest lap. Moss misread it, and drove steadily to win the race, without making any great effort to put in a fast lap. That extra point would have been the difference between the coveted title and yet another runner-up spot.

Hawthorn by the narrowest of margins

Moss drew a blank at Monza, succumbing this time to gearbox failure. Hawthorn was leading the race in the latter stages, when a clutch problem allowed Brooks to come through and win. Hawthorn hung on for second, and he now had 40 points from six races, the best six finishes counting for championship purposes. Moss had only finished five times and he stood on 32.

The final round was another new venue, the Ain Diab circuit in Casablanca. With an eight-point deficit, Moss had to win and set the fastest lap to have any chance. He did exactly that, and took a maximum nine points to finish on 41. But for Moss to win the title, Hawthorn had to finish no better than third. The Ferrari team had the tactics worked out to perfection. Phil Hill, in only his second Formula 1 drive, held on to second place, then eased off to allow Hawthorn through. His six points here meant that the four gained in Argentina could be discounted. It gave him a final tally of 42. Hawthorn had won just once in the series, compared with Moss's four wins, but his consistency had brought him the championship by a single point.

There was even worse news to come for Vanwall. Lewis-Evans had crashed out of the race and suffered terrible burns. He died before he could reach hospital.

Hawthorn killed after retirement

Hawthorn was not the jubilant winner of the spoils, however. He had been considering retiring from racing even before the German Grand Prix. The death of Peter Collins now made that a certainty. He announced the decision shortly afterwards, but didn't live to enjoy the pursuits outside racing. On 22 January, 1959, Hawthorn the Farnham Flyer was killed when his Jaguar collided with a lorry. He was 29.

Left: Moss was in top form in 1958, but reliability problems meant that he lost the championship to Hawthorn by a single point.
Previous page: Advisory capacity only. Hawthorn in conversation with Bruce Halford before a race at Brands Hatch, December 1958.

Hawthorn second at Monza

Right: Hawthorn is guest of honour at a reception held at the Park Lane Hotel, London.

Below: Mike Hawthorn on his way to second place at Monza in the penultimate round of the championship. He was now odds-on favourite for the world title, but the lustre of success was already tarnished by the deaths of Luigi Musso and Peter Collins.

Opposite: Moss is dubbed the "Master of Aintree" after edging out Jack Brabham to win the International 200 race at the Liverpool track in April. It was his third victory in the event, following wins in 1954 and 1956.

Ecstasy then tragedy for Peter Collins

Right: Peter Collins grimaces as he wipes his face after victory in his Ferrari (opposite below). Two weeks later at the Nürburgring tragedy struck. Peter Collins' Ferrari went off the track at 100mph. He died in the resulting crash.

Below left: Moss is a blur as he makes a Le Mans-style start at Goodwood. Victory that day came in an Aston-Martin; in the championship series he once again drove for Vanwall.

Below right: Brabham gives his Cooper's Climax engine a tune-up. It wasn't a great year for the 32-year-old Australian, but the rear-engined revolution wasn't far away.

Opposite above: Jack Brabham drove for Cooper in 1958, the team's first full season in Formula 1. He was largely out of luck, 4th place at Monaco being his best finish in the championship.

1959
Brabham's thrilling climax

After taking second and third places in the 1958 championship, Stirling Moss and Tony Brooks must have anticipated another competitive season with Vanwall. But team boss Tony Vandervell shocked everyone when, in January 1959, he announced his withdrawal from racing on the grounds of ill health. Brooks went to Ferrari, while Moss hedged his bets between two teams. In some races he drove one of Rob Walker's Cooper-Climaxes; in others he struck a deal which allowed him to drive a front-engined BRM.

Success for Brabham

The Argentinian Grand Prix was cancelled this year, so the championship got under way at Monaco. Moss was in the thick of the action straightaway, tussling for the lead with Jean Behra's Ferrari and the Cooper-Climax of Jack Brabham. Moss and Behra both retired, leaving Brabham to notch his and Cooper's first victory. Tony Brooks was second, with Brabham's team-mate Maurice Trintignant third.

Brabham's success was no great surprise. The Cooper was a much better car than the one in which Moss had won the Argentine Grand Prix the year before. Brabham had been with Cooper since his arrival from Australia in 1955, and became the team's top works driver when it made the step up to Formula 1 in 1957. There had been some encouraging results in 1958, Cooper's first full season in Grand Prix racing. 1959 was to be the breakthrough year for both Brabham and the impressive rear-engined car.

First win for BRM

At Zandvoort it was the turn of another British marque to taste success. BRM had been involved in Formula 1 since 1950, but had never recorded a win. Joakim Bonnier changed all that, fighting off the Cooper challenge of Brabham, Moss and Masten Gregory to secure a fine victory for the Bourne team.

The best Ferrari had managed at Zandvoort was Jean Behra's fifth place, but in two of the next three races the sheer speed of the Maranello cars proved decisive. At Rheims Tony Brooks and Phil Hill made it a one-two for the Scuderia, with Brabham having to settle for third.

Behra killed on "lethal" circuit

A strike in Italy meant that Ferrari was unable to follow up its Dutch success. This left the British teams to battle it out in their home Grand Prix at Aintree. Brabham came out on top, having led all the way. Moss chose to drive the front-engined BRM again, and things went much better this time. He took second, a whisker ahead of Cooper's up-and-coming Bruce McLaren.

Ferrari were back in time for the German Grand Prix, which for the first time was staged on Berlin's high-speed Avus track. The circuit's steeply-banked section was regarded as lethal by many of the drivers, and it did indeed claim a life: Jean Behra was killed in the sports car race which preceded the main event.

The Grand Prix itself was split into two 30-lap heats. Brooks won both to take overall first place. New Ferrari driver Dan Gurney was second, with Phil Hill making it a clean sweep for the team in third.

For the two laps that he lasted in Germany Moss had driven the Cooper. Hans Herrmann had entered the race in the BRM, but crashed out after a brakes failure. The car was destroyed, and Moss now drove Coopers for the rest of the season. It seemed to change his luck, for he dominated the next race, the Portuguese Grand Prix at Monsanto. Moss was on top form, lapping the entire field. Masten Gregory's Cooper was a distant second, ahead of Gurney's Ferrari.

The Moss bandwagon rolled on at Monza. The powerful Ferraris had been expected to dominate, but Moss was at his wily best. He sat on the tail of Phil Hill, concentrating on conserving his tyres by smooth acceleration and gentle cornering. Hill, like all the Ferraris, had to stop for new rear tyres. Moss hit the front and finished the race with his original tyres. Hill was relegated to second, but Brabham was back in the points in third. It put the championship in the melting pot with just one round to go: Brabham had 31 points, Moss 25.5. Tony Brooks was also in with a chance. His 23 points meant that he, too, could overhaul Brabham by winning the final round and setting the fastest lap.

Brabham's championship at a push

The decider was in the United States, that country's first ever championship event, with the exception of the Indianapolis 500. It took place on the Sebring airfield track in Florida, but not until December. The title contenders had some three months in which to plan and prepare.

The showdown was anti-climactic as far as Moss was concerned. He took pole and was out of the blocks first, but transmission failure put him out of the race after just six laps. Brabham took over in front and held it to the last lap. There he ran out of fuel, and his car ground to a halt 500 yards from the line. Not for the first time he pushed his Cooper to the finish, earning fourth place for his trouble. Brabham's team-mates Bruce McLaren and Maurice Trintignant crossed the line first and second, but it was Brooks's third place that was critical. Four points was enough for him to snatch second place in the championship from Moss; but it wasn't enough to prevent the quiet, unassuming Jack Brabham from taking his first world crown.

Brilliant Coopers

Right: Brabham was pushed all the way to the title. Going into the last round at Sebring Tony Brooks and Stirling Moss were also in with a chance of winning the championship.
Below: The deaths of Musso and Collins in 1958, together with Hawthorn's retirement, pushed Phil Hill up the Ferrari pecking order in 1959.
Below right: Phil Hill and Tony Brooks spearheaded the Ferrari challenge in 1959. Only on the fastest circuits could the sheer power of the Maranello cars get the better of the brilliant Coopers.
Previous page: Stirling Moss and Maria-Teresa de Filippis, the premier woman driver of the era.

Brabham's world crown

Right: After early-season problems, Moss scored back-to-back wins in Portugal and Italy to give himself yet another chance of winning the elusive title.

Below: Jack Brabham and the car which broke the mould of Formula 1 racing: the rear-engined Cooper-Climax.

Opposite above: Jack Brabham led the victorious Cooper team in 1959, the year of the great rear-engine revolution.

Opposite below: Brabham celebrates after winning the British Grand Prix at Aintree.

1960
Brabham and McLaren one-two

In the final season of the 2.5-litre formula, reigning champion Jack Brabham got off to an inauspicious start. He retired from the opening race in Argentina with transmission trouble, then in Monaco he was disqualified for receiving assistance from marshals after he spun off.

Brabham's young team-mate, Bruce McLaren, continued to impress, and it was he who made the early championship running. He won in Argentina, although he was helped by the fact that race leaders Stirling Moss and Jo Bonnier both hit mechanical trouble. Moss returned to the fray in Maurice Trintignant's Cooper to finish third.

Tragedy at Spa

Moss's new rear-engined Lotus 18 hadn't been ready in time for Argentina, but it appeared at Monaco, and he drove brilliantly in the wet to win from McLaren. Moss was on top form yet again in the Dutch Grand Prix at Zandvoort. Challenging race leader Jack Brabham, he suffered a puncture, and by the time the wheel was changed he found himself relegated to 12th place. He finished an excellent fourth. Brabham led all the way, beginning an amazing run of success that would prove decisive in the title race; Moss, by contrast, after three classy performances was now to run out of luck in the most dramatic circumstances.

The Belgian Grand Prix at Spa was marred by a series of appalling accidents. Moss broke both his legs after a wheel came off his Lotus during practice. In the race itself there were fatalities in two separate incidents, both involving young British drivers. Alan Stacey was hit by a bird, while Chris Bristow shot off the road while battling for position in his Cooper-Climax.

Jim Clark's first championship points

The race was won by Brabham, with McLaren second. Back in fifth place was Jim Clark, notching his first championship points. Clark had made an impressive debut at Zandvoort, where he vied for fourth place with Graham Hill before succumbing to gearbox trouble.

Brabham made it a hat-trick of wins on the fast Rheims circuit. The Ferraris of Phil Hill and Wolfgang von Trips were both in contention for the lead, but both suffered from transmission failure to give Brabham his third success.

Surtees makes debut

Brabham made it four in a row at Silverstone, although Graham Hill took most of the plaudits. After stalling his BRM on the line, Hill stormed through the field to take the lead, only to spin off with just seven laps to go. Brabham profited and gratefully accepted maximum points, while John Surtees, who was also in his debut year, took a creditable second place. The motorcycling champion had received a number of approaches when it became known that he wanted to make the transition from two wheels to four, but it was Lotus's Colin Chapman who had acquired his services. Silverstone was Surtees's best finish of the year, although his best performance, arguably, came in the following race in Portugal. On that occasion Surtees built up a 10-second lead over Brabham, before being forced out of the race with a split radiator. Brabham was once again the man to profit, and his fifth consecutive victory assured him of a second world title with two races still to go.

Moss back after serious injury

Incredibly, Stirling Moss was back at the wheel for the race in Oporto, and was running second at one point. He was eventually disqualified for pushing his car in the wrong direction following a spin.

The championship may have been already decided when the circus rolled on to Monza, but there was controversy in store. The British teams boycotted the event, protesting over the inclusion of the banked sections of the circuit, considered by many to be dangerous. This left Ferrari to sweep the board on home territory, Phil Hill winning his first championship race. A meaningless victory with a depleted field rounded off a dismal season for Ferrari. The team didn't bother to contest the final round, the United States Grand Prix, which this year was staged at Riverside. Moss won the race to end the series on a high note and reflect on what might have been had he not missed those mid-season races. His victory also meant that Climax-engined cars had won every race, Monza excepted. Ferrari certainly saw the writing on the wall, and their dogged persistence with front-engined cars was about to come to an end.

Left: Moss prepares for the Aintree 200 race. He had a very successful year in Formula 2, driving a Porsche. He was aboard a Lotus in the championship, but his season was blighted by injury. *Previous page:* Stirling Moss (centre) ended a frustrating season with a win in the United States. Graham Hill (right) ended his disappointing year with yet another retirement. He finished only one race all season in his BRM.

Surtees's debut in Monaco

Left: John Surtees made his debut for Colin Chapman's Lotus team at the Monaco Grand Prix. His race lasted just 17 laps.

Below left: John Surtees was second behind Jack Brabham at Silverstone, giving him his first podium finish less than two months after his Formula 1 debut.

Below right: Moss made a remarkable recovery from his injuries and was back in action at the Portuguese Grand Prix. His race ended in disqualification, while Brabham was confirmed champion.

Brabham's maximum haul

Below: Jack Brabham's five wins gave him maximum points in the championship, equalling Ascari's achievement of 1952.
Right: The veteran and the novice. 1960 was the sixth successive year that Moss finished in the first three in the Drivers' Championship. New boy Surtees had one podium success in his debut season – second place in the British Grand Prix.
Opposite above: Phil Hill won his first Grand Prix at Monza, driving a Ferrari. His task was made easier by a mass boycott of the race by the dominant British teams.
Opposite below: Graham Hill hoists daughter Brigitte aloft, with wife Betty looking on. His first season with BRM was dogged by ill luck.

Moss back on track after breaking legs

Right: Moss is back on his feet less than a month after breaking his legs in the Belgian Grand Prix. He is pictured at Battersea Heliport, on his way to Silverstone for the British Grand Prix. His role there was confined to race starter, but he was back behind the wheel for the following round.

Below right: Bruce McLaren shows off the trophies received for winning the 1960 curtain-raiser in Argentina. Team-mate Jack Brabham overhauled him in mid-season, with McLaren finishing the year as championship runner-up.

Below left: Surtees was steeped in all things mechanical from an early age. He can't resist tinkering with the Climax engine, even if he isn't quite dressed for the part.

Opposite: Colin Chapman (right) had two future champions at Lotus in 1960. John Surtees (centre) was immediately competitive after making the switch from motorcycle racing. Jim Clark (left) was signed as a Formula 2 driver that year, but was promoted after the death of Alan Stacey.

1961
Ferraris in control

1961 saw the introduction of a 1.5-litre Formula, and with it a resurgence in Ferrari's fortunes. Obviously less than pleased with recent performances, Ferrari prepared meticulously for the new campaign. The introduction of the rear-engined V-6 "sharknose" paid off handsomely, while the British teams struggled with cars using dated 4-cylinder units which had a very modest power output.

Ferrari's assault on the championship was spearheaded by American sports car ace Phil Hill, his compatriot Ritchie Ginther and the bearded German Wolfgang "Taffy" von Trips. It was Moss who won the season opener at Monaco, though, beating the Ferraris into second, third and fourth. Dan Gurney came in next, bringing a new name into the Formula One frame – Porsche. It was a virtuoso display by Moss, and widely regarded as one of the greatest drives of his career. This was because he went into the race with a two-fold handicap: as well as having the outdated Climax engine under the bonnet, Moss was forced to use the old, square-shaped Lotus 18. The arrival of the new model - the 21 – had been delayed, owing to a contractual wrangle. On fast circuits Moss would find himself hopelessly off the pace, but at Monaco the skill factor made up for it and he took the flag just 3.6 seconds in front of Ginther, with Hill and von Trips well behind.

Phil Hill and Wolfgang von Trips neck and neck

Moss would be similarly impressive later in the series at the Nürburgring, but for the most part the 1961 title race was about the battle between Hill and von Trips. At Zandvoort von Trips got home just nine-tenths of a second ahead of his team-mate and rival, to give Germany its first Grand Prix winner for 22 years. Jim Clark was also working miracles to squeeze out all he could from his uncompetitive Lotus. He took third, while Moss scraped home ahead of Ginther. Zandvoort carved a special niche in the history books that day, for it was the first time in a championship event that an entire field – 15-strong on the day – completed a race without incident.

It was a clean sweep for Ferrari at Spa, the team occupying the first four places. It was Hill from von Trips this time, with Ginther in third and Olivier Gendebien in fourth. Gendebien was a Belgian who had occasional drives for the Prancing Horse team during the year. The fact that Ferrari's fourth driver could get into the frame illustrates the team's dominance at the time.

Baghetti wins in debut race

Another piece of history was made in the French Grand Prix at Rheims. Hill, von Trips and Ginther all retired from the race, but it was a Ferrari which once again crossed the line first. The young Italian driver Giancarlo Baghetti, making his Grand Prix debut, was a narrow winner in his privately-entered Ferrari. He remains the only man to win a Grand Prix on his first outing.

It was another one-two-three for Ferrari in the British Grand Prix at Aintree, von Trips leading Hill and Ginther home in torrential rain.

There was no going through the motions at the Nürburgring for Moss. As at Monaco, he broke the Ferrari stranglehold with masterful driving and clever tactics. He knew all the intricacies of the difficult 14.2-mile circuit, but it was in tyre selection that Moss made a carefully calculated gamble which paid off brilliantly.

Black day as championship leader killed

There was no objection to the combined road and banked Monza circuit this time. Von Trips went into the race with 33 points, four ahead of Hill, and looked all set to clinch the title. On only the second lap, however, tragedy struck. His Ferrari collided with Clark's Lotus, and both went off at Vedano Corner. Clark emerged unscathed but von Trips was killed instantly. Twelve spectators also lost their lives in one of motor racing's blackest days. Phil Hill went on to win the race, and took the world title in the unhappiest of circumstances.

Ferrari withdrew from the United States Grand Prix at Watkins Glen. Moss and Brabham vied for the lead, but when both retired, Innes Ireland took over and held on to the finish in his Lotus. It was his first Grand Prix win, a feat he was never to repeat. Tony Brooks gave BRM their best finish of the year in third place, after which he decided to call it a day. Brooks had never won the championship, and was overshadowed by some more illustrious names of his era, but he had six Grand Prix wins to his name and was widely regarded as a highly accomplished and professional racing driver.

Left: BRM tried desperately to get its new V-8 car ready for Graham Hill to drive. It was meant to debut at Monza, but caught fire in practice. Hill was forced to end the season with the old 4-cylinder model.

Phil Hill takes the world crown for Ferrari

Right: Ferrari's assault on the championship was spearheaded by American sports car ace Phil Hill who won the title following the death of Wolfgang von Trips.

Below left: John Surtees drove a Cooper for the Yeoman Credit team in 1961. For the new Inter-Continental Formula race at Silverstone he took the wheel of Tony Vandervell's new rear-engined Vanwall. The "Old Man" himself is on hand as Surtees eases himself into the car.

Below right: It was a tribute to Stirling Moss's skill that he was the only driver of a British car to give Ferrari a run for their money in 1961. Here he is seen in the revolutionary 4-wheel-drive Ferguson, preparing for the Gold Cup race at Oulton Park.

Surtees in a spin

Opposite: Surtees at the wheel of the new Vanwall in the Daily Express Trophy Race, one of the new Inter-Continental Formula events. He recovered from a spin to finish fifth. Despite a good showing, it never raced again.

Left: Bruce McLaren finished the season in joint seventh place with Jim Clark.

Below: The Oulton Park Gold Trophy is filled with champagne for Graham Hill, who won the race in the new E-Type Jaguar. In the championship he drove an outdated car and scored just three points all season.

1962
Graham Hill takes world crown

Graham Hill had four fairly frustrating years since his Grand Prix debut in 1958. His two years at Lotus were bedevilled by the unreliability of the cars he was given to drive. When he moved to BRM, things initially looked no better on that score, the reliability record of the Bourne cars being almost as bad as that of Lotus. There were slow but sure signs that both team and driver were getting things right in 1960 and 1961, although in the latter year all the teams struggled when they came up against the powerful Ferraris. At the start of the 1962 season, the record books showed that Hill, far from actually winning the drivers' title, hadn't even got into the top six in any year.

That was all about to change. By 1962, BRM's new V-8 unit was ready and hopes were high. However, it faced stiff opposition from the rival Climax V-8, which most of the other teams adopted.

Moss's career ends in mystery smash

Hill's first Formula One win with BRM came at the Easter Goodwood event. His victory was overshadowed by a terrible crash involving Stirling Moss. Moss had been passing Hill on a fast stretch of the circuit when he unaccountably left the track, his Lotus piling head-on into a grass bank. The cause of the crash remains a mystery to this day. Moss sustained appalling injuries, and although he made a full recovery, his career was over. He had done everything except win the coveted world crown. He had never been out of the top three in the previous seven years, including finishing runner-up four times in succession.

After another non-championship victory at Silverstone, Hill and BRM went to the Dutch Grand Prix in Zandvoort in buoyant mood. Their optimism was not misplaced, for Hill took the lead early in the race and crossed the line first, giving BRM only their second-ever championship win.

Ferrari surpassed

Hill was ahead at Monaco before being forced out with engine trouble. Bruce McLaren brought his Cooper home first, ahead of Phil Hill. The reigning champion was still driving for Ferrari, in almost an unchanged car. That was one of the problems: Ferrari had peaked in 1961, then stood still, while the new British V-8s caught up and passed them. Phil Hill's second place at Monaco was to be his best of the season. There was considerable unrest in the camp, and Hill cut a dispirited figure through to the end of the year, when he finally broke with the Italian team.

Clark beset with mechanical problems

Jim Clark took the honours in Belgium. Like Graham Hill, Clark was now free of the shackles imposed on him by the uncompetitive 4-cylinder car fielded by Lotus in 1961. Clark not only benefited from having the new V-8 Climax unit, but there was a new car as well: the Lotus 25. Colin Chapman developed the revolutionary 25, whose monocoque chassis was to revolutionise racing car design. Clark had looked well set at both Zandvoort and Monaco, but mechanical problems in both races had finished his chances. At Spa things came right, and Clark notched the first of his 25 Grand Prix wins. Hill had to make do with second place on that occasion.

Aintree was the scene of the British Grand Prix, and Clark was in imperious form. He led from start to finish, set the fastest lap, and in the title race put himself within a point of Hill, who could only finish fourth.

Hill then scored back-to-back wins at the Nürburgring and Monza. Clark, on the other hand, suffered in both races. In Germany he stalled on the line, gave furious chase to bring himself within striking distance of the leaders, but with fuel running low he was forced to ease off and content himself with fourth place. At Monza he had to retire with engine trouble.

Four wins for Hill

Clark bounced back to win at Watkins Glen, but unfortunately for the Scot, Hill claimed second spot. Going into the final race - East London, South Africa – Hill was now nine points clear of his rival. Clark needed to win to have any chance of the title, and then only if Hill failed to score. In that scenario, Clark would have won the championship on the basis of a greater number of victories. Clark took pole, and was indeed leading the race, but there was to be no fairytale ending for the Scot. Engine failure again put paid to his hopes, and it was Hill who came through to win the race. His four wins and two second places put him on 42 points, 12 ahead of Clark. The championship was his.

Left: Jack Brabham at the wheel of his Lotus during practice for the British Grand Prix at Aintree, where he finished 5th. This was the last race before the team unveiled its own new Grand Prix car, the Brabham BT3.
Previous page: Having recovered from his Goodwood crash, Stirling Moss offers a word of advice to champion-elect Graham Hill. Four wins help to give him the title by 12 points from Jim Clark.

Moss's career at an end

Above: Trapped in the wreckage of his car, Moss is conscious but badly injured. Although he makes a full recovery, his racing days are over. The cause of the accident remains a mystery.

Clark - the mercurial Scot

Right: Several months after the Goodwood crash and Stirling Moss is on his way to hospital yet again. This time he has to undergo an eye operation at St Thomas's, London.

Below: Jim Clark accepts the trophy and garland from Stirling Moss after winning the Gold Cup race at Oulton Park. The mercurial Scot had his first championship wins in 1962, but four retirements hampered his chance of taking the title from Graham Hill.

Opposite: Who better to promote a new film in which cars feature prominently than Graham Hill? The world champion takes on a keen opponent in a publicity stunt for the comedy "The Fast Lady".

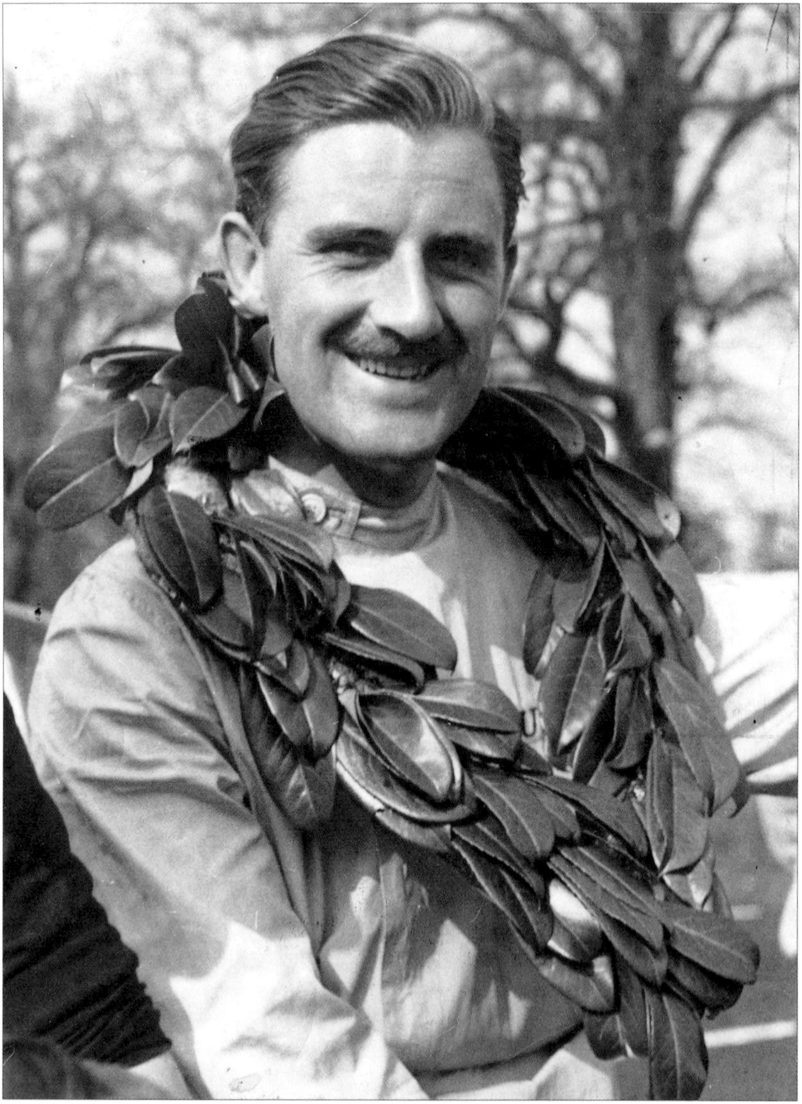

1963
Maximum points for Jim Clark

Jim Clark and Lotus had been beaten into second place in both the drivers' and the constructors' championship in 1962. The following year saw Clark in devastating form on his way to a maximum points haul, only the second time in the history of the event that such a feat had been achieved. The 1963 championship was a ten-race series, with the best six scores counting; when Albert Ascari recorded his maximum in 1952, it was the best four finishes out of eight.

Porsche decide to quit

There had been a lot of behind-the-scenes action since Hill had been crowned 1962 champion. Two teams had decided to call it a day: Porsche and Bowmaker-Yeoman. Porsche's withdrawal left Californian Dan Gurney free to drive for the Brabham team. The end of Bowmaker-Yeoman meant that John Surtees was open to offers, and he joined Ferrari.

It was a very turbulent period for the Maranello team. Engineer Carlo Chiti had walked out at the end of the 1962 season and set up his own team, ATS. Several Ferrari staff went with him, including drivers Phil Hill and Giancarlo Baghetti. It wasn't to prove a successful operation. The V-8 cars the team put out were very poor, with obvious consequences as far as Hill and Baghetti were concerned: neither took a single point in the series. The ATS team lasted just one year.

Seven wins out of ten for Clark

On the track Clark took the chequered flag first in seven of the ten races, so that he actually had the luxury of discarding a victory in taking his best six championship finishes. An analysis of what happened to the Scot in the three races he failed to win shows how his domination could have been even more overwhelming than it was. One of those was the opening race at Monaco, where he was leading from Graham Hill, then spun off with a seized gearbox. Hill went on to win, the first of what would be five Monaco successes in a row.

On the other two occasions where Clark missed out he was similarly unlucky. At the Nürburgring he was hampered by a misfiring engine, yet still managed to finish second behind John Surtees. Clark's misfortune helped Surtees to a breakthrough first championship victory, and Ferrari's first success since Monza two years before. Clark's other "failure" came at Watkins Glen, where he lost a lap and a half in the pits with battery trouble, yet still managed to finish third. Graham Hill took the race from his team-mate Ritchie Ginther. The BRM pair would end the year on 29 points each - 25 behind Clark's maximum of 54 – with Hill awarded second place by dint of those two wins in Monte Carlo and the United States.

The Flying Scot

After Monaco, Clark recorded four straight wins, at Spa, Zandvoort, Rheims and Silverstone. Of these, perhaps the Dutch race best epitomised the level of Clark's performance that year. He was fastest in practice, led the race from start to finish – lapping the entire field in the process – and became the first man to lap the Zandvoort circuit at over 100mph.

The "Flying Scot" secured the title with three races still to go. Of the other contenders, Surtees could count himself rather unfortunate. Apart from his win in Germany, he had notched a fourth place at Monaco, third at Zandvoort and second at Silverstone – where he passed Hill on the last lap, the 1962 champion running out of fuel agonisingly close to the finish. Surtees failed to finish in any of the last four races, however, and had to content himself with fourth place in the championship, on 22 points.

Best of his era

As far as Hill himself was concerned, he too had his share of ill fortune. He finished in just six races - those two victories at Monaco and Watkins Glen, plus three third places and a fourth in Mexico. During the season BRM introduced their own monocoque design, hoping to emulate the brilliant success of the Lotus 25. But the new car handled badly, and Hill was forced to revert to the old model.

With a little better luck, both Surtees and Hill may have got a little closer to Clark in the title race, but they would still have been vying for the runner-up spot. The Scot's mercurial performances in 1963 put him on a higher echelon; he was already well on his way to forging for himself the reputation as the greatest racing driver of his era.

Left: Jack Brabham had an indifferent year in 1963 and considered giving up racing to concentrate on team management. Had he done so he would have missed out on a third world crown.
Previous page: Graham Hill finished a distant runner-up behind Jim Clark in the 1963 championship. BRM introduced its own monocoque car, but it wasn't a success and Hill was forced to revert to the older model.

Seven wins for Clark

Left: Jim Clark takes a more leisurely mode of transport, having just clinched the world crown. Clark dominated the championship, with 7 wins, a second and a third in the 10-race series.

Above: All the fun of the fair. With his racing days behind him Stirling Moss is in great demand at celebrity events. Here a bearded Moss is one of the guests at a Star Gala Day at Battersea Festival Gardens.

The Grand Prix Drivers' Association

Above: Members of the Grand Prix Drivers' Association pose for the camera before convening a meeting. Sitting are current champion Graham Hill (left) and the Scot aiming to wrest the title from him, Jim Clark. Standing (left to right) are: Trevor Taylor, Bruce McLaren, Tony Maggs, Innes Ireland, Lorenzo Bandini, Jack Brabham, Jo Bonnier, Phil Hill, Tim Hall, Masten Gregory, Dan Gurney, Chris Amon, John Surtees, Ritchie Ginther.

Opposite above: Graham Hill with his children, Brigitte, 4, and 3-year-old Damon at Silverstone before the Grand Prix. Hill came 3rd in the race behind Jim Clark. The Scot was well on his way to succeeding Hill as champion.

Opposite below: Will the real world champion stand up? Graham Hill and Jim Clark are among the top drivers present at a publicity luncheon in Manchester. With three races still to go Clark is already out of sight in the championship. This produces some good-humoured banter over when exactly the Scot should assume Graham Hill's mantle. Clark insists it should be at the end of the year; Hill is happy to concede the honour immediately. Pictured are (back row, left to right) Mike Hailwood, Bob Anderson, Graham Hill, Jim Clark, Ritchie Ginther. Front row (left to right) Rob Walker, Jo Bonnier, Innes Ireland.

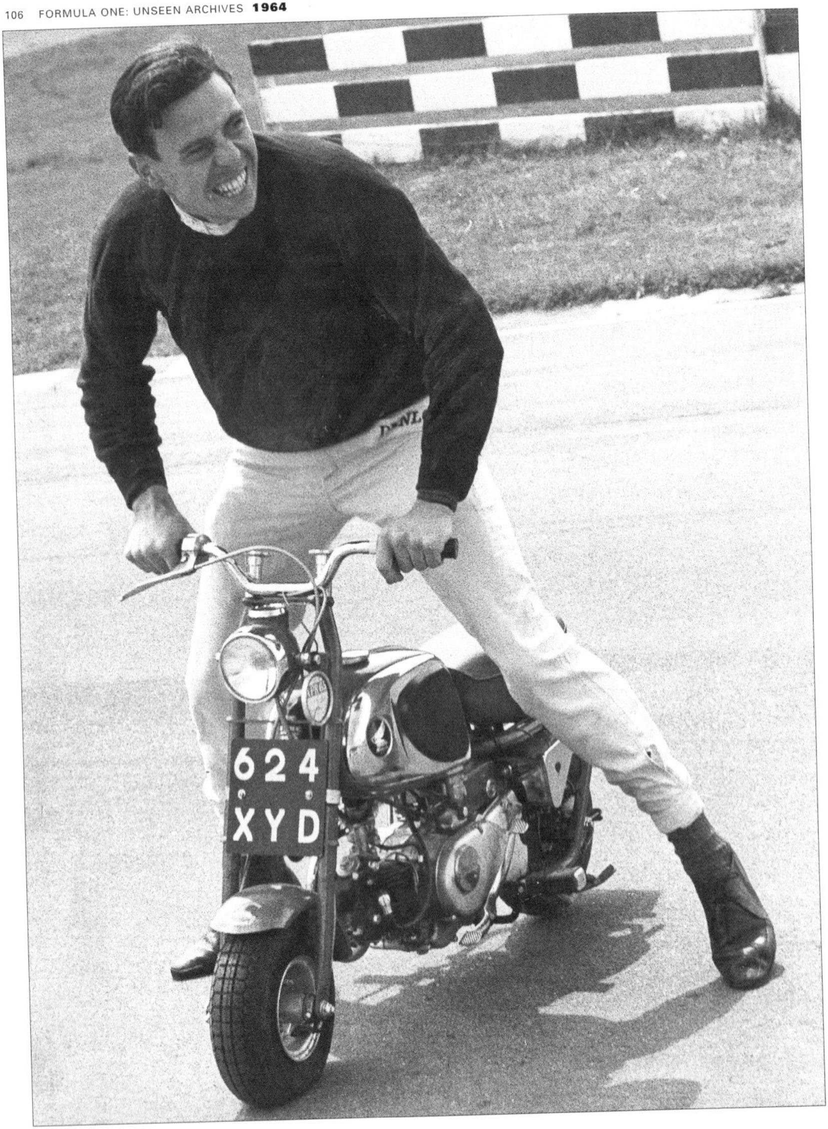
624
XYD

1964
Surtees wins on four wheels

1964 saw the closest championship race for years, with three British drivers vying for the title as the circus reached its final stop in Mexico. Clark and Hill were again in the shake-up, both looking to take their second world crown. The third contender was the man who had seven motorcycling world titles to his name – John Surtees. Four years after making his Grand Prix debut, Surtees was in with a chance of becoming the first man to take world crowns on both two wheels and four.

For the 1964 campaign Ferrari had produced a new V-8 engine for the existing 1963-model chassis. It was hoped that this hardware, together with Surtees's burgeoning skills at the wheel, would prove to be a match for the British teams which had dominated the previous two seasons.

Mike Hailwood off the mark

The early steps were faltering ones, Surtees retiring in three of the first four rounds of the championship. His only success was at Zandvoort, where he finished a distant second behind Clark – although he was at least the only driver in the field that the Scot failed to lap!

Earlier, in the traditional Monaco curtain-raiser, it had been another motorcycling ace, Mike Hailwood, who made his mark. He finished sixth to claim his first championship point.

At Spa there were several dramatic reverses of fortune. Dan Gurney looked set to give Brabham maximum points, but ran out of fuel with victory tantalisingly close. Graham Hill profited from the situation, but only briefly, for the BRM's fuel pump failed. Bruce McLaren now found himself in front, but there was to be one final twist as he, too, ran out of fuel, his car spluttering to a halt 100 yards from the finishing line. Jim Clark was the unlikely winner of the race – and he ran out of gas on the slowing-down lap!

British Grand Prix at Brands Hatch

Gurney made up for his disappointment in Belgium by winning the French Grand Prix at Rouen. Hill was second, and Gurney's team boss, Jack Brabham himself, was third. Brabham was trying to take more of a back seat on the driving side, giving himself more time to oversee team business. But each time he tried to ease himself out of the cockpit and behind a desk, events conspired to keep him involved.

The British Grand Prix was staged at Brands Hatch for the first time. Clark set a new lap record to win the race, chased hard by Hill. Surtees was now back in the points again, finishing third. After his early-season disappointments, Surtees now began a run of solid performances and consistent points scoring. He needed them, too, for at the halfway mark in the series Clark led with 30 points, with Hill on 26. Surtees was well adrift on 10.

Jochen Rindt debut in Austria

Surtees began his surge by winning on the winding 14.2-mile Nürburgring circuit, a minute clear of Hill. All three title contenders were among the host of retirements in the next race, run on Austria's rough Zeltweg circuit. That country's first-ever Grand Prix went to Ferrari's number two driver, Lorenzo Bandini. However, it was perhaps more noteworthy for marking the debut of Jochen Rindt, on home soil.

Surtees on top

Surtees came out on top at Monza, following a thrilling battle with Clark and McLaren. Victory was made all the sweeter by the fact that Clark failed to finish, while Hill didn't even get out of the blocks, owing to a jammed clutch.

Going into the final round in Mexico, Hill now led the table on 39, with Surtees up to 34. Clark was still stuck on 30, but with a glimmer of a chance of retaining the title if he won in Mexico. Hill was clear favourite, though. Third place would have been good enough for him, and that was the place he held until an ill-tempered joust with Bandini's Ferrari saw both cars spin off.

Hill's exit improved Surtees's title hopes, and these were further boosted when the desperately unlucky Clark, leading the race on the penultimate lap, succumbed once more to engine trouble. With Clark out of the race, Surtees moved into third, and was waved through into second by Bandini, where he finished behind Gurney. It was enough to give Surtees the championship by a single point from Hill.

The unsavoury circumstances surrounding the final race cannot detract from Surtees's marvellous achievement. He had become the first man to take world titles on both two wheels and four, a feat which remains unequalled to this day.

Left: Graham Hill at Spa, Round 3 of the championship. With a victory and a 4th place already, Hill added to his points tally by finishing 5th in Belgium.
Previous page: Jim Clark takes a leaf out of John Surtees's book and tries his hand on a different mode of transport. After a sedate 15 mph run on the 50cc machine it's back to business at Brands Hatch.

That's my boy...

Above: With two rounds of the championship to go, Graham Hill takes a break in Majorca with wife Betty and children Brigitte, 5, and 4-year-old Damon.

Left: 2-year-old Garry Brabham gets an impressive if predictable present from his father. On the track Jack was again outscored by his American team-mate Dan Gurney.

Romance of the track

Right: After a decade of single-minded
determination on the track, Stirling Moss
finds time for romance. He is pictured on his
wedding day.

Below: John Surtees during practice for the
British Grand Prix. He finished 3rd in the
race, and at that point had amassed just 10
points from the first five rounds of the
championship.

Opposite top: Jackie Stewart's performances in
Formula 2 caught the eye of many teams. He
chose to make the step up to Formula 1 in
1965 at BRM.

Opposite bottom: Dan Gurney jousts with Jim
Clark in the early stages of the British Grand
Prix. Gurney's Brabham hit trouble and
finished well down the field; Clark led for the
entire 80-lap distance.

Titanic battle

Above: A crowd of over 100,000 witnesses a titanic battle between Clark and Hill at Brands Hatch.

Opposite top: Jim Clark during practice for the British Grand Prix. Victory in the race extended his lead over Graham Hill to four points at the halfway mark. Reliability problems meant that Clark's season fizzled out thereafter.

Opposite bottom: Clark takes the chequered flag 2.8 seconds ahead of Graham Hill's BRM in the British Grand Prix.

Great rivals first and second

Opposite top: Graham Hill pulls out all the stops during practice for the British Grand Prix at Brands Hatch. He takes a place on the front row of the grid, with Clark on pole. The two great rivals finish the race in that order.

Opposite below: All smiles as Clark gives the thumbs up to his hordes of fans. The dignitaries involved in the presentation ceremony include Earl Mountbatten (right).

Above: Graham Hill tries not to take offence as his 4-year-old son Damon tries a miniature Lotus for size. Damon's hero is Lotus driver and dad's big rival, Jim Clark. At least Hill senior can be confident that the 20cc replica Lotus, costing £112, will be no match for his 1500cc, 200 bhp BRM, costing £10,000.

1965
Clark, 'Prince of speed', wins again

Jim Clark had had desperately bad luck in 1964, lack of reliability undoubtedly costing him his second world title. But in 1965 he managed to finish in six races - the crucial number, for the championship was once again decided on the best six finishes in a ten-event series. Not only was the Lotus's reliability better, but it was also fitted with a new and more powerful 32-valve version of the Coventry-Climax engine. These two factors combined made Clark unstoppable in the 1965 championship.

Stewart the rising star

The South African Grand Prix had been held over to New Year's Day to provide the first race of 1965, instead of the finale to the 1964 season. Clark immediately set the tone for a series he would dominate to such an extent that the races invariably turned into a scramble for the minor placings. In South Africa, Clark started on pole and also set the fastest lap. It was Surtees and Hill who followed Clark home, a reprise of the three protagonists who had contested the previous year's title decider. Claiming his first championship point with a creditable sixth place on his debut was Jackie Stewart. Stewart was a rising star, and had had offers to join Lotus and Cooper, as well as BRM.

Clark was forced to miss Monaco, as the Lotus team was keen to contest the Indianapolis 500. The 500 had not constituted part of the Formula One championship since 1960, and Clark had no great affection for it. Yet he won there, in a record speed and having led for 190 of the 200 laps. Although he was naturally delighted with the victory, Clark could now concentrate on his main goal: winning his second Formula One title.

Graham Hill: 'King of Monaco'

In his absence Hill made it a hat-trick of wins at Monaco and was dubbed the "King of Monte Carlo". Clark went one better in the Belgian Grand Prix, heralding his return to the title race with his fourth successive win at Spa. In stormy conditions Clark led all the way, while Stewart made it a one-two for Scotland. The two men repeated the performance at the French Grand Prix, held for the first time at Clermont-Ferrand. Stewart was fast emerging as future champion material, and in this race another driver destined to scale the heights quietly notched his first points – Denny Hulme. The New Zealander was an established Formula Two driver at Brabham, and was regarded so highly that the team occasionally entered a third car for him during the 1965 series. His fourth place in France was followed by a fifth at Zandvoort, immediately starting to repay the Brabham team for the faith they had in his potential.

Consecutive wins for Clark

Clark continued his devastating form with wins at Silverstone and Zandvoort. The Dutch race was comfortable enough, Clark winning once again from Stewart to make it three consecutive wins there. The British Grand Prix was a much closer affair, however. Suffering a loss of oil pressure, Clark expertly nursed his Lotus home barely three seconds ahead of Hill.

Stewart finishes third

Clark claimed his sixth win of the year at the Nurburgring – and with it his second world title. There were still three rounds of the championship to go, but Clark was already out of sight. It was just as well, for he failed to finish at Monza, Watkins Glen and Mexico. The highlight of these final rounds was Jackie Stewart's fine win in Italy. His victory came courtesy of a mistake by Graham Hill in the penultimate lap, but was none the less impressive for that. He had amassed 33 points in his first season to finish 3rd, seven points behind Hill.

Clark's maximum points haul

But 1965, the last year of the 1.5-litre Formula, was all about one man. Clark's maximum haul of 54 points – repeating his feat of 1963 – established him as the greatest driver of his era. Like Fangio who was so dominant throughout the fifties, Clark had all the natural talents. He was an instinctive driver who was born to his craft. His 1965 world crown and Indianapolis victory saw him confirmed as the new Fangio. Nicknamed 'The Prince of speed', he set a pace that few could match either in practice or in the race.

In recognition of his achievement he was made freeman of Duns, the village where he had spent most of his life.

Left: Jochen Rindt made his Formula 1 debut with Brabham in 1964. The following year, his first full season at the top level, he drove for the Cooper team. *Previous page:* Clark takes the champagne prize for clocking up a ton during practice for the Race of Champions at Brands Hatch. It was the first time that the Kent circuit had been lapped at more than 100 mph. In the race Clark made a mistake and went off the track, one of the few errors in a season full of virtuoso performances.

Reliability problems for Brabham

Above: Jack Brabham in action at Brands Hatch. Reliability problems meant another poor season for the Australian, but he clinched a new engine deal which was to transform the team's fortunes.

Left: Graham Hill looks tired before a Formula 2 race at Crystal Palace.

The Champions have a ball

Right: Jim Clark relaxes at the Daily Mail Race of
Champions Ball, held at London's Park Lane Hotel.

Top and above: Surtees had just three podium finishes in
1965, and finished 5th in the championship. In September he
sustained severe injuries during practice for the non-
championship Canadian Grand Prix. Many thought he
would never race again, but he was back in action early the
following year.

Opposite top: In 1965 Graham Hill finished runner-up in the
championship for the third successive year. He notched 40
points, which had been enough for Surtees to take the title a
year earlier.

Opposite below: 26-year-old Jackie Stewart enjoyed a mete-
oric rise in 1965. A string of fine performances was capped
by a first championship win at Monza.

Clark champion by fourteen points

Above: Jim Clark had recently sealed his 14-point championship win over Graham Hill when the two met up with another famous speed merchant, Donald Campbell. The occasion was the Man of the Year luncheon at the Savoy Hotel, London.

Right: John Surtees arrives in London three weeks after his horrific crash at Mosport. He suffered spinal injuries, a broken pelvis and ruptured kidney, but confirmed that he was determined to return to racing.

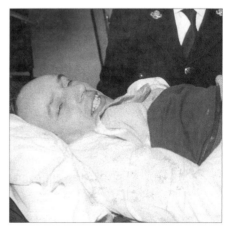

Relaxing in the Monaco sunshine

Above: The Stewarts, Mosses and Bruce McLaren take in the Monaco sunshine before the Grand Prix. Stewart came 3rd in the race, which was won by his BRM team-mate Graham Hill. *Left:* Clark crosses the line ahead of Graham Hill in the British Grand Prix. It gave him his 4th win in five races. He had missed the Monaco race as Lotus wanted him to compete in the Indy 500.

1966
Brabham wins - in a Brabham

Even when Jack Brabham was reigning world champion, he had plans well in hand to form his own racing company. His decision to go off and build his own Grand Prix car didn't endear him much to the team with which he'd won successive world crowns, Cooper. They felt that Brabham had gained a great deal of knowledge, which he would now be deploying in direct competition to them.

The new car made its first appearance in 1962. The following year, American driver Dan Gurney joined the team, and his accomplished driving, together with Brabham's own waning form, had made the Australian consider giving up racing to concentrate on team management.

Denny Hulme joins Brabham

Gurney won two Grands Prix in 1964, but 1965 was a lean year for the Brabham team, mainly down to lack of reliability. For the start of the 1966 campaign, which brought with it the new 3-litre Formula, the team was better prepared than most. The Brabham cars would be powered by an Australian-built V-8 Repco engine that proved to be a model of reliability. After a 3-year association, Gurney also harboured thoughts of setting up his own outfit. He left Brabham to head up the Eagle team, and his place was filled by New Zealander Denny Hulme.

Brabham didn't set the world alight in the early part of the season. At Monaco, in a race with a high casualty count, he fell victim to gearbox trouble. Another early victim was Bruce McLaren who, like Gurney, had decided to branch out on his own. Monaco was the first time that McLaren had run a car under his own name. Jackie Stewart won the race, one of only four classified finishers. His victory gave BRM its fourth Monaco success in a row.

Surtees and Rindt battle at Spa

Very wet conditions at Spa saw the 15-strong field reduced to just seven after a series of first-lap incidents. Surtees and Rindt battled it out and finished in that order, with Brabham in the points but a distant fourth.

From that point on the wins started to roll in. At Rheims Brabham set a record in averaging over 136mph to win ahead of Ferrari newcomer Mike Parkes. Hulme took third that day, and the team went one better at Brands Hatch, Brabham leading all the way to cross the line 1.6 seconds in front of his number two.

Brabham notched his third win in a row at Zandvoort. He took the race from Graham Hill, while Clark just held on for third place from Stewart.

The Brabham bandwagon now rolled on to the Nürburgring. Brabham had never won in Germany, but he put that right this time with a magnificent victory in the wet. John Surtees followed him home, now driving a Cooper-Maserati. Surtees had begun the season with Ferrari, who had produced a very competitive new V-12 unit for the campaign. But simmering friction between Surtees and the Ferrari team boss Eugenio Dragoni led him to join Cooper after his win at Spa. Surtees was to finish second in the championship, driving the rather less impressive Cooper. He may well have gone one better if he had remained with the Scuderia for the entire season.

Three times world champion

As the circus moved on to Monza, however, it was Brabham who had the title within his grasp. He led here briefly, too, before retiring with an oil leak. But those with a chance of catching him also fell by the wayside. Italian sports car ace Ludovico Scarfiotti won the race for Ferrari, but more importantly, Brabham was confirmed as world champion for the third time.

There was another retirement for Brabham in the penultimate race at Watkins Glen. Jim Clark won, his Lotus by now fitted with the new H16 engine. It was the only victory of the series in a frustrating year for the Scot. Surtees took the final honours in Mexico, with Brabham and Hulme occupying second and third places. It left Brabham 14 points clear of Surtees in the final table.

Brabham's third title, in his forty-first year, brought him an OBE. (He would later become the sport's first knight.) After receiving the award at Buckingham Palace, reports emerged that Brabham's car wouldn't start, and he was forced to effect some oily repairs wearing top hat and tails!

Left: Surtees made a remarkable recovery from the injuries sustained at Mosport the previous September. Not only was he back competing at the start of the new campaign, but he won the second championship race at Spa.
Previous page: Graham Hill is welcomed home by Betty and children Brigitte and Damon after winning the Indianapolis 500.

Rindt the number one

Top: Jochen Rindt became the number one driver at Cooper after Bruce McLaren left to set up his own team.

Above: Graham Hill was one of many drivers involved in accidents on the opening lap at Spa. His car was undamaged, but Hill stopped to help his BRM team-mate Jackie Stewart.

Surtees splits with Ferrari

Right: John Surtees began the year with Ferrari, but walked out after a row. He finished the season in an inferior Cooper-Maserati, yet still finished the championship in second place. Leaving Ferrari probably cost him the world crown.

Below left and opposite below: New Zealander Denny Hulme was promoted to Brabham's Grand Prix team in 1966 following the departure of Dan Gurney. He enjoyed considerable success in his first full season in Formula 1 appearing on the podium in every race he finished.

Middle right: Denny Hulme in action in a sports car event at Silverstone.

Friendly rivalry

Above: No hard feelings. A pit lane error caused Jim Clark (left) to think he was leading the Indy 500, when in fact he was lying second to Hill. Clark showed that the two were still best of friends by joining the Hills at their house in Mill Hill for a surprise party. Stirling Moss (right) gets the full story of the race, while 7-year-old Brigitte is happy with a cuddle from dad.

Opposite bottom right: Jack Brabham gears up for the new season, his team's cars now powered by the excellent V-8 Repco engine.

Stewart crashes in treacherous conditions

Below left: 12 June: Helen Stewart accompanies husband Jackie to hospital after his frightening accident at Spa. In treacherous conditions Stewart's BRM went off the track at high speed, one of a spate of first-lap crashes.

Right: Helen Stewart visits Jackie in hospital as he recovers from the injuries.

Below right: Less than two weeks after the crash at Spa, Stewart leaves hospital. He was back in action at the British Grand Prix on 16 July, having missed just one championship race.

Opposite above: There's a champagne celebration at the Hills' house after Graham's victory in the Indianapolis 500. Jim Clark, who was second in the race, doesn't look too upset about missing out on the £55,000 prize money.

Opposite below: Denny Hulme on his way to second place at Brands Hatch behind team-mate and team boss Jack Brabham.

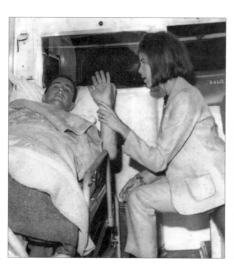

Brabham takes the championship

Right: Brabham's win at Brands Hatch puts him 10 points ahead in the title race. In France two weeks earlier he became the first man to design, build and drive a Formula 1 car to victory in a Grand Prix.

Below: Jack Brabham at the wheel of the Repco-engined car in which he won four races on his way to the 1966 title.

Opposite page: Jack Brabham takes centre stage after the British Grand Prix, his second win of the year. He was now in the veteran class, having turned 40 three months earlier.

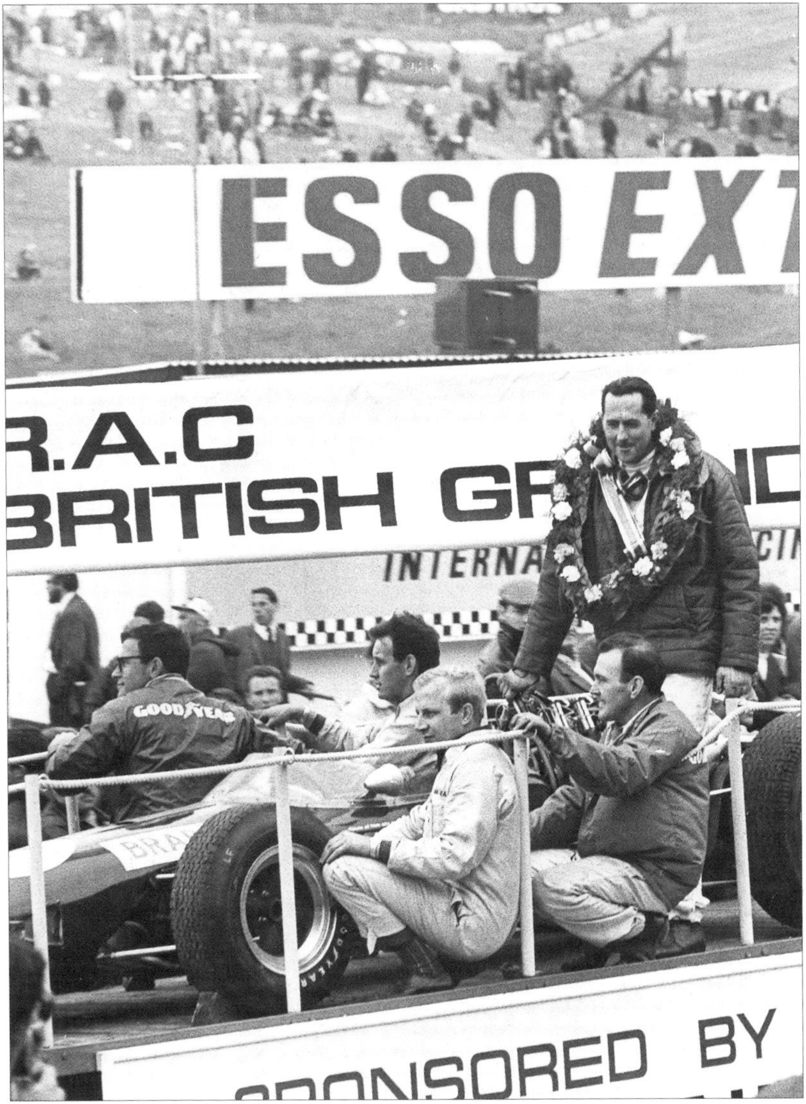
ESSO EXT
R.A.C
BRITISH GR
INTERNA
CIN
GOODYEAR
SPONSORED BY

1967
Brabham first and second

The superiority of the Brabham team continued for one more season. Brabham and Hulme capitalised on the fact that the stunning new Lotus 49 experienced a lot of early teething troubles. The Lotus was the car of the future, but for the 1967 championship the less sophisticated Repco-Brabham was able to prevail. Its reliability was the key, for while the Lotuses along with most of the other rivals were far quicker on paper, the Brabham cars were excellent workhorses and less temperamental.

Denny Hulme, who the previous year had finished fourth in the title race behind Brabham, now stepped out of the number two shadow to pip his team boss in the 1967 championship. It was the first "team double" since Hill and von Trips in 1961. Only Jim Clark would get anywhere near to challenging them, and his chances were blighted by a desperate run of bad luck.

Cooper-Maserati win first round

Unusually, both Brabhams experienced problems in the opening round, at the new Kyalami track in South Africa. But it was typical of the season that both limped home in the points. Hulme, who had led for 60 laps, finished 4th, with Brabham 6th. Privateer John Love almost pulled off a sensational win in an outdated Cooper-Climax. Unfortunately, he ran out of fuel late in the race and had to content himself with second. The race was won by Pedro Rodriguez, giving a flying start to the team he had only recently joined, Cooper-Maserati.

For Hulme the pattern of the season would be solid scoring rather than spectacular successes. He would win just two races in the series, the first of them coming at Monaco. That victory, his first Grand Prix success, must have been sweetened by the fact that he came home over a lap in front of Graham Hill, who had such a brilliant record in the street classic. The result was overshadowed by a horrific crash in which Lorenzo Bandini was killed. On the 82nd lap Bandini's Ferrari struck straw bales and burst into flames. Bandini was trapped and suffered appalling injuries. He died shortly afterwards.

At Zandvoort Lotus finally showed off the new Ford-powered 49 model. It was the car that had enticed Graham Hill to leave BRM and spearhead Lotus's assault on the title with Jim Clark. It hadn't been ready for the first two races, forcing Hill and Clark to compete in the old 2-litre Lotus 33. In Holland it was immediately clear that the new car was something special. Hill led early on, but retired to leave Brabham in front. Clark then came through to register a brilliant win for the new car on its first outing. Unfortunately for Lotus, Hill's experience rather than Clark's was to set the pattern for the year. Between them, the pair were to finish in just nine races out of 22 championship starts. By contrast, Brabham and Hulme grabbed the minor placings at Zandvoort, establishing that team's pattern of being regularly in the points.

Poor year for Lotus

Spa was another typical example of Lotus's ill-fated year. With Hill already out of the race, Clark was leading, only to be forced into the pits with spark plug trouble. Unusually, both Brabham and Hulme retired in Belgium, and Dan Gurney gave his Eagle-Weslake car its first and only success.

In the French Grand Prix, run on the Bugatti track at Le Mans, both Clark and Hill were going well until the Lotus 49s gave out again. The Brabhams dominated the race on this occasion, the boss himself taking centre stage, with Hulme second and Jackie Stewart a lap adrift in third.

British Grand Prix - Clark wins five out of six

Clark enjoyed a trouble-free race at Silverstone and duly won, his fifth success in six years in the British Grand Prix. Hulme and Brabham took second and fourth respectively, with another New Zealander, Chris Amon, continuing to make a name for himself with a third place in his Ferrari.

Normal service resumed for Clark at the Nürburgring: he was out after just three laps with a broken suspension. Hill was faring even worse. His retirement in Germany was his sixth out of the seven races thus far. Hulme and Brabham made it another one-two for the team, with Amon third once again. In the Formula 2 section of the race, young Belgian star Jackie Ickx drove his Matra brilliantly before suffering suspension trouble. Before his retirement, he actually held overall 4th place, ahead of several Formula 1 cars.

At the inaugural Canadian Grand Prix it was much the same story. Clark looked set to win, only to exit with ignition trouble. Brabham and Hulme took the points yet again.

Monza proved to be the most dramatic race of the year. Clark suffered early problems as usual, but this time pulled back a huge deficit, breaking the lap record repeatedly. His amazing recovery took him into the lead, but he ran short of fuel on the final lap. In an exciting final half-lap, Brabham passed Surtees to lead, but the latter retook it at the death to win by just 0.2 seconds. Clark struggled home in third.

Hulme wins world crown with 51 points

It finally came right for Lotus at Watkins Glen. Clark and Hill came home first and second, although even here they both had problems late in the race. Ironically, although it was a good day for Lotus, another solid third place for Hulme enhanced his title hopes still further.

There was another win for Clark in the final round in Mexico, but there was also another third place for Hulme. It was enough to give him the title with 51 points, five ahead of Brabham, who had finished second in the race. Clark had accumulated 41 points to finish a frustrating third. Of the six races where he finished, Clark had won four. Hulme, on the other hand, won just twice, but scored three second places and three thirds.

Clark remained the virtuoso star, but Hulme was undoubtedly a polished performer, thoroughly deserving his moment of glory and place in the champions' hall of fame.

Above: Denny Hulme on his way to second place behind Clark at Silverstone. He won only two races, but consistent performances saw him take the title from Brabham.
Left: Graham Hill gets away from the frustrations of the season by taking to the skies.
Previous page: The Lotus team gets to work on Jim Clark's car at Silverstone. By now the car was fitted with the Cosworth engine, which was to win more than 150 Grands Prix over the next 15 years.

Brabham outgunned by Hulme

Above: The Brabham-Repco dominated the championship for one more year, but this time Jack was outgunned by team-mate Denny Hulme.

Middle: John Surtees continued to drive a Lola-Ford in Formula 2 races, while staking his hopes for Grand Prix success on the V-12 Honda.

Below: Jackie Stewart was BRM's number one driver in 1967, following Graham Hill's move to Lotus. Stewart would soon want away, too, for the BRMs were uncompetitive and unreliable.

Only second for Hill in Monte Carlo

Left: Graham Hill and his wife Betty, pictured before the Monaco Grand Prix. He finished second in Monte Carlo, but suffered a succession of mechanical failures during the rest of the season.

Below: John Surtees joined the Honda team in 1967. The V-12 Honda had great potential but needed much development work. Surtees took joint-4th place in the championship with 20 points.

1968
Clark killed at Hockenheim

The change to rear-engined cars at the beginning of the 1960s had brought with it a welcome improvement in safety, however slight. Only six drivers had lost their lives in the decade to date. The 1968 championship brought two further fatalities, and the year was made even blacker by the deaths of Mike Spence and Ludovico Scarfiotto in other events on the motor sport calendar.

It was fitting that Jim Clark won the opening round of the series, at Kyalami. It was also fitting that the victory – his 25th in just 72 Grands Prix – took him one ahead of the great Fangio. His place in the history books was assured when he took part in a Formula Two race at Hockenheim on April 7th. Clark was killed when his Lotus 48 left the track on a gentle right-hand bend and went into trees. It was a tribute to him that few of his peers could contemplate driver error as the cause of the crash.

Sponsorship arrives

Lotus, the only team for whom Clark had driven, was left to pick up the pieces. Rising star Jackie Oliver was brought in to team up with Graham Hill. Hill had finished second to Clark in South Africa, and it was a stark reality that his chances of winning the title now increased considerably.

Kyalami was the last race in which Lotus sported its famous green and yellow livery. By the time of the next race, Colin Chapman's outfit had become Gold Leaf Team Lotus, and the car was bedecked in red, white and gold. The age of sponsorship in Formula One had arrived.

Spain was back on the championship calendar for the first time since 1954. A pre-race accident put Stewart out of contention for several races, and he lost vital ground which was to prove crucial in the latter stages.

King of Monte Carlo

Hill then further enhanced his reputation as the "King of Monte Carlo" by scoring his fourth Monaco success. After two wins and a second place, Hill now had a run of bad luck which saw him fail to finish in the next four races. The first of these was Spa, where his main rival Stewart returned to the fray. The Scot looked certain to give Matra their first win in Belgium – he was 25 seconds ahead of Bruce McLaren with just two laps left. But he ran out of fuel, and McLaren was able to bring home the car which bore his name for its debut victory.

Although it wasn't to be a successful year for Ferrari and Brabham, these two marques were at the forefront of experiments with rear-mounted aerofoils. It was a trend which would soon become the norm.

Brilliant Stewart at Spa

After his misfortune at Spa, Stewart drove brilliantly in the wet at Zandvoort. On his way to victory he lapped the entire field, except for Beltoise in the works Matra.

The French Grand Prix at Rouen was also run in atrocious conditions. It also brought another fatality, when Jo Schlesser's Honda crashed out of the race and burst into flames. Stewart was less happy with his Dunlop wets here, and finished third. Ickx led for 59 of the 60 laps to give Ferrari their first win since Monza 1966. It would be another two years before a Grand Prix would be won by a car powered by anything other than a Ford engine.

The Lotuses of Hill and Oliver both led for a time in the British Grand Prix at Brands Hatch, but neither finished the race. Stewart was desperate for points, but the circuit put too much strain on his injured wrist and he could do no better than 6th. Rob Walker's Lotus, driven by Jo Siffert, won the race, holding off the Ferrari challenge of Amon and Ickx.

There was more torrential rain and a heavy mist for the running of the German Grand Prix. Stewart was now happy with the special Dunlop rain tyres fitted to his car. There was still the wrist problem, though, and he was acting against doctors' advice by continuing to race. He was determined to continue, however, and in Germany his plan was to get in front so that he could have clear track ahead of him. It worked brilliantly, and he took the flag 4 minutes ahead of Hill. More importantly, he was now within four points of Hill in the championship.

Late surge from Hulme

Engine trouble forced Stewart out at Monza, but Hill's Lotus lost a wheel, so the balance of the title race remained unchanged. Hill then slightly extended his lead over the Scot at the Canadian Grand Prix. Both drivers were hampered by suspension trouble, but Hill managed 4th, while Stewart could only finish 6th. Reigning champion Denny Hulme scored back-to-back wins in these two races, a late surge that would help him to finish third overall this time round.

Second world crown for Hill

US star Mario Andretti was given a works Lotus-Ford for the race on his home territory at Watkins Glen. Andretti and fellow-countryman Bobby Unser had practised at the Italian Grand Prix, but were disqualified from the race for taking part in an event in America within 24 hours of Monza. At Watkins Glen Andretti made an immediate impact, setting the fastest lap in practice. He led in the early part of the race, but was overhauled by Stewart. Watkins Glen became the Scot's third success of the series, but Hill finished second. It meant that Hill would take a three-point lead into the final race in Mexico.

The Matra and Lotus vied for the lead in the early stages of that title decider. It had the makings of going right to the wire. But there was an anti-climax as Stewart's engine – and with it the Scot's title hopes – fizzled out. He finished 7th, while Hill drove impeccably to take the race, and with it his second world crown.

Top: John Surtees on his way to 5th place in the British Grand Prix. Surtees stayed with Honda in 1968 and believed it was only a matter of time before the car was a success. Honda didn't wait to find out, pulling out of racing at the end of the year.
Above left: Despite winning the 1967 world title with Brabham, Denny Hulme joined McLaren the following year. He had teamed up with fellow-Kiwi Bruce McLaren for the 1967 Can-Am series. Robin Herd designed the McLaren car which brought Hulme and team boss McLaren considerable success in 1968.
Above right: Graham Hill's record lap time of 107.31 mph at Brands Hatch earns him 100 bottles of champagne.
Previous page: Denny Hulme leads the way in a competitive practice for the British Grand Prix at Battersea.

Siffert's record win

Jo Siffert's wife lends a hand with the prizes after her husband's victory at Brands Hatch. Siffert's win made him the first Swiss Grand Prix winner since 1949.

Above: Siffert crosses the line at Brands Hatch. Note the addition of the spindly aerofoil. This season saw several teams experiment with "wings" to generate extra downforce.

Opposite: Siffert takes the applause of the crowd after his victory.

Swiss ace Jo Siffert wins at Brands Hatch

Above: The Lotuses of Graham Hill and Jackie Oliver occupy the front row as the British Grand Prix gets under way. Neither finished the race, which was won by Jo Siffert.

Opposite above: Earl Mountbatten takes a draught from the trophy won by Jo Siffert at Brands Hatch.

Opposite below: The new M7A brought Bruce McLaren and Denny Hulme considerable Formula 1 success in 1968. The duo also dominated the Can-Am series. Pictured is the M8A, in which Hulme won the Can-Am championship.

Stewart joins Ken Tyrrell

Left: Jackie Stewart joined Ken Tyrrell's Matra team in 1968. Although he lost the championship to Graham Hill, he missed two races and carried a wrist injury for much of the season.

Opposite above left: Denny Hulme casts an eye over the Chevrolet-powered M8A, which he drove in the 1968 Can-Am races. He beat team boss Bruce McLaren into second place in the prestigious 6-race series.

Opposite above right: Jack Brabham's team went from top dogs to also-rans in a single year. With a hopelessly unreliable new Repco engine Brabham finished just one of the 12 championship races. His new team-mate Jochen Rindt completed two.

Opposite below: Graham Hill on his way to a fastest lap in qualifying for the British Grand Prix at Brands Hatch. He failed to finish in the the race, however.

Below: McLaren breakthrough. The team began the season with the BRM-powered M5A. This was soon replaced by the Robin Herd-designed M7A, powered by the Ford V-8 engine. Both Hulme and McLaren performed well in the new car.

Baby you can drive my car...

Below: Graham Hill (right) and Jim Clark (centre) show themselves to be good sports in a send-up of the Fab Four. *Opposite:* Graham Hill is honoured with an OBE after winning his second world title. Proud wife Betty and children Brigitte and Damon accompany Graham to Buckingham Palace for the investiture. *Left:* 8-year-old Damon Hill gets a close-up view of an OBE as Graham attaches it to his lapel.

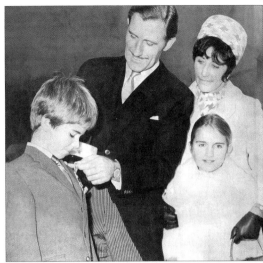

1969
The flying Scot

For Jackie Stewart the disappointment of missing out on the 1968 championship soon gave way to an optimistic view of the next campaign. His runner-up spot had been achieved despite losing points through injury, and that bemusing fuel miscalculation at Spa. With no such mishaps, the prospects for the new year looked good. And they were further boosted by the fact that Stewart would have a new Ford-powered Matra for 1969. The Scot already felt he had the best car around; the new MS80 promised to be even better.

Exit Honda, Cooper and Eagle

Matra withdrew its works team at the end of the previous season, leaving its Formula One involvement in the hands of Ken Tyrrell. Three other teams departed the scene at the end of 1968: Honda, Cooper and Eagle.

Stewart dominated the first championship race, at Kyalami, in spite of the fact that the new car wasn't quite ready and the previous year's car had to be dusted off for the race. Stewart's closest challenge – brief though it was – came from American racing star Mario Andretti. Andretti was continuing his occasional flirtation with Grand Prix racing when other commitments allowed. On this occasion, he was contesting the lead with Stewart before his Lotus gave out with transmission trouble.

Hill and Rindt foiled

Stewart won again in Barcelona, although he needed some good fortune this time. He recovered well after a poor start, picking his way through the field and clawing back lost ground. But his victory was also partly down to some bad luck on the part of those ahead of him. Chris Amon was particularly unfortunate, for he was well ahead when his Ferrari failed him. The Lotuses of Hill and Rindt both crashed out of the race, with the cause put down to the aerofoils that the cars sported. Hill escaped unscathed, but Rindt's injuries forced him to miss Monaco.

The great "wings" debate was one of the hot topics of the year. Most teams had adopted aerofoils, but following the worrying incidents in Spain they were banned at Monaco. Stewart again looked well set, sharing the lead with Amon. But when both retired, Graham Hill came through to score a fifth Monte Carlo success. It would be Hill's only win of the year, and one of the few moments to savour for Lotus, which was an unhappy camp this season. Monaco also proved to be a good day for the independents. Piers Courage, driving a Frank Williams-entered Brabham-Ford, was second, with Jo Siffert, in a Walker-Durlacher, finishing third.

Stewart back in command

The Belgian Grand Prix was cancelled because of a wrangle over safety measures. The circus thus moved on to Zandvoort, where Rindt recovered from his injuries to take pole. He led the race until driveshaft failure put paid to his chances, and Stewart was left to claim a third win. Several cars sprouted "wings" again, although they were smaller and less imposing than those which had attracted criticism.

Stewart was in commanding form again in France. The Scot's latest triumph contrasted starkly with the plight of BRM, whose slow and unreliable V-12 made John Surtees and Jackie Oliver regular whipping boys in a miserable season. Not at Clermont-Ferrand, though, where BRM didn't even bother to enter.

Stewart and Rindt were involved in a ding-dong battle at Silverstone until the Austrian was forced into the pits with a loose wing. This victory showed Stewart's unflappable temperament, for he had had a high-speed crash in practice and was forced to take over team-mate Jean-Pierre Beltoise's car in the race. Both Lotus and McLaren were showing off their innovative four-wheel-drive cars at Silverstone, with mixed results. John Miles had a smooth ride and brought his Lotus home in 10th place, while Derek Bell's McLaren lasted just five laps.

Civic reception for champion Stewart

Stewart was beaten into second place at the Nürburgring, hampered by gearbox trouble. Jackie Ickx won, giving Brabham its first win of the season. Jack Brabham had signed the young Belgian after Rindt decided to depart for Lotus the previous year. While Jack himself had an indifferent, injury-hit year, Ickx was impressive, and was now lying second in the championship with 22 points. Stewart was almost out of sight, though, on 51, and the Scot removed any remaining doubt at Monza. An extraordinarily close slipstreaming battle ended with Stewart just heading home Rindt, Beltoise and McLaren. The title was now his, and a civic reception awaited in Dumbarton.

With the pressure off, Stewart's last three races saw him retire twice, and manage only 4th in Mexico. Ickx prevailed in Canada, while Rindt finally notched his first win in the United States. In that race, at Watkins Glen, Graham Hill was badly injured after a tyre blew on the straight as he was heading for the pits. A long convalescence looked on the cards, but Hill resolved to be back at the wheel for the start of the 1970 season. He made it, but there were to be no more Grand Prix successes in his career. Monaco 1969 was to be the last time that Hill would wear the victor's laurels.

Flying Scot

Top left: Flying Scot. Stewart celebrates after winning the Race of Champions at Brands Hatch in March. Stewart won six of the 11 championship races in 1969 and took the title by 26 points.
Top right: 22-year-old Brazilian Emerson Fittipaldi was a Formula 3 champion in 1969, and already taking the eye as a future star of Grand Prix racing.
Above: The superb new Matra MS80, the car in which Stewart dominated the world championship.
Previous page: Jackie Stewart relaxes with his wife Helen before the British Grand Prix at Silverstone. A 140 mph crash in practice the day before didn't faze the Scot, who cruised to his fifth win of the season in the race.

Aerofoil "wings" failure

Below: Aerofoils were the subject of much controversy in 1969. The crashes which put Jochen Rindt and Graham Hill out of the Spanish Grand Prix were the result of "wings" failure.

Right: Graham Hill wins the Evening News prize of 100 bottles of champagne after setting the fastest lap during practice for the Race of Champions at Brands Hatch. He pours wife Betty a glass.

Opposite above: Jochen Rindt wins a Formula Two race at Thruxton. The Austrian ace also had his first Grand Prix victory in 1969, but it was generally an unhappy year both on and off the track.

Opposite below left: A serene-looking Helen Stewart. Having known Jackie since childhood, she had considerable first-hand experience of the triumphs and tragedies of motor racing.

Opposite below right: Of the eight races that Stewart finished in 1969, he won six and came 2nd and 4th in the other two. He clinched the title with three races still to go.

New car
fit for a champion

Below: Everything has to be just right in the world champion's new car. Jackie Stewart tries the new March 701 for size. Stewart agreed to drive the March after an internal wrangle caused a split from Matra. *Right*: Prime Minister Harold Wilson meets Graham Hill at a Sportsmen and Sportswomen's lunch, held at London's Savoy Hotel. *Opposite*: Six weeks after his horrific crash at Watkins Glen Graham Hill is in jocular mood as he hands his crown to new champion Jackie Stewart. The presentation ceremony took place at the Savoy Hotel, London.

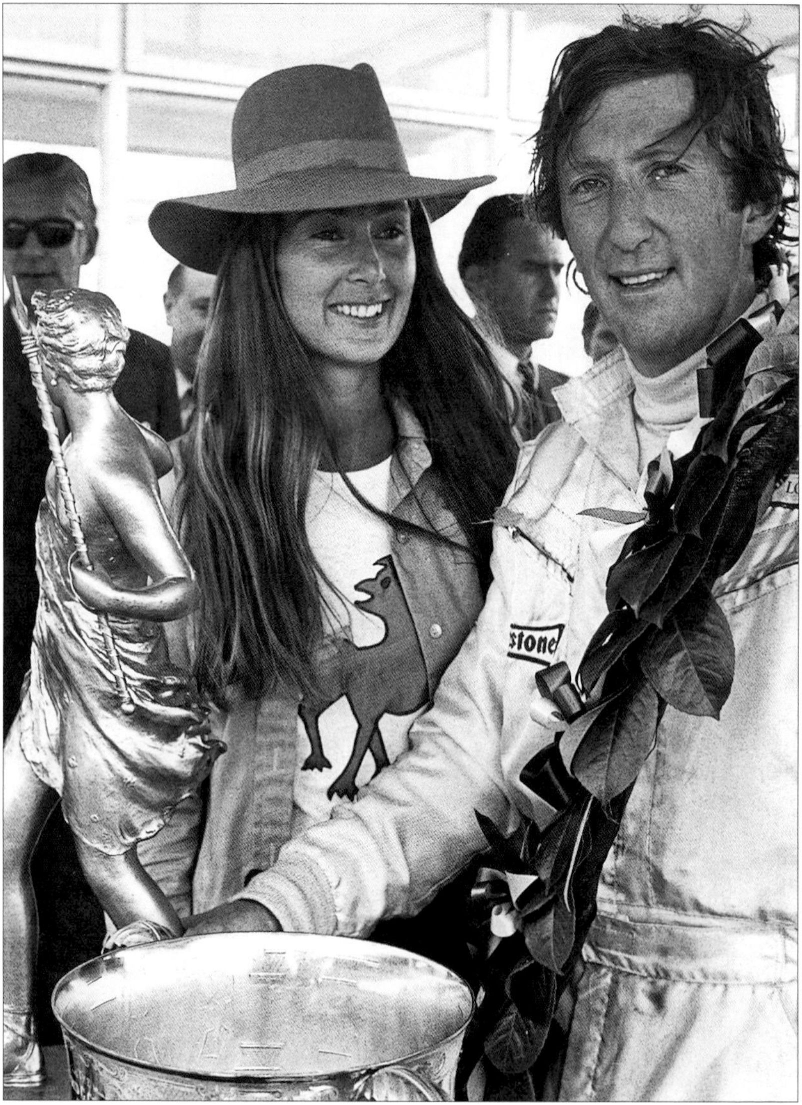
stone

1970
Tragedy for champion Rindt

Jochen Rindt had had a frustrating five years in Formula One. Following his debut in a one-off drive for Rob Walker in the Austrian Grand Prix of 1964, he had spent three seasons contracted to the largely uncompetitive Cooper stable. In 1968 he was a free agent and opted to join Brabham, the team which had won back-to-back championships. He was again unlucky, as the new Brabham car for 1968 wasn't a success. Desperate to emulate the kind of impact that the likes of Stewart and Ickx had made, Rindt moved to Lotus for the 1969 championship. Once again he was unfortunate. There were several retirements, and that aerofoil-induced crash in Spain. After four long years he at least notched his first win, at Watkins Glen, but he still felt that his natural ability should have brought him greater success.

Rindt is the Lotus number one

For the 1970 season the signs began to look favourable. Graham Hill, following his terrible accident the previous year, vowed to race on, but not with Lotus. The pair had had joint status the previous year; Rindt was now the undisputed number one at Colin Chapman's outfit. Chapman had also prepared a new car, the Lotus 72, with which Rindt could mount a serious challenge on the title.

In the opening round, at Kyalami, the Austrian received a hefty bump from Jack Brabham early in the race. He carried on despite the damage, but engine trouble then put paid to his chances. 43-year-old Brabham, now in his 23rd year of racing, enjoyed a splendid win in his new Brabham-Ford BT33. Graham Hill was also as good as his word: he claimed a point by finishing 6th, marking an amazing recovery from the injuries sustained in the United States the previous year.

Stewart races with March

The new Lotus made its debut in Spain. It sported many technical advances, but almost inevitably there were early teething problems. Rindt retired with ignition trouble. The race was won by reigning champion Jackie Stewart. There had been a parting of the ways between the Tyrrell outfit and Matra at the end of 1969, and Stewart was racing the new March 701. March Engineering, headed by Max Mosley, Alan Rees and ex-McLaren designer Robin Herd, thus found itself in the winner's enclosure at just the second time of asking. It was a remarkable start for the new concern.

McLaren killed while testing

Monaco provided a sensational finish. "Black Jack" Brabham was comfortably ahead in the latter stages, with Rindt who had been forced to revert to the old Lotus 49 driving increasingly quickly in an attempt to hunt him down. Brabham got the danger signal from the pits and responded, but Rindt was relentless, and was on the Australian's tail going into the last lap. Under severe pressure Brabham overshot his braking on the final bend and Rindt swept through to victory.

Rindt retired at Spa, a race which saw BRM back on top after several poor seasons. Sponsored now by Yardley, BRM's first success since 1966 came courtesy of a superb performance from Pedro Rodriguez. The McLarens had withdrawn from the race as a mark of respect for Bruce McLaren himself, who had been killed a few days earlier while testing his Can-Am car.

The revised Lotus 72 made a brilliant reappearance at Zandvoort. Rindt took the lead on the third lap and held it to the chequered flag. The Austrian's elation quickly turned to sorrow, however, when he learned of the death of his great friend Piers Courage. Courage's de Tomaso had crashed and exploded in the early part of the race. The news prompted Rindt, who now led the championship, to consider retiring. He decided that a mid-season withdrawal was out of the question.

Three in a row for Rindt

The Austrian extended his lead in the championship by winning the next three races. The first of these was in France, where he came through after Ickx's Ferrari and Beltoise's Matra both hit trouble.

At Brands Hatch Brabham shadowed Rindt for much of the race and succeeded in passing him, only to run out of fuel on the final lap. Rindt, who had all but settled for second place, crossed the line an unlikely winner. But there was more drama to come, as a protest regarding the height of the Lotus's aerofoil was initially upheld, and Brabham – who had coasted over the line in second – was declared the winner. That decision was itself later reversed and Rindt was reinstated as the victor.

It was John Surtees's first season running his own Grand Prix team. At Brands Hatch he showed off his new car, the TS7, which made a promising start before succumbing to engine trouble. Another feature of the British race was the performance of the young Brazilian Emerson Fittipaldi. He had been given Team Lotus's old 49c car to drive and finished a creditable 8th.

A safety wrangle at the Nürburgring meant that the German Grand Prix moved to Hockenheim for the first time. Rindt again came out on top, a narrow winner over Ickx.

Ickx was on form again in Austria, and with his team-mate Clay Regazzoni the pair made it a Ferrari one-two. Ickx was now the clear threat to Rindt. As the circus moved on to

Monza, the Lotus camp knew that a win there would give Rindt an unassailable lead; any other result would leave him in Ickx's sights.

In final practice for Monza, on 5 September, Rindt's luck finally ran out. Feted for his sheer speed in a racing car, but sometimes criticised for a reckless streak which took him too close to the edge too often, Rindt was killed when his Lotus lurched into a crash barrier. He was 28. Lotus withdrew from the race, which was won by Regazzoni in his first season in Formula One.

Rindt posthumous champion

Lotus scratched from the Canadian Grand Prix, too, the first of a trio of trans-Atlantic races which finished the series. Ickx was the only man who could overhaul Rindt's 45 points, and then only if he won all three final rounds. The Belgian succeeded in Canada, and in the final race in Mexico, but he could finish only 4th at Watkins Glen. Rindt was confirmed as the first posthumous winner of the Drivers' Championship.

Above: Not for the first time Jack Brabham planned to retire before the start of the 1970 season. His failure to entice Jochen Rindt to join the team meant that Brabham once again had to climb into the cockpit.
Left: Jackie Stewart and Ken Tyrrell. Both men walked away from Matra International at the end of 1969. They went into the new season as team boss and number one driver in the new Tyrrell Racing Organisation.
Previous page: Jochen Rindt and wife Nina after his fortuitous win at Brands Hatch.

All change at the top

Right: Reigning champion Jackie Stewart won just one race in 1970. His victory in the Spanish Grand Prix gave the new Tyrrell team success in only its second outing.

Below: Graham Hill takes his hat off to Jackie Stewart, the victor in the Race of Champions.

Opposite top: Jack Brabham in action during his 23rd and last season of racing. The 43-year-old veteran showed that he was still competitive, with a win in South Africa and three other podium finishes.

Opposite bottom: Denny Hulme's season started quite brightly. In the new McLaren M14A he was 2nd at Kyalami and 4th at Monaco. However, later that year, he suffered bad burns when his car caught fire during practice for Indianapolis. He was still recovering when Bruce McLaren was killed at Goodwood..

Hill's departure puts Rindt as Lotus No 1

Right: Jochen Rindt (right) enjoyed a much better relationship with Colin Chapman (left) after Graham Hill departed and the Austrian became number one Lotus driver.

Below: Champagne time again as Jochen Rindt wins the French Grand Prix. He was in the middle of a scintillating run of success which brought him 5 wins in 6 races.

Opposite above: Mario Andretti drove one of the new March 701s in 1970. It didn't do much to help him fulfil his dream of making an impact in Formula 1. He scored just 4 points for finishing 3rd in Spain.

Opposite below: A Ferrari mechanic shows that it helps to be a contortionist as he works on Jacky Ickx's car at Brands Hatch. It was to no avail; the Belgian failed to finish.

Brabham running on empty

Top: Rindt leads Brabham at Brands Hatch. The Austrian snatched victory after Brabham ran out of fuel on the last lap.

Above: Running on empty. An unlucky Jack Brabham splutters across the line in second place at Brands Hatch.

Bruce McLaren killed at Goodwood; Rindt killed at Monza

Left: 2 June: The tyre-marks bear gruesome testimony to the accident that claimed Bruce McLaren's life. McLaren was testing his new Can-Am car at Goodwood when it left the track and hit a bank at high speed.

Below: Jochen Rindt and the Lotus 72. Although it brought him 4 straight wins, the new car had many teething problems. At Monaco Rindt reverted to the old 49c model and gave a virtuoso performance to pip Brabham on the last lap. In final practice for Monza, on 5 September, Rindt was killed when his Lotus lurched into a crash barrier. He was 28.

1971
Tyrrell on the march

1970 had been a frustrating year for Jackie Stewart. Early on he had realised that the March was inferior to the Matra in which he'd won the title in 1969. More importantly, it was uncompetitive in comparison to the new offerings from Lotus, Ferrari and Brabham. Even before the end of that campaign in which Stewart could manage only a shared fifth-place Ken Tyrrell was planning ahead. There was a new car under development, and Stewart drove it in the final three rounds of the 1970 series. Although he failed to finish on each occasion, the car looked promising.

By the time the 1971 championship got under way, the car had been further refined, and a second had been prepared for Stewart's young team-mate, Francois Cevert. The ubiquitous Ford Cosworth engines should have put all the teams deploying them on a fairly level footing. In fact, the difference was quite marked. In 1971 Stewart's Tyrrell-Ford proved to be more powerful and reliable than rival machines using the same unit.

Ferrari threat

Ferrari looked a distinct threat to all the Ford-powered cars. The new flat-12 engine had been very successful at the back end of the 1970 season, and it began 1971 in the same vein. Mario Andretti won the opener, at Kyalami, some 20 seconds ahead of Stewart. It was Andretti's first Grand Prix success, and it marked a big step on the way to fulfilling a lifelong ambition.

Andretti had been a superstar of American racing for many years, but he was desperate to reach the top in Formula 1. The reason lay in his Italian roots, and the man he hero-worshipped as a boy, Alberto Ascari. 12-year-old Andretti had been at Monza in 1952 to see Ascari claim his sixth win and his first world title. Before then he had hoped to become a racing driver; afterwards he simply had to be.

Andretti's attempts to make the breakthrough into Formula 1 went back to 1968. His efforts thus far had been frustrated by a combination of bad luck and uncompetitive cars. Signing for Ferrari the team his hero had driven for was the fillip he needed. Informed opinion was that Andretti was champion material in the right car. Informed opinion was right, but after this dream start in South Africa, Andretti would come back to earth with a bump. His day was still several years away.

It was with the Spanish Grand Prix that Stewart began to steamroll his way to the title.

He took over the lead from Jacky Ickx's Ferrari on the 6th lap and stayed there, crossing the line 3.4 seconds ahead of the Belgian. Stewart's third win in a row in Spain had given the Tyrrell team its maiden success.

Stewart dominant at Monaco

The Scot was on form again at Monaco, dominating the race from start to finish. Stewart took the honours, but there were many plaudits for the second-place man, the young Swede Ronnie Petersen. Petersen had impressed as he battled his way past Siffert and Ickx to finish 25 seconds behind the winner in his works March-Ford 711. Ickx took third after Siffert retired.

Bad weather at Zandvoort led to a blip in what was to be a spectacular run of success for Stewart. The Tyrrell had suffered engine problems during practice, and there was no time to set the car up for the wet conditions. Stewart merely went through the motions and trailed home 11th. Ickx, by contrast, gave a masterclass in wet-weather driving and came out on top after a race-long battle with another expert in such conditions, Pedro Rodriguez, in the BRM. These two were a lap ahead of the field.

Rodriguez killed in Germany

The venue for the French Grand Prix was the new Paul Ricard circuit, near Marseilles. Stewart won again, and Cevert followed him home, much to the delight of the home fans. Emerson Fittipaldi put up a great show in third place. He carved his way through the field but just failed to catch the Frenchman.

Before the next race, at Silverstone, Pedro Rodriguez was killed in a minor sports car event in Germany. He had won only twice in his eight-year career in Formula 1, but he was regularly in the points. A fine driver, particular in distance sports car racing and in wet conditions.

Clay Regazzoni, the greatest talent to emerge in 1970, took pole at Silverstone, and led in the early stages. Stewart then took over, and as so often, dominated from the front. Petersen gave another fine showing to finish second, half a minute behind the Scot. Fittipaldi finished third once again.

The Nürburgring brought another top two finishes for Tyrrell. Stewart won, but Cevert had the honour of setting the fastest lap. Ickx was Stewart's closest rival, as he had been in 1969, but he still only had a theoretical chance of catching the Scot. Stewart crashed out of the Austrian Grand Prix, but Ickx also failed to finish. It meant that on one of his few unsuccessful days Stewart had made sure of his second world title. Jo Siffert won the race for BRM. The Swiss driver's second ever win had been a while in coming, for his first success had come in the British Grand Prix of 1968.

Two Austrians made their first Formula 1 appearance on home territory. One was Helmut Marko, who drove a steady but unremarkable race to finish 11th. The other fared rather worse, retiring in his rented March-Ford after just 20 laps. His name: Niki Lauda.

Thrilling duel

Stewart was out of luck again at Monza in a race that was memorable for its blanket finish. Just 0.61 seconds covered the first five cars across the line. It was Peter Gethin who squeaked home first in the tightest Grand Prix finish ever. He had begun the season with McLaren but had had an unhappy time of it and had just moved to BRM. Petersen, Cevert and Howden Ganley were three of the others in the shake-up, finishing 2nd, 3rd and 5th respectively.

With the title in the bag, Stewart's season seemed to be fizzling out. In the penultimate round in Canada, however, he got the better of a thrilling duel with Petersen. Conditions were terrible and the race was halted after 64 of the scheduled 80 laps. The blond Swede had edged in front on several occasions but had to settle for second in the end.

Stewart had enjoyed six wins on his way to the title. The final race at Watkins Glen added icing to the cake for the Tyrrell team. Francois Cevert took the lead from Stewart on the 14th lap and held on to win from Siffert and Petersen. He became the first Frenchman to win a Grand Prix since Maurice Trintignant's victory in Monaco in 1958. It also meant that Tyrrell had won seven of the eleven championship rounds.

Petersen and Cevert were undoubtedly the two finds of the season. They finished second and third in the final table, with 33 and 26 points respectively. The fact that Stewart had garnered 62 points underlines how far ahead of the field he was that year.

The season finished on another tragic note. In a specially arranged Grand Prix at Brands Hatch Jo "Seppi" Siffert was killed when his BRM crashed and caught fire.

Above: Emerson Fittipaldi on his way to 3rd place at Brands Hatch. Stewart won, with Petersen 2nd.
Previous page: Colin Chapman (left) and the Lotus crew check with Fittipaldi on the performance of the Lotus 72.

Stewart concentrating on his second world crown

Right: Emerson Fittipaldi, fifth in Monaco after retirements in the first two rounds.

Below: Fittipaldi shares a glass of champagne with his wife Maria Helena.

Opposite: Jackie Stewart's powers of concentration bring him his second world title and come in handy on the golf course.

1972
Fittipaldi pips Stewart

1971 had been one of the least successful seasons for Lotus and Colin Chapman. The team took its eye off the ball by flirting with a gas-turbine car. Meanwhile, the Lotus 72 proved no match for the Tyrrells, Ferraris and March 711. Emerson Fittipaldi had done well under the circumstances. He was injured for part of the season, and suffered numerous mechanical troubles; yet he managed a second place and two thirds to finish sixth overall in the 1971 championship.

All that was about to change. A lot of work in the close season, together with some eye-catching new livery, and the car was reborn as the John Player Special. The famous black and gold colours would make the car a classic. More important was the fact that it was now as quick and reliable as any of the opposition.

Chapman had spotted Fittipaldi's potential early on, and promoted him to the Formula One ranks after the untimely death of Jochen Rindt in 1970. Chapman knew that if he could come up with the right car, Fittipaldi was capable of doing the rest.

Jackie Stewart won the opening race in Argentina, suggesting that Tyrrell was going to be the team to beat yet again. But Stewart's year was to be affected by a stomach ulcer. It was a mark of the Scot's talent and character that he would still record four victories in the series, but this time that wouldn't quite be enough.

McLaren back to winning ways

Fittipaldi had retired with suspension trouble in Argentina. He then took second in South Africa, behind Denny Hulme. Hulme had got off to a fine start in the title race, his win in South Africa coming hard on the heels of a second-place finish behind Stewart in Argentina. It marked a welcome return to form for McLaren, who hadn't won a race for three years. The team had concentrated its efforts on the Indianapolis 500 and the Can-Am races the previous year. Now, under Yardley's sponsorship, the focus was firmly back on Formula One.

Fittipaldi's charge began with a victory in the Spanish Grand Prix at Jarama. Monaco followed, where appalling conditions caused many spectacular slides. The man who mastered the conditions best on the day was Jean-Pierre Beltoise in his BRM. His victory was to be that marque's last ever success. Fittipaldi had a far from happy race, but he stayed in contention, concentrating on avoiding mistakes. At times he had virtually nil visibility, but his efforts were rewarded by a third place, after Stewart's Tyrrell fell back with wet electrics.

The Brazilian's second win came in the Belgian Grand Prix at the new Nivelles circuit, a race which Stewart's ulcer caused him to miss. The Scot was back in time for the French race at Clermont-Ferrand. He won, with Fittipaldi second. The same pair contested the British Grand Prix at Brands Hatch, but Fittipaldi came out on top this time. The championship was shaping up into a two-horse race. As they headed for the next round at the Nürburgring, Fittipaldi led with 43 points, to Stewart's 27.

Jacky Ickx notches eighth victory

In the German Grand Prix Fittipaldi was chasing the Ferrari of Jacky Ickx, when oil leaked from his gearbox and ignited. Ickx notched his eighth Grand Prix victory; it was also to be his last. The Belgian's team-mate Clay Regazzoni was second, giving Ferrari their first one-two since the same pair had finished in that order two years earlier in Canada. Stewart failed to finish and was unable to make up any ground on Fittipaldi in the championship.

Fittipaldi bounced back in Austria. He took the lead from Stewart at around the half-distance mark and never lost it. He was pressed all the way to the line but by Denny Hulme, not Stewart. The Scot trailed away to finish only 7th and out of the points. Hulme's team-mate Peter Revson finished third, giving him his third podium finish of the year. The Revlon heir had signed a two-year deal with Yardley-McLaren, and was hoping to make an impression in Formula One second time round. He had had his first taste of Grand Prix racing back in 1964, with a few outings in a Lotus. Most of the intervening time had been spent establishing himself in Indy Cars and the Can-Am series.

Fittipaldi now led Stewart by 52 points to 27. The title was nearly safe for the Brazilian, but not quite. The next race was Monza, and as in 1971, Chapman was concerned about competing there. He feared that the ongoing investigations surrounding Jochen Rindt's death might result in a summons for him and the impounding of his cars if he set foot on Italian soil. He eventually received assurances that this wouldn't happen. After all the agonising it certainly wasn't a wasted trip. Fittipaldi took up the running after the Ferraris of Ickx and Regazzoni both retired. Easing off he crossed the line 14 seconds clear of Hailwood.

61 points was now an unassailable lead. With just two races to go Denny Hulme was his nearest challenger on 31. Fittipaldi didn't add to his tally in the final rounds, in Canada and the United States. Stewart finished strongly to win both. That was enough to take second place from Hulme, but he was still 15 points adrift of the Brazilian. The new champion also put himself into the record books by becoming the youngest ever holder of the title: he was just 25 years 273 days.

Surtees bows out eight years after title success

Left: John Surtees bowed out of racing in 1972. His 111 races had brought him six wins and one world title.

Below: Denny Hulme wins the bubbly after setting the fastest lap in the Race of Champions. The Kiwi had a champagne moment in the championship, too, with a victory at Kyalami. It was his and McLaren's first success since 1969.

Previous page: Graham Hill, president of the Midget Auto Racing Club, gets a helping hand from Stirling Moss as he squeezes into one of the tiny single-seaters. In his second championship season with Brabham he scored just 4 points.

Five championship wins for Fittipaldi

Right: Emerson Fittipaldi wearing the victor's laurels, a common sight in 1972. Apart from 5 championship wins, his other successes included the Rothmans £50,000 race and the Race of Champions, both at Brands Hatch, and the Daily Express Trophy race at Silverstone. As a youth Fittipaldi raced motorcycles and go-karts in his native Brazil. In 1969 he came to Europe to further his ambitions, signing up with the Jim Russell Racing Drivers' School.

Below: The natural drama of motor racing has made it the subject of several feature films. For acclaimed director Roman Polanski (right) and Jackie Stewart the immediate theme is pure comedy.

Petersen and Lauda off the pace in the March

Above: The STP March team in 1972 consisted of Ronnie Petersen (centre) and Niki Lauda (right), the latter in his first full season in Formula 1. The March was a poor car and both soon wanted away.

1973
Victory for Stewart and Tyrrell

The same teams and personnel who had battled for supremacy in 1972 were up there again the following year. Fittipaldi and Stewart were the main features, for Lotus and Tyrrell respectively; Ronnie Petersen and Francois Cevert were very able supporting acts for the same teams. Petersen and Cevert had shot to prominence from nowhere in 1971, but both had disappointed somewhat the following year. As far as Petersen was concerned, the March hadn't been competitive, and he was the only one of the four who decided that fresh pastures were needed if he was to make an impact. His move to join Fittipaldi at Lotus certainly strengthened Colin Chapman's line-up, and the Swede's personal performances in 1973 vindicated his decision.

First blood to Lotus

First blood went to Lotus and Fittipaldi as the reigning champion won both South American races. He was rather fortunate in Argentina, for Cevert had held the lead for much of the race. Fittipaldi took over when it mattered, and Cevert and Stewart had to settle for the minor placings. Brazil was somewhat easier, for he led all the way. He hadn't taken pole, however. That honour had gone to his team-mate Petersen, but the Swede failed to finish, as he had in Argentina. Bad luck was to be a recurring theme for him.

After two podium finishes behind his Brazilian rival, Jackie Stewart had his first win, in South Africa. Stewart was already considering retiring from the sport and was desperate to regain his crown and bow out at the top. He did it the hard way at Kyalami, for a crash in practice put him well down the grid. Peter Revson pipped Fittipaldi for second. Interestingly, it was Revson's team-mate Denny Hulme who was giving the new McLaren M23 its first outing. Hulme had taken pole in a machine that was to be very successful for McLaren over the next few years. But while he could finish only 5th in the race, Revson, driving the old M19, took second. Both drivers would race the new machine from now on.

Fittipaldi made it three wins out of four in Spain, with Cevert a distant second. Brake problems did for Stewart in the middle of the race. Petersen also failed to finish, and was again desperately unlucky. He had taken pole, and set the fastest lap as he led for 56 of the 75-lap race. Gearbox trouble allowed Fittipaldi to take a lead which he held to the end.

The great see-sawing battle continued as Stewart now had back-to-back victories, in Belgium and Monaco. Cevert was second at Zolder, giving Tyrrell their first one-two of the year. Fittipaldi finished a distant third. These were the only three to complete the full 70 laps in a race that saw a spate of accidents.

The championship top six

The top six finishers at Monaco was to mirror exactly the final championship table. Stewart won narrowly from Fittipaldi. After four retirements from five starts, Petersen finally had some luck and finished third, ahead of Cevert. The McLarens of Revson and Hulme came fifth and sixth, proving themselves the strongest of the other contenders. Back in ninth place was James Hunt, who was making his debut in a March 731 for Hesketh Racing, the team of the eccentric aristocrat Lord Alexander Hesketh.

Denny Hulme won for only the second time in four years as the Formula One circus went to Sweden for the first time. The New Zealander spoiled the party for local hero Petersen. Petersen had taken pole and led up to lap 78 out of 80. A puncture allowed Hulme to win, while Petersen just held on to take second place from Cevert.

Impulsive Scheckter

It finally all came right for Petersen at the French Grand Prix. This time it was his turn to capitalise on the misfortune of others. The unlucky person in this case was a future champion, Jody Scheckter. The South African was an occasional third driver for McLaren in 1973, and France was only his third Grand Prix outing. The raw talent that McLaren had spotted looked set to make a dramatic early impact. But he crashed out, having led to the three-quarter mark, and Petersen accepted the victory.

Scheckter was regarded as an impulsive, if not hot-headed talent in the early days. This was very much in evidence in the next race, at Silverstone, where he went off on the first lap and took out 13 other cars. Revson won after a restart, with Petersen edging out Hulme for second. James Hunt had escaped the early trouble and was in the points for the second time: his fourth place here following a sixth in France.

There had been no major casualties in the Silverstone pile-up, but tragedy followed at Zandvoort. Roger Williamson's March crashed in flames, and the best efforts of David Purley couldn't prevent another fatality for the sport. Stewart and Cevert finished first and second, and repeated the feat at the Nürburgring.

Monza decides the championship

Lotus needed to respond and they did. Petersen led in the opening stages in Austria, then allowed Fittipaldi through. But a broken fuel line put paid to the Brazilian's hopes a few laps from the end, and Petersen won in spite of the tactical ploy. The tactics employed in the next race were to have much wider implications.

Monza turned out to be the championship decider. Petersen and Fittipaldi were running first and second, as they had in Austria. But this time Petersen didn't allow his team-mate through, apparently on Chapman's instructions. It seemed to be a tacit acknowledgment that Petersen ought to be number one in such circumstances. In the races where he had not been dogged by bad luck the Swede had been consistently quick, and that appeared to be receiving recognition from the team. The Lotuses duly finished first and second, but it wasn't enough to prevent the title going to Stewart. Fourth place put the Scot on 71 points, enough to seal his third world championship.

Revson won the penultimate round in Canada. Stewart had finished fifth in that race, his 99th. He was all set to sign off in grand style in the United States. He didn't make the 100, for he withdrew from the race after Francois Cevert was killed in practice. Stewart never raced again. His five wins that year made a total of 27. That put him two ahead of Jim Clark on the all-time list, and it was a record that would stand for fourteen years.

Petersen won the academic final round, and finished the season on 52 points. He had won four races, but perhaps more interesting was the fact that he had taken nine poles and led in 11 of the 15 races. With all his bad luck he still finished just three points behind Fittipaldi in the final table. It was hardly a surprise that the Brazilian felt the mood of the camp and left to join McLaren at the end of the season, determined to prove he wasn't a spent force.

Above: Leaving for the final race of the season at Watkins Glen are (left to right) Helen Stewart, Emerson Fittipaldi and Maria Helena Fittipaldi. The Brazilian was already certain of finishing runner-up in the championship.
Previous page: Jackie Stewart edges one step closer to his 3rd world title by winning the German Grand Prix. Helen adds her congratulations.

Disappointment for Fittipaldi

Right: Smiling and relaxed: the reigning champion began the defence of his title with 3 wins from the first 4 races.

Below left: Watch your back. The season which started so well for Fittipaldi turns to disappointment as Lotus swings its efforts behind Ronnie Petersen (right).

Below right: Denny Hulme at the Nürburgring, where he finished well down the field. His 6th season at McLaren produced one victory, in Sweden.

Opposite: Helen Stewart will soon be able to dispense with the clipboard and stopwatch as husband Jackie decides to retire from motor racing at the top.

1974
McLaren's first world title

A world energy crisis was the backdrop for the 1974 championship. The whole series looked to be under threat at one point, but those concerns turned out to be misplaced and fans were treated to a dramatically close race for the title. No fewer than seven different drivers took the top spot on the podium during the course of the season, with three men still in with a chance of winning the championship going into the final race.

The drivers' merry-go-round was as active as ever in the close season. Fittipaldi's acrimonious split with Lotus saw him move to McLaren, a team now backed by Texaco and Marlboro. There he joined forces with Denny Hulme, now in his seventh year with the team. The Brazilian's Lotus berth was taken by Jacky Ickx, with Ronnie Petersen staying on there.

Perhaps the most interesting changes were at Ferrari. Clay Regazzoni had spent three seasons at Ferrari, before joining BRM for what proved to be a dismal 1973 campaign. There he teamed up with Niki Lauda, with whom he struck up a good working relationship. Regazzoni and Lauda between them accumulated just five points in 1973. Ferrari hardly fared much better with Jacky Ickx and Arturo Merzario at the helm. The team was keen for Regazzoni to return to the fold, and Lauda made the decision to go with him.

Denny Hulme's swansong

The veteran Denny Hulme took the opening honours in Argentina, in what was to be the New Zealander's swansong year. He came by the final win of his long career rather fortuitously, however. Local hero Carlos Reutemann had led virtually all the way in the impressive Gordon Murray-designed Brabham BT44. But luck deserted him two laps from the line when he ran out of fuel.

On home territory in Brazil it was Fittipaldi who prevailed. Like his team-mate Hulme, he had a slice of luck. A tight mid-race tussle with Petersen ended when the Swede suffered a puncture. Fittipaldi must have enjoyed giving Lotus an early sign that they had made a mistake in effectively switching their primary allegiance to Petersen the previous year. As far as McLaren was concerned, it simply meant back-to-back wins as the circus moved to South Africa.

Carlos Reutemann had held the lead in both of the first two races. It finally all went right for him at Kyalami, and he claimed his maiden Grand Prix victory. The race was overshadowed by the death of Peter Revson in practice. Revson had enjoyed some success in partnering Denny Hulme at McLaren the previous year.

Lauda and Regazzoni scored a one-two success for Ferrari in the Spanish Grand Prix. It was all smiles then, but as the season developed successfully for both drivers, there would be the same kind of ill feeling that had been generated at Lotus the year before.

Quiet start for Scheckter

Regazzoni led for the first half of the Belgian Grand Prix, having taken pole. But it was Fittipaldi who won, a fraction of a second ahead of Lauda, with Regazzoni back in fourth. In third place that day was Jody Scheckter. Scheckter had made a quiet start, his third place in Belgium followed a fifth in Spain but he was to play a part in the final shake-up for the title.

Ronnie Petersen became the fifth different winner in six races when he came out on top at Monaco. His victory in Monte Carlo coincided with Lotus's decision to revert to the ageing but competitive 72 model. The team had trialled the new 76 in the previous three races, but it had been a huge disappointment. Scheckter took second in Monaco, while Regazzoni continued his impressively consistent form by finishing fourth.

The see-sawing theme to the season continued in Sweden, with Scheckter and Depailler giving Tyrrell their first win. Neither Ferrari finished that day, but the Scuderia bounced back in the Dutch Grand Prix, where Lauda once again led Regazzoni home.

Third pole in a row for Lauda

The Ferrari 312B3s were up there again in the French Grand Prix. Lauda took pole and led in the early stages. But Petersen took over on lap 17 and stayed in front for the remainder of the 80-lap race. Lauda then took his third pole in a row at Brands Hatch. He led for 69 of the 75 laps, but he delayed coming into the pits for a tyre change and suffered a puncture. Jody Scheckter was the man to profit from Lauda's miscalculation, the South African holding off Fittipaldi for the remaining six laps of the race.

Lauda was earning himself the reputation of being the quickest driver around. Of the 15 championship races he would take pole position no less than nine times. But his rise to prominence had been relatively swift and the season would reveal other crucial mistakes which a more experienced driver wouldn't have made. In fact, the next error came in the very next race, at the Nürburgring. The Austrian failed to warm up his tyres, and his race ended on the first lap in a bump involving Scheckter. The South African still went on to finish second, but the race was comfortably won by Regazzoni.

Regazzoni in the lead

With four races to go Regazzoni led the table with 44 points, to Lauda's 38. The Swiss driver would later point this out in defence of his view that the team should have swung behind his tilt for the title. The fact that Ferrari didn't share this view was to have major repercussions. Lauda retired from the Austrian Grand Prix; Regazzoni finished fifth. Carlos Reutemann gave the Brabham another success at Osterreichring, having dominated the race.

It was at Monza that Ferrari went into self-destruct mode. Lauda led for 30 laps, then Regazzoni for 10. Regazzoni felt that Lauda was in a position to cover him and give him the best possible chance of picking up maximum points. As things turned out, both Ferrari drivers went all out to win and both retired with engine trouble. To make matters worse, three of the Ferrari pair's chief rivals took the top honours: Petersen, Fittipaldi and Scheckter, who finished in that order.

Fittipaldi wins the title in the final race

Lauda made another costly mistake in the penultimate race in Canada. He shot into the lead and held it up to the three-quarter distance. But he skidded out of the race and allowed Fittipaldi to win. Regazzoni was again critical of Lauda's tactics, particularly as it meant that the Brazilian had now drawn level with him going into the final round at Watkins Glen.

Jody Scheckter also had a slender chance of taking the title. But that disappeared when he failed to finish in the United States. It was thus a straight fight between Fittipaldi and Regazzoni. Regazzoni experienced terrible handling problems. He only needed to finish ahead of Fittipaldi to take the title, but in a car he later descibed as "uncontrollable" that was never going to happen. Reutemann won the race, but Fittipaldi's fourth place was enough to bring him his second championship.

Above: Lauda in action at Brands Hatch. Going into the race he led the championship by 4 points from his Ferrari team-mate Regazzoni.
Previous page: James Hunt and fiancée, ex-model Susie Miller.

Lauda off the mark in the Spanish Grand Prix

Right: 25-year-old Niki Lauda and the Ferrari 312B3 was the quickest combination on the circuit in 1974. The first two of his 25 Grand Prix wins came during this season. He won his first Grand Prix in Spain at Jarama. He was followed home by team-mate Regazzoni.

Below: James Hunt looking mean and moody astride a motorcycle. A volatile character, he had already earned himself the nickname "Hunt the Shunt" for the many prangs he had been involved in. Hunt emerged as the natural successor to Jackie Stewart as Britain's top racing driver.

Fittipaldi and McLaren

Top: Emerson Fittipaldi joined McLaren in 1974. His second world title and McLaren's first came after the closest championship for a decade.

Above: Turning point. Lauda led at Brands Hatch when a puncture forced him into the pits. There he was impeded by an official's car. Instead of winning, he finished only 5th.

US Grand Prix decides the title

Opposite above: Exchanging their racing gear for cricketing whites are Jody Scheckter (left), Denny Hulme (third left) and Peter Gethin (right). The occasion is the annual charity match between the drivers and the Lord's Taverners. Helen Stewart captures on film the highlights of the event, which the drivers lost.

Opposite below: Scheckter and the Ford-powered Tyrrell 007. The South African was one of three drivers who went into the final round with a chance of taking the title. He retired on lap 44 leaving Fittipaldi, who finished in fourth place, to secure the title.

Above: Ronnie Petersen plays chauffeur to Jacky Ickx in the run-up to the British Grand Prix. Despite the smiles, the two Lotus drivers had had 10 retirements between them in the first 9 rounds of the championship.

Scheckter wins British Grand Prix for Tyrrell

Above right: Jody Scheckter takes the trophy and the applause after winning at Brands Hatch, his second victory of the season. Delighted team boss Ken Tyrrell (right) joins in the celebrations.

Right: Before turning his attention to motor sport, Jackie Stewart was a British shooting champion. He shows wife Helen some of the finer points, but she declares it all very dull compared with motor racing.

Above: Jacky Ickx captured in reflective mood during practice for the British Grand Prix. He qualified only 12th, but finished 3rd, equalling his best performance of the season.

Opposite: James and Susie Hunt on their wedding day.

1975
Lauda takes title from Fittipaldi

Niki Lauda and Clay Regazzoni both stayed at Ferrari for 1975. The latter was now the clear number two, something which must have irked him somewhat. Regazzoni felt that if Ferrari and Lauda had swung behind his bid for the title in 1974, he would have been going into the new campaign as reigning champion. As for Lauda, he was just as quick, but a year older and wiser. He was determined to learn from his mistakes of the previous year. In fact, he was totally focused on winning the world crown.

Fittipaldi made a strong start in defence of his title. He won in Argentina, and followed it up with a second place in Brazil. It could have been very different, though. Jean-Pierre Jarier was so nearly the early pace-setter. He stunned everyone by taking pole in his Shadow in both races. Unfortunately, he didn't get a start in Argentina, the car failing him on the warm-up lap; and in Brazil he was leading till eight laps from home, when his fuel metering unit gave out.

Turning point of the season

Ferrari had had a quiet start. Lauda and Regazzoni had just squeezed into the points in both South American races, but already they were behind their arch-rival Fittipaldi. However, for the third race of the series, at Kyalami, Ferrari played its ace: the new 312T model made its debut. Designed by Mauro Forghieri, the new car had a transverse gearbox which improved weight distribution. Ferrari didn't win in South Africa, that honour went to Jody Scheckter but it was the crucial turning point of the season. The teething problems were relatively minor. Lauda, who finished fifth in the race, enthused over its handling.

Both Ferraris were on the front row in Spain, but they were prevented from setting the pace. Lauda's race was over almost as soon as it started, following a shunt from Mario Andretti. Regazzoni also got caught up in the ensuing chaos. Worse was to follow later in the race. The spate of accidents had taken out many of the cars, and Embassy Racing's Rolf Stommelen found himself an unlikely leader. Then, on the 25th lap, his car somersaulted over a barrier and killed four spectators. Earlier, practice had been disrupted when the Grand Prix Drivers Association lodged a protest about the safety of the circuit, particularly the barriers. Those fears were now tragically realised. The race was stopped soon after the incident and half points were awarded. Jochen Mass had been leading, from Ickx and Reutemann. Montjuich Park, 1975 did yield an interesting statistic for the annals of the sport: Lella Lombardi became the first woman to score a championship point. Her sixth place gave her half a point in the revised scoring.

Lauda makes a charge

Lauda's charge began in earnest at Monaco. He enjoyed a three-second win over Fittipaldi that day, and followed it up with slightly more comfortable winning margins over Scheckter and Reutemann in Belgium and Sweden respectively. He had to settle for second place in the Dutch Grand Prix, however. On a drying track James Hunt made a brave decision with his Hesketh's tyres and it earned him a narrow one-second win over the Austrian. Hesketh's triumph was to be short-lived, for the cost of running a team without a major sponsor was proving impossible. Hesketh was forced to quit at the end of the year, and although the name carried on, it wouldn't be such a force again.

Lauda avenged that defeat in France, edging out Hunt. There was only a couple of seconds in it at the finish, but Lauda had dominated, having taken pole and led from lap 1 to lap 54. Silverstone was the next venue, a race which was also curtailed. A heavy downpour caused a dozen cars to slide off. Of the top six finishers, only two were still running when the red flag was waved. Fittipaldi was ahead at the time.

Williams' team in the points

Lauda suffered a puncture in Germany, which meant only a third-place finish, well behind Reutemann and Jacques Laffite in the Williams. Laffite's second place provided a welcome boost to Frank Williams' outfit, which was striving to keep its head above water at the time.

There was more bad weather for the Austrian Grand Prix. Mark Donohue, of the Penske team, had already lost his life in the warm-up. The race itself had a courageous and popular winner in Vittorio Brambilla, although he too crashed over the line in his works March. Half points were again awarded for the curtailed event.

Regazzoni got the better of his team-mate for only the third time in the season at Monza, the penultimate race. But Lauda's third place was enough to put him out of sight as far as the championship was concerned. He capped it with another victory, his fifth, in the final round at Watkins Glen. That put him 19.5 points clear of Fittipaldi.

Single-minded Lauda takes the title

Lauda was phlegmatic about his achievement; for him it was the natural outcome for the effort he and the team had invested. Regazzoni had a somewhat different view. He felt that Lauda's driven, single-minded attitude had been the key, and that was what other aspiring champions had to emulate.

1975 ended on a sad note, with the death of Graham Hill and several members of his Embassy Racing team. Hill had run the team for two years, and had announced that he was retiring in order to concentrate on management. In November, he was piloting the light aircraft bringing the team home from Paul Ricard. The plane crashed in fog near Elstree airfield. Along with Hill and several members of the crew, the talented young driver Tony Brise lost his life. Hill had left his mark on the sport. He was the only driver to have won the world title, the Indianapolis 500 and Le Mans. His 176 Grands Prix was also a record, one which would stand until 1990, when Ricardo Patrese set a new mark.

Above: James Hunt, who drove for Hesketh in the 1975 season, gives a few pointers on driving technique. Hunt's only win of the year was in the Dutch Grand Prix.
Previous page: Jacky Ickx (left) and Ronnie Petersen, Lotus team-mates in 1975. It was a poor year for Lotus wiho scored no victories. Ickx made their only two podium finishes.

Advice from the best

Opposite: In 1975 Jody Scheckter (left) was in his second year with the Tyrrell-Ford team. Who better to offer advice than Jackie Stewart, winner of two world titles for Ken Tyrrell's team.

Below left and right: Jody Scheckter is the focus of attention for the photographers. It wasn't a great season for the South African; he had just 3 podium finishes in the 14-race series.

Left: Hunt finished a creditable fourth in the world championship, pointing the way to better things to come. In his Hesketh car he achieved a total of thirty-three points.

Hill and his team killed in plane tragedy

Left and below: Officials examine the wreckage of the Piper Aztec in which Graham Hill and five others died. Hill was piloting the aircraft on its return from Marseilles, where he and his team had been testing a new car. The plane came down in thick fog on Arkley golf course, just three miles from its destination, Elstree airfield.

Opposite above: Niki Lauda and girlfriend Micki de Rauch.

Opposite below: Hunt relaxes away from the pressures of the circuit. At the end of the season he was set to replace Fittipaldi at McLaren.

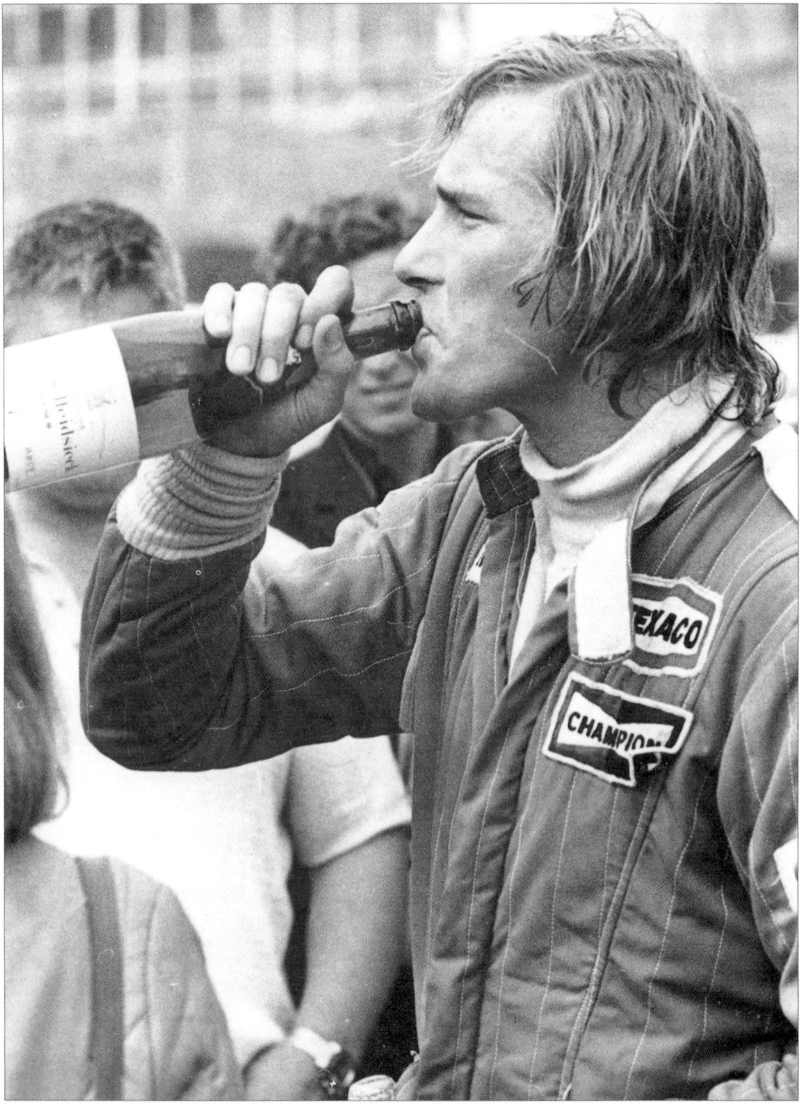
TEXACO
CHAMPION

1976
Hunt "the Shunt" by one point

The 1976 championship turned out to be the closest since John Surtees pipped Graham Hill for the title twelve years earlier. Niki Lauda dominated the first part of the season, James Hunt the second, and there was a final-round showdown between the two in Japan. Those bald facts don't come near to doing justice to the drama on the track, and they don't even begin to address the controversies that raged behind the scenes.

The season began with Lauda in prime form, picking up where he had left off the year before. There were wins in Brazil and South Africa, followed by a second place behind team-mate Regazzoni in the US West Grand Prix at Long Beach. Hunt, by contrast, had two retirements, and ran second to Lauda at Kyalami.

Hunt, a 29-year-old former public schoolboy, was now fronting for McLaren, who had snapped him up after Hesketh's withdrawal at the end of 1975.

The season's first big drama was played out in the fourth round, at Jarama. Lauda was again the early leader, in spite of the fact that he was still recovering from two broken ribs. The injury was sustained in a vehicle, but not quite a Formula One car: Lauda was at the wheel of a tractor when it overturned. Whether or not he was still feeling the effects of the injury, Hunt overtook him on lap 32 of the 75-lap race, and held on to cross the line first. But he was then sensationally disqualified after it was discovered that his car was 1.8cm too wide. Lauda was awarded first place, and stretched his lead to 27 points. McLaren put in an appeal, but that was to take many weeks to resolve. The decision, when it finally came, was to reverse the earlier ruling and reinstate Hunt.

Tyrrell's six-wheel wonder

It was business as usual in Belgium, Lauda and Regazzoni finishing well ahead of the field. The pair were now running the Ferrari 312T2, a revised version of the car in which they had enjoyed so much success. A more revolutionary change in hardware was taking place at the same time in the Tyrrell camp. They were giving the six-wheeled P34 its second outing at Zolder. Scheckter brought it into a respectable fourth place, and it would reach even greater heights before the season was out. The car was merely flattering to deceive, however, and it was not to prove a lasting success.

Lauda continued his sparkling form in Monaco, where he beat off the challenge of both Jody Scheckter and Patrick Depailler in the six-wheelers. Tyrrell then had their finest hour with their new concept by taking first and second in Sweden. It confounded all the sceptics, but that was to be a very early pinnacle of success for the innovative P34; it would never win another race.

Lauda well ahead

Lauda was third in Sweden. Hunt also finally picked up a point in sixth, having retired in both Belgium and Monaco. The Austrian's lead now stood at a massive 47 points, and it is doubtful that the bookmakers were accepting any fresh bets on his retaining the title. The next race, in France, was the final round in the first half of the championship. It was to mark the turning point in the respective fortunes of the pair. Hunt won at Paul Ricard, while Lauda had his first piece of bad luck of the year, mechanical trouble forcing him out of the race. It was immediately after this win that Hunt and McLaren received the welcome news regarding the Spanish Grand Prix. Lauda's lead was suddenly reduced to 27 points.

The championship had been split into two halves since 1968, with drivers having to derive points from a stipulated number of races in each half. In 1976 it was the best seven results from the eight races which made up the first half of the season, then the best seven finishes from the remaining eight rounds in the second half.

Lauda badly burned

The second phase kicked off at Brands Hatch, with more controversy. Regazzoni tried to get a flyer at the start, and there was a collision involving both Hunt and Lauda. Hunt won the restarted race, with Lauda second. But between the shunt and the restart Hunt had had repairs to his car. Another inquiry was instigated, and two months later Hunt and Lauda received the second vital ruling affecting them that season. This time it went against the Englishman. He was disqualified, and maximum points were awarded to Lauda.

The Nürburgring, 1 August 1976, is etched in the sporting memory as the day that so nearly cost Lauda his life. The dreadful accident occurred on the second lap. Lauda cut a corner tight and ran over a kerb. He wrestled to keep control of the Ferrari but it went into a full spin. The car hit a bank, then bounced back onto the track, where it burst into flames. With Lauda unconscious inside, the car was hit by at least two more drivers. Others then managed to stop and help until the ambulance crew arrived. Lauda was later given last rites, but within a few days he was off the danger list. His recovery thereafter was nothing short of astonishing, and he reappeared in his Ferrari just five weeks after the crash.

Hunt won the restarted German race to put himself within 14 points of Lauda. There were then just two races in Austria and Holland before Lauda rejoined the fray. Hunt was in the points in both, taking fourth at Osterreichring and winning at Zandvoort.

The Austrian race provided John Watson with his first ever win. The victory did cost the Ulsterman his beard, though, after a bet with team owner Roger Penske. Watson would go on to bigger and better things, but for Penske it was to be their only taste of Formula One glory.

Lauda was back for Monza on 12 September, his championship lead now down to just two points. It wasn't vintage Lauda. He was still recovering, and an eye infection was an added impediment on the day. But with incredible fortitude and determination he took fourth place. He was buoyed by the fact that Hunt had retired from the race, so he actually increased his lead. But Monza was more significant for its psychological effect. He had made a spectacularly early return to racing and proved he could still perform at the highest level.

Hunt stripped of points

McLaren now received the news that Hunt was to be stripped of the points from the Brands Hatch race. If anything, it galvanized the team, for Hunt now took back-to-back victories in Canada and the United States. Lauda was out of the points at Mosport Park, and could manage only third at Watkins Glen. Going into the last race, the first Japanese Grand Prix, Lauda led by three points.

Conditions were terrible on that late October day at Fuji. If the surface water on the track wasn't bad enough, there was also fog impeding the drivers' visibility. There was uncertainty over whether the race should be run at all, but the pressures to go ahead were too great to resist. After just two laps Lauda had had enough and returned to the pits. For him the conditions put the race beyond the usual calculated risk. His comment was that he prized life more highly than any world title. Many understood and applauded the decision; some were unhappy and thought Lauda was finished.

For Hunt the objective was now simple: finish in the first three and the championship was his. He led for 61 of the 73 laps, but a tyre change put him back in fifth. With the laps fast running out he managed to claw his way up to third, and held on to take the title by a single point.

Above: Regazzoni's Ferrari is flipped round to face the oncoming traffic. Hunt becomes embroiled in the mêlée and the race is stopped.
Previous page: James Hunt set a Brands Hatch lap record in the Race of Champions in March, then beat it four months later during practice for the British Grand Prix. He went on to cross the line first in the championship race, only to be controversially disqualified.

Read all about it - Hunt's dramatic victory in Japan

Above: Hunt finds out how the dramatic championship-decider in Japan has been reported. Hunt's victory gave him the title by just one point from Niki Lauda who withdrew from the race after two laps because of the appalling conditions. The race was run on a track covered in surface water and in thick fog. Hunt finished the race in third place behind Andretti and Depailler.

Opposite below: Hunt poses with the McLaren M26, the car in which he would defend his title.

Opposite top: James Hunt and his new love Jane Birbeck share a moment of domestic bliss.

Left: Niki Lauda: many understood and applauded his decision to withdraw in Fuji on a waterlogged circuit. However, some were unhappy and thought he was finished.

Come in James - your time is up...

Left: Lauda decides it's time to take evasive action as Hunt's McLaren gets perilously near. The light-hearted moment was in stark contrast to the rollercoaster drama of the championship.

Bottom: Carlos Reutemann (No 7) and Carlos Pace (No 8) remained with Brabham in 1976, the team's cars now running under Alfa-Romeo power. After amassing 61 points between them the year before, with Ford engines, the two managed a total of just 10 points in 1976.

Opposite top: Stars are fans too. James Hunt takes the role of keen spectator on this occasion.

Opposite bottom: Adulation for James Hunt: world motor racing champion.

1977
Lauda repays Ferrari loyalty

Among those who harboured doubts about Niki Lauda's future in Formula One was Enzo Ferrari. He had on his hands the man who had delivered the world title in 1975, Ferrari's first win in eleven years. But he also had the man who some felt had let the title slip from his grasp in 1976. He eventually decided to give the Austrian the benefit of the doubt and confirmed him as the driver to lead Ferrari's attack in 1977.

Lauda's partner for the new season was Carlos Reutemann. The Argentinian, now in his sixth season in Formula One, had four Grand Prix wins to his credit. Three of them had come in 1975, but that had only been good enough for a distant third place behind his new team-mate Lauda in the final championship table.

Scheckter the Wolf

After three years at Tyrrell, Jody Scheckter decided to join the new Wolf team. This new concern became only the third in the event's 28-year history to win at the first time of asking (the others were Alfa Romeo in 1950, and Mercedes in 1954). Watson, Hunt and Carlos Pace had all led in Argentina, but Scheckter took over five laps from home to win from Pace's Brabham. Watson and Hunt both retired, as did Lauda, and Reutemann flew the flag for Ferrari in third.

Ferrari's newcomer did even better at Interlagos. He set the pace from the halfway mark and had a 10-second cushion over Hunt at the finish. Lauda was third that day. The Austrian then announced that he wanted his title back by winning at Kyalami, his first victory since the Nürburgring crash. The South African race was overshadowed by another tragedy. Tom Pryce crested a brow in his Shadow and was confronted by the sight of a marshal, who was crossing the track in order to reach a retired car. Pryce had no time to react and both men were killed instantly.

The race at Kyalami offered an interesting footnote for the record books: when Larry Perkins brought his Rotary Watches Stanley BRM home in 15th place, it was to be the last time that that illustrious name in motor sport would qualify to start a Formula One race.

Before the next round of the championship, at Long Beach, Carlos Pace was killed in a plane crash. He had won only once, his home Grand Prix in 1975, but proved more than once that with the right car he was a competitive driver.

Mario Andretti edged out Lauda by a second at Long Beach. This marked a continued resurgence in Lotus's fortunes. The Lotus 77 had now given way to the 78, occasionally dubbed the "wing car". Sidepods on either side of the cockpit channelled air under the car to create huge amounts of downforce. "Ground effect" wasn't a new idea, but Chapman and Lotus had put the theory into very successful practice.

Lauda mystery in Spain

Lauda was mysteriously missing from the Spanish Grand Prix at Jarama. There were rumours of an injury, but relations between driver and team were certainly cooling and an argument couldn't be ruled out. Lauda could ill afford to miss many races, for the Ferrari 312/T2 was no longer quite so dominant, as the new Lotus confirmed. Indeed it was Andretti on target again in Spain, taking pole and leading for the entire 75-lap distance.

Scheckter gave Wolf its second win of the season at Monaco, a race which marked the 100th Grand Prix success for the famous Cosworth DFV engine. Lauda was second once again. For him the season was a succession of canny races. He needed to show all his skill, too, for there were niggling handling problems with the Ferrari. The saving grace was its reliability. If the car could get round, Lauda had the ability to get in the points, and it was this consistency which was so important over the season.

Lotus's Achilles' heel

The Lotus eclipsed the Ferrari yet again at Zolder, but this time it was Andretti's team-mate Gunnar Nilsson who took the honours ahead of Lauda. The Austrian's fifth podium finish came after an astute change of tyres as he sensed a change in the prevailing conditions. The next race, Sweden, showed the Lotus's Achilles' heel. Andretti took pole, and led for 67 of the 72 laps, setting the fastest lap in the process. Five cars then overhauled him in the dying stages, and the American emerged with just one point to show for his efforts. The French Grand Prix was one of Andretti's good days. This time it was his turn to capitalise on the misfortune of another, namely, John Watson. The Ulsterman had led virtually all the way, only to have the lead snatched from him on the 80th and final lap. It was incidents such as this which earned Watson the reputation for being desperately unlucky during this period in his career.

Hunt wins at Silverstone

James Hunt had been having a terrible time of it, with three retirements and just two podium finishes all season. He was to have more luck at the back end of the season, and it started on home territory at Silverstone. He was involved in a close tussle with Watson for two-thirds of the race, until the latter's Brabham developed a fuel injection problem. Lauda finished second to Hunt; it was almost like old times. But in truth even a big improvement in Hunt's form over the final seven races wasn't going to be enough to put him in the final frame.

One of those who failed to finish at Silverstone was Jean-Pierre Jabouille. He was driving a Renault, that marque making a return to racing after a gap of almost 70 years. The team returned in dynamic style, too, for it was showing off the 1.5-litre RS01, the first turbo-charged car to feature in a Formula One race. Perhaps predictably it was the turbo which gave out and brought an early end to the race for Jabouille, but within seven short years the entire grid would be made up of turbo-powered cars.

Lauda won only his second race of the year at Hockenheim, then in Austria took his fifth second place. That race provided the Shadow team with their only win, with Alan Jones at the helm. It was welcome news after the events at Kyalami.

Another win followed for Lauda at Zandvoort, but the continued success was by now barely masking the discontent within the team. Before Monza where he finished second yet again, this time to Andretti he made it clear that his days at Ferrari were numbered. A fourth place in the next round, at Watkins Glen, gave Lauda an unassailable lead in the championship. Having achieved what he had set out to do, Lauda walked away from Ferrari. A medical problem was one reason cited, the sacking of a chief mechanic was another. There was certainly little love lost, and Lauda signed for Bernie Ecclestone's Brabham team.

Jody Scheckter won the penultimate race in Canada, and Hunt rounded off an indifferent season by winning in Japan, the scene of his finest hour twelve months earlier. Scheckter finished runner-up to Lauda in the championship, but it was Andretti who might easily have run the Austrian a lot closer. He had scored four wins to Lauda's three, but had lost valuable points through a spate of collisions and engine failures.

Left: James Hunt and Jane Birbeck relax during preparations for the Monaco Grand Prix. He retired in the race, the 6th round of the championship. With just one podium finish so far, it was already looking a tall order for Hunt to retain his title.

Previous page: Niki Lauda accepts the International Award for Valour in Sport, in recognition of the courage he showed after his horrific Nürburgring injury. The unassuming Austrian ace is quick to point out that his art is based on skill and practice, not courage.

Lauda makes his move

Above: Monaco, what does the future hold? Not marriage, according to James Hunt. He says that he and girlfriend Jane Birbeck are blissfully happy as they are. Under British law Hunt is still married to Susie, despite the fact that she has now gone through a wedding ceremony with actor Richard Burton.

Opposite above left: Mr and Mrs Jody Scheckter swap the race track for the tennis court at Queen's Club. The South African left Tyrrell after 3 years to join the new Wolf team.

Opposite above right: Niki Lauda during practice at Silverstone. James Hunt beat him into 2nd place in the race, but the Austrian was steadily racking up the points needed to take Hunt's crown.

Opposite below left: Hunt celebrates his Silverstone success with champagne. He was now lying 5th, behind Lauda, Scheckter, Andretti and Reutemann. They would finish the season in the same order 7 races later.

Opposite below right: Andretti took the revolutionary Lotus 78 to four victories in 1977. With greater reliability he would have run Lauda close for the title.

From one champion to another

Opposite: Niki Lauda was well on his way to his second title by the time the circus arrived at Silverstone. Barry Sheene was in a similar position in the world 500cc motorcycle championship.

Right: Jacky Ickx's Formula 1 career was on the wane. Following a huge crash at Watkins Glen in 1976, Ickx made just one appearance for the Ensign team in 1977. He did have his third successive win at Le Mans that year, however.

Below: Carlos Reutemann in action at Silverstone. The Argentinian had six podium finishes during the year but was overshadowed by his Ferrari team-mate Lauda.

1978
Andretti leads Lotus one-two

Niki Lauda officially joined Bernie Ecclestone's Brabham team at the end of August 1977, although it later transpired that the deal had been struck more than three months earlier. Carlos Reutemann was promoted to the status of Ferrari's number one driver, with French-Canadian Gilles Villeneuve filling the other slot. Villeneuve had been taken on for the back end of the 1977 season, after Lauda's dramatic walk-out. A former snowmobile champion, he had made his Formula One debut at the beginning of that season, for McLaren. McLaren didn't take up the option on Villeneuve's contract, however, and when Ferrari expressed an interest, he was a free agent to join the Scuderia.

The team Ferrari had to beat was going to be Lotus. They, too, had one change in their line-up. Andretti was still there but Gunnar Nilsson left to join the new Arrows team. Unfortunately, his career was tragically cut short by cancer; he succumbed to the disease before ever contesting a race for Arrows.

Petersen rejoins Lotus

Ronnie Petersen took over Nilsson's berth at Lotus. The Swede had had a lean time of it in recent seasons, scoring just 23 points in the previous three campaigns. He knew he would be running as second-string to Andretti in 1978, but it was still a wise decision to rejoin Lotus, for it put him back on top, where he belonged.

First blood went to Lotus, Andretti leading from start to finish in Argentina. Lauda followed him home, but the Brabham's Alfa Romeo engine was to be a bone of contention for the entire season. Lack of success was variously put down to the engine itself, the preparation of the cars, and even a demotivated Lauda.

Reutemann then brought Ferrari an early indication that they could manage quite well without the world champion by winning the Brazilian Grand Prix. Back came Lotus at Kyalami, Petersen this time edging out Patrick Depailler's Tyrrell on the last lap.

The season's battle lines were being drawn up between Lotus and Ferrari. Reutemann won from Andretti in the US West Grand Prix at Long Beach. The next race, at Monaco, was the only race in the entire series in which neither Ferrari nor Lotus registered a single point. Petersen and Villeneuve retired, while Reutemann and Andretti finished out of the points. Patrick Depailler, the nearly man on so many occasions, took advantage of the fact and eased home ahead of Lauda.

More improvements by Chapman

Ironically, that race was a turning point for Lotus, for it was the last time that both Andretti and Petersen featured in the 78 model. In the following round, at Zolder, Andretti drove the 79, an improved version of an already impressive car. Colin Chapman's latest idea involved putting the fuel in a centrally-located tank to the rear of the cockpit. This allowed for a narrower chassis, which in turn meant that the ground-effect principle operated even more efficiently.

Andretti duly won in Belgium, with Petersen following him home in the old 78 model. The duo followed it up with another one-two in Spain, although now both drivers were in 79s. The last round in the first half of the championship season saw Lauda score his first win of the season. It was a controversial success, though, for Lauda's Brabham was fitted with a large rear-mounted fan. This was the brainchild of designer Gordon Murray, who was attempting to create the kind of downforce that Lotus was working on but by a different method. The ingenious idea was for the fan to draw air from underneath the car. That reduced the air pressure, creating a vacuum effect which sucked the car tight onto the road surface.

Lauda's victory at Anderstorp prompted an immediate outcry from rival teams. The Brabham didn't appear to contravene the letter of any law, but the spirit was seriously breached. The innovation was immediately banned by the FIA, although the result in Sweden was allowed to stand. The "fan car" never raced again.

After the threat of innovative Brabham had been removed, Andretti and Petersen made it business as usual with yet another one-two at Paul Ricard. Reutemann won the British Grand Prix at Brands Hatch, but he was helped by the fact that neither Andretti nor Petersen finished the race. Petersen was performing in an exemplary manner as number two to Andretti. There were times during the season when the Swede was quicker, but he respected the terms of the contract. In atrocious conditions in Austria, however, Andretti crashed out right at the start, and Petersen came home ahead of Depailler and Villeneuve to score his second and final win of the season.

High Court ban for Arrows

The race at Osterreichring was notable for the introduction of the new Arrows car, the A1. The car with which the fledgling team had started the season had been banned by the High Court. The court ruled that the car was similar enough to the Shadow DN9 to constitute an infringement of copyright.

Andretti was back on form at Zandvoort, so Petersen duly reverted to his usual role of second-place man. As the circus moved to Monza, the title was between the two Lotus men. Petersen crashed heavily in the warm-up and had to start the race in the old 78 model. He was then involved in a huge start-line pile-up. Andretti won from Villeneuve in the restarted race, but they were both sensationally penalised for jumping the start. Lauda thereby inherited his second win of the year. This victory, together with the controversial win in Sweden, gave Lauda a slightly flattering fourth position behind Reutemann in the final table.

Ronnie Petersen dies from crash injuries

Andretti was now confirmed as champion, but the moment lost its lustre when he heard that Petersen, a close friend as well as team-mate, had died. The Swede's injuries had not been considered to be life-threatening, but an embolism had developed, which proved fatal.

Reutemann scored his fourth win of the year at Watkins Glen on his way to third place in the title race.

Villeneuve was a popular home winner in the final race of the season in Canada. 1978 was all about Lotus, however. Petersen, the quickest driver of his era, had fulfilled his contract and finished runner-up as a result. For Andretti, meanwhile, the title was the culmination of a 10-year dream. The realisation of that dream was somewhat tarnished by the death of Petersen, and also, ironically, by the fact that he had won in the outstanding car of the day. The Lotus 79 was indeed a superb car, but Andretti's achievement was none the less impressive for that.

Left: James Hunt and the McLaren M26. 1978 was a disastrous year for both team and driver. McLaren failed to follow the "ground effects" trend and Hunt slumped to 13th in the championship, scoring just 8 points.
Bottom: Alan Jones at the wheel of the 500 horsepower Williams FW06 in the Brazilian Grand Prix. He finished out of the points that day, but the Patrick Head-designed car showed great early promise.
Previous page: Colin Chapman gets some feedback from Mario Andretti after a practice session at Silverstone. Lotus was undoubtedly on the up with its innovative 78 model, the first to employ the "ground effects" principle.

Sponsorship and Andretti take a grip

Opposite top: By the late 1970s, every available space on cars, helmets, overalls and umbrellas is taken up with legends and sponsors' names. Mario Andretti not only kept dry during practice for the French Grand Prix, but went on to win the race.

Opposite below: Mario Andretti won 6 races on his way to the 1978 title, emulating the achievement of his hero Alberto Ascari in 1952. Ascari's 6 wins constituted a clean sweep, while Andretti's victories came in a 16-race series. It was the fulfilment of a dream, coming 10 years after he made his Formula 1 debut.

Right: Lauda finished 4th in the 1978 championship. Worse was to follow, with Brabham in a period of decline. The Austrian ace would soon be complaining of a lack of motivation and questioning his future in the sport.

Below: Jody Scheckter's second season in the Wolf-Ford wasn't as fruitful as the first, but he did enough to persuade Ferrari to sign him as their number one driver for 1979.

Motor racing stunned by Petersen's death

Below: Ronnie Petersen was back at Lotus and back to his best in 1978. Honouring his commitment to run as Andretti's number two undoubtedly cost him points. However, his British Grand Prix ends on the 6th lap with a fractured fuel pump.

Opposite: Motor racing is stunned by the death of Ronnie Petersen, following a crash at Monza. The pall-bearers at the popular Swede's funeral are (left, front to back) Ake Strandberg, Emerson Fittipaldi, James Hunt and (right, front to back) Jody Scheckter, Niki Lauda, Tim Shenken.

Right: Carlos Reutemann wins the British Grand Prix after a thrilling duel with Niki Lauda. Rumours are already abroad that Ferrari are planning to replace the Argentinian with Jody Scheckter. Reutemann's victory doesn't make the team think again. It was the best season of his career, but earned him only 3rd place behind the mighty Lotuses.

1979
Scheckter edges out Villeneuve

Carlos Reutemann may have won four races on his way to third place behind the two Lotuses in 1978, but he wasn't popular with the Ferrari hierarchy. The judgment was that he was talented but erratic, prone to the occasional expensive mistake. It was he who bore the consequence of failure in 1978 and was shown the door by Ferrari.

Reutemann, predictably, asserted that the Lotuses that had beaten him were, quite simply, superior cars. If that was so, his axing from the Maranello team provided him with a golden opportunity, for it allowed him to join Lotus, where he teamed up with Andretti.

Scheckter joins Ferrari

Ferrari went into the new season with Jody Scheckter partnering the mercurial Villeneuve. The South African should have joined Ferrari the year before, but the Wolf team had taken up its option on his services and Ferrari had to wait. The deal was announced long before the 1978 campaign was over.

The season got off to a very disappointing start for Ferrari. Scheckter had an accident in Argentina and managed only sixth in Brazil. Villeneuve fared little better in South America; with just two points for finishing ahead of his team-mate at Interlagos. The star of these opening races was Jacques Laffite and Ligier. Laffite won both, with his team-mate Patrick Depailler following him home in Brazil. The change in fortunes at Ligier coincided with the team switching from a Matra engine to Cosworth V-8 power. Also, among the number of Lotus imitators in 1979, Ligier was probably the team that had best adapted the "ground effect" principle in its JS11 car. The impact was immediate but not lasting.

Williams chase Ferrari

The next two races, at Kyalami and Long Beach, were to be a fairer representation of the season's pattern. The Ferraris took one-two in both, but it was the putative second-stringer Villeneuve who took the top honours. At Kyalami Ferrari's new car, the 312-T4, was introduced. This car wasn't to be without its teething troubles, but they were ironed out as the season went on. It was powerful and reliable, and it needed to be. As the early challenge from Ligier faded, strong opposition was provided by Williams and the turbo-powered Renault.

Back came the Ligier in Spain, Depailler leading from start to finish. Lotus, who had swept the board in the drivers' and constructors' championship in 1978, took first and second at Jarama. It was a rare good day for Reutemann and Andretti. The Lotus 80, the successor to the all-conquering 79, was plagued by problems. Reutemann was finding out the hard way that Lotus had peaked the year before, and he was joining the team at the wrong time. Lotus quickly realised the mistake and the 80 was dropped. That was little comfort for Reutemann and Andretti, for the 79 was no longer the quickest car. It would be three long years before Lotus would win another race.

James Hunt bows out

Scheckter won the next two races, in Belgium and Monaco. These were significant wins, for Ferrari was considering swinging all the team's efforts behind Villeneuve's bid for the title. The short-term gain was thus in the South African's favour. But more significant in the longer term was the debut of the Williams FW07. This car took the ground effect principle to a different level. Alan Jones was winning at Zolder, when a problem with the car's electrics wrecked his chances. Regazzoni then pushed Scheckter all the way at Monaco, losing out by just half a second. It was advantage Scheckter, but Williams, now backed by Saudi Arabian money, was firmly on the march.

Monaco also saw James Hunt bow out of the sport. After his sixth retirement in seven races in the Wolf, the former champion decided it was time to call it a day.

Turbo-charged Renault

At the French Grand Prix it was the other looming threat to Ferrari that took centre stage. Renault's perseverance with turbo-charged cars finally paid off as Jean-Pierre Jabouille crossed the line first in the RS10. His team-mate Rene Arnoux just lost out to Villeneuve for second place. These two had a ding-dong battle, their cars often touching as they passed each other repeatedly. Villeneuve was ahead when it mattered, squeaking home a quarter of a second ahead of the Frenchman.

The opposition to Ferrari became even more intense in the second half of the season. Regazzoni and Arnoux came home first and second at Silverstone. Regazzoni, now 39, thus had the honour of bringing Williams its maiden victory. His team-mate Alan Jones then hit a purple patch to build on that success. The Australian had taken pole and led for 38 of the 68-lap British Grand Prix before retiring with water pump trouble. He then proceeded to win four of the next five races to dominate the latter half of the season.

However, Scheckter was in the points in every one of these races: second behind Jones at Zandvoort, and fourth in Germany, Austria and Canada. That was to prove vital in terms of the championship. For Scheckter was no longer the blood-and-guts driver with plenty of raw edges. There was now more finesse to his driving. He was still quick, but his performances were consistent and measured.

As the championship was to be decided on the best four finishes from the first seven races, plus the best four finishes from the final eight rounds, Jones's superb run wasn't going to be enough to bring him the title. In fact, as the circus moved to Monza only Scheckter and Villeneuve could take the crown. Team orders were issued and Villeneuve duly followed them and protected race leader Scheckter. The South African won the race and with it the championship.

Jones won the penultimate round in Canada. It was in practice for the Montreal race that Niki Lauda followed Hunt's example and decided he'd had enough after a frustrating season at Brabham. Villeneuve rounded off the season with a win in the US East Grand Prix at Watkins Glen, putting him four points behind Scheckter in the final table.

Comfortable first and second for Ferrari

Ferrari had thus emulated Lotus's achievement of 1978 by taking first and second in the drivers' championship and comfortably winning the constructors' title (the points system for the latter changed this year to include each car from a constructor that finished in the top six in any race).

Scheckter enjoyed his moment of glory, but admitted that the technological refinements in the Formula One car were now making it more difficult than ever for a driver to compete in a car that was off the pace. Whether he had the Williams FW07 or the turbo Renault in mind isn't clear, but his comment was to prove accurate in the coming years.

Left: Packing his bags. James Hunt bows out of motor racing halfway through the 1979 season. After 7 races for the Wolf team 6 of which ended in retirement he decides to decamp to his Spanish home with girlfriend Jane Birbeck.

Bottom: Hunt may no longer be a top Formula 1 star, but he remains a big draw on the PR circuit. A keen photographer himself, Hunt is the perfect celebrity for the launch of a new amateur club in London.

Previous page: After a dismal year with Brabham in a totally uncompetitive car, Niki Lauda decided he'd had enough. He didn't even complete the season, walking out at Montreal, the penultimate race of the season.

Jody Scheckter's world crown

Opposite bottom: Scheckter wins the 50th Grand Prix in Italy at Monza on his way to the world championship for Ferrari.

Opposite top: How the mighty are fallen. Twice world champion Emerson Fittipaldi's loyalty to the family team came at a price: he registered just a single point from the 15-race series.

Left: Gilles Villeneuve winning the Race of Champions at Brands Hatch a week after he had won the Long Beach Grand Prix. Villeneuve finished the season second to Scheckter in the final table.

Below: John Watson (centre) left Brabham to join McLaren in 1979. The move initially brought the Ulsterman little success as McLaren struggled to keep pace with the latest technological developments.

1980
First top spot for Williams

After Alan Jones's stunning performances in the Williams at the back end of the 1979 season, it was no surprise that he featured prominently in the new campaign. Perhaps less predictable was the rise to prominence of the Brazilian Nelson Piquet. Piquet had been Brabham's second driver behind Lauda in 1979, his first full season in Formula One. After Lauda's controversial walk-out at Canada, the 26-year-old found himself elevated for the second time in less than twelve months; he was now Brabham's number one.

Brabham had finally said goodbye to the 12-cylinder Alfa Romeo engine, closing an unhappy chapter in the marque's history. The team now reverted to Ford power in the BT49, and that decision, together with Piquet's skill behind the wheel, gave Brabham its best season for a decade.

Jones won from Piquet in the curtain-raiser in Argentina. Third that day was Keke Rosberg. He had stepped into James Hunt's shoes in the Wolf team when the Englishman retired part-way through the 1978 season. For 1979 he had signed for Fittipaldi. He was a top driver just waiting for a competitive team to take him on, but his time was still some way off.

Arnoux the new French talent

Rene Arnoux scored back-to-back wins in Brazil and South Africa in the new Renault, the RE20. Arnoux was a product of a government-backed scheme to find new racing talent in France in the 1970s, reminiscent of Argentina's approach thirty years before. Arnoux's rise to the highest echelons of motor sport had been prodigious. However, he failed to capitalise on these early successes, and it would be another two years before his next victory.

Nelson Piquet scored his first win in the US West Grand Prix at Long Beach. He did it in style, taking pole, leading from lap 1 to 80 and setting the fastest lap in the process. The race was marred by an accident which ended the career of Clay Regazzoni. Regazzoni had been replaced at Williams by Carlos Reutemann, the second time in his career that that had happened. The Swiss had rejoined Ensign, the team he had raced for in 1977 after leaving Ferrari. At about the two-thirds distance at Long Beach the throttle of Regazzoni's car jammed open and he hit a concrete wall at full tilt. He survived, but severe spinal injuries left him confined to a wheelchair.

Coming home in fifth place at Long Beach was Jody Scheckter in the latest Ferrari, the 312-T5. Those two points were to be his final tally for the season, marking an amazing reversal of fortune for Ferrari. Nor did Villeneuve fare much better, garnering just six points for his year's efforts.

Jones wins in France and Britain

Another new name headed the rostrum in the Belgian Grand Prix at Zolder. Didier Pironi, like Arnoux, had been schooled as a racing driver in the early 1970s. After two successful seasons in Formula One with Tyrrell, he had joined the Ligier team for the 1980 campaign. Although Jacques Laffite was the official team leader, Pironi matched him throughout the year. Only two points separated them at the end of the season, although they would both finish well adrift of Jones and Piquet.

Williams took top honours in the next three rounds. Reutemann had his first success for two years at Monaco, after Pironi, who had led for the first fifty laps, crashed out of the race. Then Jones won the French and British Grands Prix to give him three victories, a second and a third from the first eight races. Following on from the successes at the end of 1979, Williams had been looking to dominate the championship. The team was certainly performing well, but with half of the season still to go there was still a threat from the Ligiers, Arnoux's Renault and, particularly, Piquet in the Brabham.

Spanish Grand Prix declared void

The Spanish Grand Prix ought to have featured between the Monaco and French races. But political in-fighting between FISA and FOCA resulted in the race which was also won by Jones being declared void as far as the championship was concerned.

The Williams team had had its share of luck in recent races. Reutemann's Monaco win had come after Pironi, who had led for more than fifty laps, crashed out. At Brands Hatch Jones had been the beneficiary after both Ligiers had spells in front but both failed to finish. In the next round, the German Grand Prix, it was Jones who was now unlucky. He suffered a puncture while leading the race and it allowed Laffite to come through in the latter stages and give Ligier their second success of the season. Reutemann took second, while Jones had to content himself with third. Piquet's fourth place on the day continued a fine run of consistency. Of the nine races so far he had been in the points seven times. This represented a 100 per cent record in the races the Brazilian finished, for he had suffered retirements in Brazil and Belgium.

The latest tragedy to hit the sport came in practice for Hockenheim. Patrick Depailler, who had only recently recovered from a serious hang-gliding accident, was killed after a high-speed crash in his Alfa Romeo.

Piquet challenging hard for Brabham

In the Austrian Grand Prix it was once again a case of France holding off the Williams threat. This time it was Jabouille in the Renault, who led from the halfway mark to cross the line less than a second ahead of Jones. Reutemann took third.

As they went to Zandvoort, with just four races to go, Jones had a healthy if not decisive 11-point lead. Arnoux took pole but Jones shot into a first-lap lead. It all went wrong for Williams then, however, as Jones had to pit with damaged bodywork. Not only was he out of the points, but Piquet won, bringing him to within two points of the lead in the title race. Jones's slender advantage became a one-point deficit after Monza. Piquet took up the running on lap 4 and held it to the end. Jones was second half a minute behind.

Piquet took pole in the penultimate race in Montreal, with Jones occupying the other front row spot. Both hurtled out of the blocks, seeking to gain a vital early advantage. Neither backed off as they approached the first corner and there was a multi-car pile-up. Jones got the jump on his rival in the restart, only to be passed by Piquet on the third lap. The decisive moment in the race and the championship came on the 24th lap, when Piquet's engine blew. Jones followed Pironi home, but the Frenchman received a 60-second penalty for jumping the start. Jones thus took maximum points. As the title was decided on the best five finishes in each half of the season, Piquet now couldn't overhaul the Australian, even with a win in the final race at Watkins Glen. As it turned out Jones used that race as a victory celebration. He won, with team-mate Reutemann second.

Following Lotus in 1978 and Ferrari in 1979, Williams had become the latest team to celebrate a clean sweep of the honours. The task now was to avoid the rapid decline in fortunes that had befallen those other two marques as they tried to retain their titles.

Above right: Already an established motorcycle racer, 19-year-old Damon Hill prepares to make the transition to four wheels in a saloon car event at Brands Hatch.
Above left: Rene Arnoux clocks the fastest time in practice for the German Grand Prix at Hockenheim.
Previous page: Riccardo Patrese hoists the trophy aloft after winning the Race of Champions at Brands Hatch. By contrast, the championship season with Arrows yielded just 7 points.

Patrese's F1 record

Above: Riccardo Patrese didn't get to spray the champagne too often in his career, just 6 times in championship races. But he takes the prize for sheer longevity: his 256 starts over 17 years remains a record.

Opposite above: Jones carried on in 1980 the way he had finished the previous campaign. The superb FW07B made its appearance in mid-season, and the Australian clinched the title in the penultimate round. It was Jones's only championship success; for Williams it was the first of many.

Opposite below: Cap that. Lady Rothermere (left) presents Alan Jones with the trophy after his victory at Silverstone. Jones's 3rd win of the year helped him to extend his lead over championship rival Piquet, who finished 2nd in the race. On the right is Mrs Rob Hermans, wife of the managing director of Philip Morris Ltd.

1981
Brabham edge out Williams pair

The 1981 championship took place against a backdrop of political wrangling. FISA and FOCA were in dispute over the decision to ban side skirts for the new season. The ruling had huge implications for the "ground effect" cars, which were predominantly British. One of the main casualties was the new Lotus 88, forcing Colin Chapman to field the old 87 model.

The top four finishers in 1980 again contested the 1981 championship, but it was a much tighter affair this time. Jones and Reutemann were still there for Williams, with Piquet again heading the Brabham challenge. Jacques Laffite continued as Ligier's number one, with the team reverting to Matra power. These four, together with the emerging talent of Alain Prost, would be the protagonists in 1981, with just 7 points separating them after the 15-race series.

Reutemann in team orders row

Jones and Reutemann started the campaign at Long Beach the way they had finished the season before. When Jones took the lead from his team-mate on lap 32, the race was all but over. This was because Reutemann's contract stipulated that he could only go for a win if he was 7 seconds ahead of Jones; otherwise he had to let the Australian through.

This agreement came apart at the seams in the next round, Brazil. Reutemann led the whole way. With four laps to go he was signalled to let second-placed Jones pass. The Argentinian disregarded the order and won, precipitating a huge row after the race. Reutemann's punishment was the withholding of his race fee. The wider implication was a breakdown in the relationship between the two drivers for the rest of the season. They were curt and professional, and that was about all.

Mansell's first podium finish

Piquet scored successive victories in Argentina and San Marino. In Buenos Aires he led the whole way to win by nearly half a minute from Reutemann. Villeneuve took pole and led in the early stages at Imola, but Piquet came through in the latter stages to win from Patrese and Reutemann.

Jones went off the track at Zolder as he tried to impose himself on Reutemann. It backfired, for with Jones out of contention his team-mate went on to win a rain-shortened race comfortably from Laffite. Third was Nigel Mansell's Lotus. It was his first podium finish in his first full season in Formula 1.

Jones was leading at Monaco with just four laps to go, when a fuel feed problem hampered him. Villeneuve came through to give Ferrari their first win for two years. He followed it up by crossing the line first in a tight finish in Spain. Laffite, Watson, Reutemann and de Angelis were hot on the Canadian's heels, with less than 1.5 seconds separating all five.

Dennis and Barnard in control at McLaren

Like Mansell, another future champion had his first taste of success in 1981. Alain Prost did even better, though, winning on home soil at Dijon. The first of his 51 victories came in a race that was split into two parts because of rain. The Frenchman came home two seconds ahead of Watson's McLaren.

It was Watson who came out on top at Silverstone. This win for the MP4 was an early marker for the huge success that McLaren would enjoy during the 1980s. Ron Dennis had just assumed control of the team, and with John Barnard in charge of design, these two men would be the linchpins in a stunningly successful era for McLaren.

Reutemann's second place at Silverstone gave him a 17-point lead in the championship. But the man who had been trying to win the title for 9 years could only score 2 points in the next three races. 5th place in Austria was sandwiched between retirements at Hockenheim and Zandvoort. Piquet won his third race of the year in Germany, inheriting the lead from Jones, who again suffered fuel feed problems. Jacques Laffite became the 7th different winner of the year when he won from Arnoux and Piquet in Austria. Piquet was second behind Prost at Zandvoort, giving him 19 points for the three races. This edged him ahead of Reutemann in the championship with three races to go.

Piquet by a single point

Prost joined Piquet on three wins by leading all the way at Monza. Jones and Reutemann finished behind him, while Piquet picked up just one point in sixth. Laffite won in Montreal from 10th place on the grid. Piquet scored just two points in 5th, while Reutemann finished out of the top six.

Despite an indifferent latter half of the season, Reutemann still led with 49 points going into the final round. Piquet was one point behind, with Laffite in contention on 43. In the unlikely surroundings of a track laid out around the Caesar's Palace car park in Nevada, Reutemann was superb in practice and took pole. In the race itself, however, he put in a lacklustre performance and finished 8th. Laffite scored just one point in 6th, and was overhauled in the final table by Jones, who stormed to victory. But it was Piquet's 5th place which proved decisive. That was enough to give him his first championship by a single point from Reutemann.

Motor racing "a pain in the neck"

Above left: Jacques Laffite having a neck massage following a gruelling race. Throughout 1981 there was growing concern about the modern, virtually suspension-less cars. Physiotherapy for neck and back injuries was now commonplace.

Above right: Rene Arnoux in his car shaking hands with fellow Frenchman Alain Prost at the Austrian Grand Prix. Arnoux was fastest in the first practice session but was second to Laffite in the actual race.

Left: Watson doubled his tally of Grand Prix victories by winning at Silverstone. The 35-year-old Ulsterman's only other success had come in the Austrian Grand Prix 5 years earlier.

Previous page: John Watson gives Jacques Laffite a customary soaking after his victory in the British Grand Prix. Carlos Reutemann was second, with Laffite third.

Piquet by one point

Left: Nelson Piquet went into the final race of the season one point behind Reutemann. But it was Piquet's 5th place at Caesar's Palace which proved decisive. That was enough to give him his first championship by a single point.

Below: November 1981: McLaren boss Ron Dennis (left) unveils his new driver line-up for the coming season. John Watson remains for the 4th year; his new team-mate is Niki Lauda, whom Dennis has persuaded out of retirement.

Opposite top: Watson and Lauda pose with the MP4, the car they would drive in the 1982 championship.

Opposite below: Watson's 9th season in Formula 1 yielded 27 points, his best ever showing. Unfortunately for Watson, McLaren's period of domination was still a couple of years away, by which time he would be replaced by Prost.

1982
Rosberg victorious in tragic year

The victories and points were even more widely spread in 1982 than they had been the year before. No fewer than 11 drivers won races, and only 23 points covered the top 10 at the end of the extended 16-race series.

Even though Williams was obviously a team on the up, both Jones and Reutemann had decided to call it a day. Jones made his announcement at the end of 1981; Reutemann took second place in the 1982 opener in South Africa, but felt there was something missing and he, too, walked away.

With most of the top drivers already committed, Williams signed Keke Rosberg. The extrovert Finn had had a disastrous couple of years with the Fittipaldi team, things becoming so bad that he stormed out in the middle of 1981. Williams offered the quick but inexperienced Rosberg a deal, and the driver was naturally delighted to be given a seat in what was one of the best cars on the circuit. His only handicap was that the team was still running the normally-aspirated V-8 Cosworth engine, bucking the turbo trend that many of the other top outfits were turning to.

Piquet and Rosberg disqualified

Prost recovered from a puncture to win the opener in South Africa. Reutemann's last completed race for Williams produced a second place, while Rosberg, the team's number two at that stage, was 5th. The Frenchman also won in Brazil, although this was an inherited victory after Piquet and Rosberg were disqualified for running underweight cars.

Niki Lauda returned to Formula 1 in 1982 after being out of the sport for two years, during which period, among other things, he had set up his own airline. His first win came in his third race back, at Long Beach. Andrea de Cesaris took pole and led until the 14th lap, when an accident put him out of the race. Lauda stayed in front for the remaining 60 laps, with Rosberg finishing second. Villeneuve crossed the line third, but his Ferrari was found to have an illegal wing and Patrese moved up from 4th to take the 4 points.

The fall-out from the disqualifications in Brazil led to a mass withdrawal by the FOCA teams from the San Marino race. There were only 14 starters, and just 5 finishers. The lead changed hands several times between the Ferraris of Villeneuve and Pironi, and Arnoux in the Renault. Arnoux departed with engine trouble at the three-quarter distance, and Pironi passed Villeneuve on the last lap to win. This manoeuvre infuriated Villeneuve, who vowed not to speak to Pironi again.

Villeneuve killed in practice

Tragically, Villeneuve's feud with his team-mate lasted just two weeks, for the Canadian was killed during practice for the Belgian Grand Prix at Zolder. In the race Rosberg had victory in his sights when he locked his brakes, allowing John Watson through. It was a moment of irony for Williams, for a deal had almost been done to bring Watson to the team instead of the Finn.

Riccardo Patrese claimed his first Formula 1 win at Monaco, a race in which the lead changed hands four times in the last three laps. Prost was ahead when he crashed out. Patrese took over, but a spin let Pironi through. His Ferrari then succumbed to an electrical problem just one lap from home and Patrese repassed the Frenchman to give Brabham their first win of the season.

Watson won a restarted race at Detroit, after which another tragedy occurred at Montreal. Riccardo Paletti was killed in a start-line accident when his Osella collided with Pironi's Ferrari. Mansell was involved in a nasty spill at the restart, his car overshooting the Alfa of Bruno Giacomelli. Piquet and Patrese made it a one-two for Brabham, though interestingly, their cars were differently powered. Piquet had the BMW turbo, Patrese the normally-aspirated Cosworth engine.

Pironi's career over

Pironi dominated the Dutch Grand Prix, then took second at Brands Hatch behind Lauda. After a 3rd place at Paul Ricard, the Frenchman led the championship on 39 points, 9 clear of his nearest rival. Hockenheim was next, and the black season got even blacker as Pironi broke both legs in a crash during practice. His racing career was over. Patrick Tambay provided Ferrari with a crumb of comfort by winning the race.

Lotus was now in a period of decline. The new 91 model performed well on fast circuits, but generally struggled against the onslaught of the turbos. Austria's Osterreichring was one of the few tracks which suited the car, and Elio de Angelis won narrowly from Rosberg, but only after much of the turbo-powered opposition was out of the race.

After a string of finishes in the points, Rosberg finally scored a win in the Swiss Grand Prix, which was held at Dijon, owing to Switzerland's ban on circuit racing. The Finn passed Prost on the last lap, the latter struggling with gearbox trouble.

Only one win for champion Rosberg

Arnoux led from start to finish at Monza. Rosberg finished out of the points that day, while Watson picked up 3 in 4th place. With Pironi out of contention, Rosberg went into the final round at Caesar's Palace with 42 points from his 9 finishes. Watson, on 33, needed a win to have a chance of snatching the title. He could only manage second, behind Alboreto's Tyrrell. Rosberg finished 5th anyway, to take the crown by 5 points. He had only won once, but a consistent run of 10 finishes in the points was the decisive factor.

Closest ever contest

Below: Former champion Niki Lauda found that he hadn't lost his touch when he returned to the Grand Prix stage at Kyalami. He finished a crditable 4th, beaten only by the turbo-powered Renaults and Reutemann's Williams.

Left: Rosberg takes pole at Brands Hatch. He failed to finish in that race, but both he and the Williams were consistent performers in 1982. He won only once, but 10 finishes in the points brought him the championship.

Previous page: Niki Lauda receives the trophy after winning the British Grand Prix. The presentation is made by Lady Rothermere. Lauda went on to finish 5th in the most evenly contested season ever: just 19 points covered the top 8 drivers.

Tragedy strikes as popular Gilles Villeneuve is 28th driver to die in Formula One

Opposite: The popular Canadian Gilles Villeneuve was killed during practice for the Belgian Grand Prix at Zolder. His car somersaulted after hitting the back wheel of a March driven by Jochen Mass. Nigel Mansell, a member of the safety committee, was distraught: "There are too many cars and they are too fast."

Above: Niki Lauda's comeback year yields two victories, at Long Beach and Brands Hatch. He was one of five drivers who won twice in 1982. Rosberg won only once, at Dijon, but a string of podium finishes gave him the title.

Left: Reigning champion Keke Rosberg pictured against a backdrop of memorabilia of his illustrious career. Prior to 1982, Rosberg had spent four years making the most of some uncompetitive hardware. When he got his hands on a Williams FW08, he showed his champion's mettle.

1983
Piquet beats Prost in head to head

Nelson Piquet had had a disappointing year as reigning champion. The turbo-charged Brabham had been quick but unreliable. Nevertheless, the Brazilian stayed on for 1983, along with Patrese.

The turbo stranglehold was even greater this time round. The famous Cosworth engine, with over 150 wins to its credit, finally had to give way as one by one the teams turned to turbo power. Brabham itself had hedged its bets by running a turbo and normally-aspirated car side by side in 1982. Concentrating on the former in 1983 was a distinct advantage to Patrese and, more importantly, Piquet.

Williams wait for Honda

The Brazilian took the opening honours in Brazil. Rosberg crossed the line second but was disqualified for receiving a push start in the pits. It was an unfortunate start for Williams. The team had cut an engine deal with Honda, but was having to continue with Ford power until the new unit was ready.

Lauda, third in Brazil, came home second in a McLaren one-two at Long Beach, finishing behind team-mate Watson. For McLaren, too, it was one of the last moments of glory before the TAG-financed Porsche turbo ushered in a new era.

Prost won his 6th race for Renault on home ground at Paul Ricard, and followed it up with a 2nd place behind Tambay at Imola. It was the beginning of a consistent run which would put the title within his grasp.

Keke Rosberg, now running in a flat-bottomed version of the FW08 to comply with the new regulations, scored a memorable win over Piquet and Prost at Monaco. He later commented that he had to drive on the absolute limit to keep his Cosworth-powered car ahead of the mighty turbos. Even then it might not have been enough had he not made the canny decision to run on slicks on a damp but drying track.

Mansell gets competitive

Prost had his 3rd pole and 2nd win of the year at Spa. Round 7 was Detroit, which provided a landmark in sports history: Michele Alboreto's win was the 155th and last for the famous Cosworth engine, which had made its debut in 1967.

Montreal saw Rene Arnoux score his first win for Ferrari since his move from Renault in the close season. Behind him was the man who had replaced him in the French team, American Eddie Cheever.

Nigel Mansell finally got his hands on the Renault-turbo car at Silverstone. After a dismal year thus far, he was immediately competitive, finishing 4th, some 40 seconds behind race winner Prost.

Arnoux kept up his title hopes by winning at Hockenheim. It had been a Ferrari front row, with Arnoux's team-mate Tambay on pole. Arnoux ought to have let his fellow-countryman have a clear run, not least because he trailed Tambay by 12 points in the championship. As it was, Tambay retired with engine trouble, but he and Ferrari would not have been best pleased by Arnoux's actions.

The Ferraris were now enjoying a good run. Tambay was again on pole in Austria. This time he got away to lead for the first 21 laps. After an oil problem put him out, his team-mate took over. Arnoux held the lead until 5 laps from home, when Prost passed him. They finished in that order, with Piquet 3rd.

Ferrari then enjoyed a one-two at Zandvoort. Piquet had led up to lap 41, when an incident involving Prost put both contenders out. Arnoux took over and held on to win by 20 seconds from Tambay.

Prost's four wins had helped him to an 8-point advantage over Arnoux, with Piquet and Tambay a further 6 points behind. Monza was disastrous for Prost. His turbo went at the halfway mark, while Piquet, Arnoux and Tambay finished 1st, 2nd and 4th respectively.

Piquet overhauls Prost for second title

Prost was 2nd in the European Grand Prix, this year staged at Brands Hatch. But Piquet dominated this race, too, crossing the line 7 seconds ahead of the Frenchman. Neither Ferrari was in the points, so it was a straight fight between Prost and Piquet in the final round, the Frenchman's lead now down to 2 points.

Piquet was on the front row, with Tambay on pole. The Brazilian got the better start and led for the first 59 of the 77-lap race. Prost could only qualify 5th and his race ended with a turbo failure on the 35th lap. He now had to hope that Piquet finished no better than 5th. The Brazilian did relinquish the lead, passed by both Patrese and de Cesaris. However, 4 points for 3rd place was enough to give him his second title.

While Piquet celebrated, Prost was roundly criticised in his home press for letting the championship slip from his grasp. It was a failure which also precipitated a swift parting of the ways between Renault and the Professor.

Hill and Senna - New kids on the circuit

Left: Damon Hill turned to car racing in 1983, having spent his youth competing on two wheels. With the media spotlight inevitably trained on him, 23-year-old Hill's baptism in Formula Ford 2000 proved to be something of a struggle.

Previous page: Ayrton Senna's Formula 3 success in 1983 brought him to the attention of several Formula 1 teams. He tested for both Williams and McLaren, but felt that Toleman offered the best opportunity at that stage of his career.

Below: The TAG Porsche cometh. John Watson puts McLaren's new turbo unit through its paces. It didn't break any records when it replaced the Cosworth engine for the final three races of the 1983 season. The following three years were quite a different matter.

Watson under pressure at McLaren

Opposite above: John Watson (left) outscored team-mate Niki Lauda in 1983, as he had the year before. However, when Prost became available at the end of the season, it was the Ulsterman who was shown the door at McLaren to make way for him.

Opposite bottom: There's a hairy moment for Elio de Angelis as smoke belches from his Lotus during practice for the European Grand Prix at Brands Hatch. It didn't stop him taking pole, but that race and the whole season were very disappointing for the Italian.

Above: Rosberg won just one race in 1983, as he had in his title-winning season the year before. This time, however, he finished well off the pace set by the turbo-powered opposition.

Piquet's "toy" brings him second world crown

Opposite below: Nelson Piquet poses in a London cab: "At my Brabham BMW team we have perhaps 100 people and spend perhaps $10m. For what? To give me a toy to play with." Playtime in 1983 brought Piquet his second world crown.

Right: John Watson didn't quite reproduce his form of the season before, but 1983 ended on a happy note when the Ulsterman was awarded the MBE.

Bottom: Rosberg in action at Brands Hatch in the penultimate round of the championship.

Opposite top: Ayrton Senna became Formula 3 champion in 1983, following a titanic and occasionally acrimonious battle with Martin Brundle.

1984
Lauda by half a point from Prost

As Piquet and Prost were battling it out for the top spot at the end of 1983, McLaren drivers Watson and Lauda were giving a quiet debut to their new TAG Porsche engine. McLaren had relied on Ford power for several seasons, latterly with little success against its turbo-charged competitors. Ron Dennis's team fielded the new unit for the last four races of the 1983 season, and although there were several retirements, the car showed undoubted promise.

Lauda stayed on for 1984 and was joined by Prost, who had finally had enough of the vilification directed at him in the French press over his performances with Renault. All of the pieces in the McLaren jigsaw were now in place: an impressive new turbo unit fitted to John Barnard's superb carbon-fibre MP4, and two top-line drivers. The results were dramatic.

The opening race in Brazil saw several drivers come to the fore. Elio de Angelis took pole in the Lotus-Renault, but Alboreto, who was beside him on the front row, got the better start. A brake problem put the Italian out after 11 laps and Lauda took over in front. When the Austrian's car succumbed to an electrical fault, the race turned into a fight between Prost and Derek Warwick, the man who had replaced him at Renault. Warwick's suspension gave out 10 laps from home and Prost scored the first in an avalanche of McLaren successes.

First points for Senna

Prost and Lauda qualified only in 5th and 8th places respectively at Kyalami, but scored a comfortable one-two success. Lauda finished more than a minute clear of his team-mate, and both were a lap ahead of Warwick in third.

Gaining his first championship point in 6th place was Ayrton Senna. Senna had tested for both Williams and McLaren but decided that at this stage in his career he was better off being a bigger fish in a smaller pond and opted to join Toleman. Even then, however, the fiercely competitive Brazilian had made it clear that he would give his all, but walk away if the car wasn't up to scratch.

Both McLarens retired at Zolder, one of just two races all season when neither Prost nor Lauda finished in the points. Alboreto took pole and enjoyed a start-to-finish victory.

Reigning champion Piquet had had three straight retirements and continued his wretched start to the season at Imola. He took pole, but his turbo failed 12 laps from the line when he was running second. Prost won, having led for the entire 60-lap distance.

Lauda's engine blew in the early stages at San Marino. He bounced back to win the French Grand Prix at Dijon. Second that day was Patrick Tambay, who, along with Warwick, made up Renault's new partnership for 1984. Nigel Mansell scored his first points of the year by finishing 3rd. He had remained at Lotus, despite considerable antagonism towards him in the post-Chapman era. Mansell's performance was certainly stoic, for it later transpired that he had been devastated by the news of his mother's death shortly before the race.

Mansell loses his grip

Mansell should have won at Monaco, in a race run in torrential rain. He had done the hard work in getting past Prost to take the lead, but lost grip on the painted white lines and slid into the Armco. More frustratingly for Mansell, the race was stopped shortly after his exit. Prost was ahead again by then and declared winner. Senna drove brilliantly. From 9th place on the opening lap he got to within 8 seconds of Prost when the race was halted. Half the distance had been covered and half points awarded.

After six retirements Piquet finally had some luck in Montreal, where he relegated the McLarens to the minor placings. The champion repeated the feat at Detroit, in a race that was restarted after a first-lap shunt involving the Brazilian and the two McLarens, which had qualified 2nd and 3rd on the grid. Martin Brundle performed heroically to finish within a second of Piquet. His achievement was short-lived as he was disqualified for a weight irregularity in his Tyrrell.

In Dallas Mansell and de Angelis occupied the front row, the first time Lotus had had that distinction for six years. Baking conditions cracked the surface, and some hastily added cement didn't set. Mansell led up to halfway, when Rosberg passed him in the Williams-Honda. The Finn went on to win, while the unlucky Mansell had transmission failure on the last lap. He fainted as he pushed his car to the line, but his efforts earned him one point as he was classified 6th.

Lauda won at Brands Hatch, inheriting the lead after Prost hit gearbox trouble at the halfway mark. At Hockenheim it was the Frenchman's turn to benefit from the misfortune of others. De Angelis and Piquet both fell by the wayside after early spells in front, leaving Prost to head Lauda home.

Lauda joins the exclusive club

Austria was a landmark race. For the first time the entire field was made up of turbo-powered cars. Lauda crossed the line 24 seconds ahead of Piquet, while Prost spun off and failed to score. Zandvoort saw the third McLaren one-two of the year. Piquet was again first away, but his miserable season continued: out of the race on the 10th lap with an oil leak. Prost took over and 61 laps later took the flag 10 seconds ahead of Lauda.

The fluctuating fortunes of the two McLaren drivers continued as Lauda won at Monza, then Prost replied by winning the European Grand Prix at the new Nürburgring.

Prost had retired in Italy, whereas Lauda took 3 points for 4th place in Germany. Going into the decider at Estoril Lauda led Prost 66-62.5. Prost took the lead from Rosberg and held on to win, but the wily Lauda drove cannily, as he had all season, and moved through to finish in second place. Prost had won seven races to Lauda's 5, but the Austrian had secured a wafer-thin half-point advantage. It earned him membership of the exclusive club of three-time winners, a club whose only other members were Fangio, Brabham and Stewart.

Top: Alain Prost takes the Daily Mail prize for setting the fastest lap during practice for the British Grand Prix. He retired in the race, which was won by his McLaren team-mate and championship rival Niki Lauda.
Above: First lap drama at Brands Hatch as Philippe Alliot's RAM and Jo Gartner's Osella make contact.
Previous page: Lauda claims his third win of the season in the British Grand Prix.

Below: Ayrton Senna made his Formula 1 debut with Toleman in 1984. He scored just 13 points, finishing 9th in the championship. That wasn't enough for the fiercely determined Brazilian, who had ensured that his contract allowed him to move on if the car proved uncompetitive.

Right: Officials help Gartner from his car, shaken but unhurt but the Osella waits for someone to extricate it from the tyre wall.

Opposite: Lauda's Brands Hatch win put him just 1.5 points behind Prost, in a season that developed into a two-horse race. Prost was younger and quicker, but the wily, experienced Lauda pipped him for the championship. Lauda's win at Brands Hatch brings his career total of Grand Prix points to a record 367.5. He overtook Jackie Stewart's haul of 360 points, although the Scot was still ahead in terms of outright victories: 27, to Lauda's 22.

1985
Prost's first victory

Niki Lauda's decision to return to racing was vindicated by his 1984 triumph. He remained at McLaren for one more season, alongside Prost, but he couldn't contain the Frenchman any longer. Nor could anyone else. After two hugely disappointing years, in which he could easily have won the title, Prost made no mistakes this time.

Prost won the opener in Brazil from 6th on the grid. Alboreto and Rosberg had occupied the front row, and both had spells in the lead in the early stages. Alboreto finished the race in second place, while Rosberg went out early with a failed turbo.

Mansell moves to Williams

The Finn had a new number two this year, Nigel Mansell moving from Lotus to replace Laffite. Mansell had finally had enough of being undermined at Lotus, and his relationship with the team's hierarchy had all but broken down. Lotus boss Peter Warr didn't think Mansell had what it took to get beyond the also-rans; the British driver joined Frank Williams' outfit and set about proving him wrong.

Mansell, like Rosberg, retired in Brazil, but he was in the points at Estoril. A bump on the warm-up lap meant that he had to start from the pit lane, yet he recovered to finish 5th. The winner that day was Ayrton Senna, whom Warr had brought to Lotus to replace Mansell. In atrocious conditions Senna took the first pole of his career and led all the way. He finished more than a minute clear of Michele Alboreto.

Senna should have made it two in a row at Imola, where he also took pole and led for 56 of the 60-lap race. The Brazilian ran out of fuel and had to watch as six drivers passed him. Instead of leaving San Marino with nine points, he came away empty-handed. Prost was also out of luck. He crossed the line first, only to be disqualified after his McLaren was found to be underweight. Elio de Angelis was the man to profit, gaining only his second win in six years of Formula 1 racing.

Senna was again quickest in Monaco, and led until he suffered engine failure on lap 13. Prost then traded the lead with Alboreto for 20 laps, before establishing an advantage that he held to the line.

Montreal was Ferrari's day. Alboreto ended a 17-race barren spell for the team, and with Stefan Johansson following him home, Ferrari had their first one-two since Zandvoort two years earlier. Both Ferrari drivers were on the podium in Detroit, too, though well adrift of race winner Keke Rosberg. The 1982 champion, and his team-mate Mansell, had experienced handling problems with the Williams-Honda. The turbo kicked in unevenly, giving a huge power surge or nothing at all. The promised new Honda engine had now arrived, however, and matters improved considerably. Rosberg took the flag a minute clear of Johansson and Alboreto.

It looked good for Williams at Paul Ricard, too. Mansell was out after a frightening 200 mph spill in practice, but Rosberg took pole. The Finn led early on, and also set the fastest lap. He had to settle for 6 points, however, as Piquet got by him on the 11th lap and kept the lead to the end.

Rosberg sets 160mph record

Rosberg was on pole again at Silverstone, becoming the first man to lap at more than 160 mph in a Grand Prix. Both he and Mansell, who hadn't fully recovered from his crash, retired at the one-third distance. The team had the chassis, the speed and the drivers; they now needed reliability. Senna led for 57 of the 65 laps, when he ran out of fuel. Prost took over and scored his third counting victory of the season, a lap ahead of Alboreto and Laffite.

Alboreto only qualified 8th at the Nürburgring, but after the early leaders Rosberg and Senna retired, he led for the last 20 laps to win from Prost. The Italian had had a marvellous run in the first nine races. This was only his second win, but he had been on the podium seven times, a 100% record, as he had retired in the other two races. He now led the championship on 46 points, 5 ahead of Prost.

The Frenchman brought the two drivers level by winning in Austria, with Alboreto 3rd. Lauda had led in the middle part of the race, then had his 8th retirement in 10 races. The Austrian was about to hang up his helmet for good. He had one last moment of glory at Zandvoort, where he scored the 25th and final win of his illustrious career.

Prost, second in Holland, went one better at Monza. As he began a fine run in the points, Alboreto's season dried up. After amassing 46 points from the first 9 rounds, the last seven would yield a string of retirements and just 7 points for the Italian.

The reliability of the Williams-Honda was now showing considerable improvement. Mansell and Rosberg were 2nd and 4th at Spa. Senna won his second Grand Prix there, giving him five podium finishes in the five races he'd completed. Prost was 3rd, racking up the points on the way to the title.

First win in 72 outings for Mansell

The same four were first home in the European Grand Prix at Brands Hatch. It was Nigel Mansell's 72nd Grand Prix and he finally tasted victory. Rosberg gave further cause for Williams optimism by coming 3rd. He recovered from a spat with Senna on lap 7, the two cars touching as the Finn tried to grab the lead. Senna again showed how competitve he was in a reliable car by finishing 2nd. Prost picked up 3 points for 4th place. He now had 72 points from the required 11 finishes and became the first Frenchman to win the coveted title.

Williams dominated the last two rounds. Mansell immediately scored a second success after taking pole at Kyalami. Rosberg, second that day, rounded off the year by winning in Adelaide. The Williams-Honda was obviously a car whose time was coming, and Senna showed what a threat he could be in the right car. There would be no comfortable 20-point margin for Prost and McLaren in the next campaign.

Above: Nigel Mansell relaxes with wife Rosanne, and children Chloe, 3, and 9-month-old Leo in the run-up to the European Grand Prix at Brands Hatch. Mansell was about to prove his detractors at Lotus and elsewhere emphatically wrong. He scored his debut victory at Brands Hatch, then followed it with another win two weeks later at Kyalami.
Left: Gary Brabham and Damon Hill pose for the cameras. A generation on from the time when their illustrious fathers regularly clashed.
Previous page: Patrick Tambay crashes out of the British Grand Prix in spectacular fashion on the first lap.

The pain of Formula One

Below: Martin Brundle gets a second opinion on his leg injuries from Formula 1 rival Jonathan Palmer, who happens to be a doctor. Brundle's wife, Liz, looks happy enough with the prognosis. Brundle was recovering from a crash during practice for the 1984 Dallas Grand Prix when he received the news that Tyrrell had been banned for the season.
Right: Brundle is out of plaster and well on the way to recovery. Liz Brundle shows the kind of pins which doctors inserted into her husband's leg.

Brundle was back in the cockpit by the start of the new season. The Tyrrells switched from Ford engines to Renault-turbo power during the year, but Brundle failed to register any points. Nevertheless, the 26-year-old was marked out by many pundits to achieve great things in the sport.

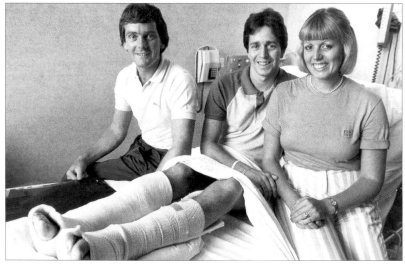

Prost's fortunate win on the way to world crown

Left: Prost acknowledges the fans after his somewhat fortunate win in the British Grand Prix. He took the lead 6 laps from home after Senna's Lotus ran out of fuel. Beside him on the podium is Michele Alboreto, who took 2nd place for Ferrari. At the halfway mark of the season Alboreto led Prost in the championship, 37-35.

Below: Prince Michael of Kent stumbles as he presents Alain Prost with the winner's trophy at Brands Hatch. Prost's lightning reflexes save the day. Prost won the championship by a comfortable 20 points from Michele Alboreto in a Ferrari.

1986
Last year for all-powerful turbos

The 1986 championship marked a watershed in the history of Formula 1, for it was the last full year in which the unfettered turbo engines were allowed to dominate the event. It had been just 9 short years since Renault was the subject of mild amusement after introducing the innovative booster. Now FISA decided enough was enough. The power the cars were generating was going off the scale, and Formula 1's governing body decreed in 1986 that they were to be outlawed. There were to be interim arrangements for 1987 and 1988, after which the sport would revert to normally-aspirated power.

1986 was dominated by four men: Mansell, Piquet, Prost and Senna. Between them they won every race except one, and by the end of the year there was a gulf of more than 30 points between them and the 5th-placed driver, Stefan Johansson.

Prost, Mansell and Senna remained with their previous year's teams. Piquet, having been with Bernie Ecclestone's Brabham team since 1978, now decided it was time for a change. By teaming up with Mansell at Williams he allied himself to the car of the year. The Honda-powered Williams was to win 9 of the 16 races and take the constructors' title by a country mile.

Senna on pole eight times

Senna took pole in Brazil, and he, Piquet and Prost all enjoyed spells in front. Piquet took over at the two-thirds mark and held on to win from Senna. Prost retired, while an accident involving Mansell meant that his race was over before it even started.

Senna was on pole again in Spain and won by a whisker from Mansell, his third Grand Prix victory. At Imola the mercurial Brazilian took his third successive pole, an honour he would hold in 8 of the 16 races. Only twice would he convert these into victories, but he showed that he was a rare talent indeed. He was unfortunate in that his Lotus-Renault was up against the formidable Williams and McLaren cars. Senna was clearly a champion in waiting.

He retired early at Imola, and reigning champion Prost scored his first win of the year. Piquet, the only other man to complete the 60-lap distance, came in second. Prost made it two in a row by also winning at Monaco. It was a double delight for McLaren as Rosberg followed him home. The Finn had had three unremarkable years at Williams following his title-winning season of 1982. The decision to join Prost in the MP4 must have looked a good

276 FORMULA ONE: UNSEEN ARCHIVES **1986**

one, but he would soon discover that he had left Williams just as they were coming up with an irresistible car.

Mansell dominates

Mansell had had a 2nd, 4th and two retirements in his first four outings. But he now hit top form, winning four of the next five races. In Belgium, Canada and France he ended the races with a 20-second cushion or thereabouts. Brands Hatch was the closest of the four, as Piquet got within six seconds of the Briton. Mansell came of age during this dominant period. Until then many regarded the former test driver as a tough and gritty competitor; now he was also championship material.

In the middle of this fine Mansell winning streak Senna came out on top in Detroit, in a race where the lead changed hands several times. The next two races saw a return to Hockenheim for the German Grand Prix and a new venue, Hungary's Hungaroring. These provided Williams with their 6th and 7th wins of the season, but this time it was Piquet who crossed the line first, with Senna second on both occasions.

Titanic battle in Hungary

The inaugural race in Hungary was the first time the Formula 1 circus had gone beyond the Iron Curtain. Any apprehensions were quickly dispelled. Some 200,000 fans converged on Budapest and witnessed a titanic battle between Piquet and Senna. The two traded the lead, which was surprising as overtaking opportunities were limited on the narrow, winding circuit. The trip to the Eastern Bloc was a resounding success and the Hungaroring was later voted Course of the Year.

Senna, Mansell and Piquet all suffered retirements in Austria. Prost didn't and duly won. This race gave some of the other drivers the chance to get in the frame. It was the Ferraris of Alboreto and Johansson and the Lolas of Jones and Tambay which followed the Professor home, though none got to within a lap of the Frenchman.

Teo Fabi took pole on home territory at Monza, as he had in Austria. The Italian's BMW-engined Benetton had awesome power in short bursts, but maintaining the pace for the duration of a race was a different proposition and Fabi regularly failed to finish. The race was another one-two for Williams, Piquet taking the flag 10 seconds ahead of team-mate Mansell. The Briton then hit back at Estoril, where he took his 5th win of the season. His bid to become the first British champion since James Hunt was back on track.

Mansell's tyre agony

The penultimate round saw a return to Mexico for the first time since 1970. This was the only race of the year where one of the "big four" didn't prevail. Gerhard Berger was the man who broke the oligopoly. The Austrian notched his first Grand Prix success as the powerful Benetton lasted the full distance. Benetton had taken over the Toleman team only that year. The step up from being being simply sponsors to running a fully-fledged racing team under its own banner had thus brought an early reward.

Mansell was in the box seat going into the final race at Adelaide. Third place would be enough to give him the title, irrespective of what his rivals did. But fate struck a cruel and dramatic blow on lap 63, when a tyre on his Williams blew. His race was over. Piquet lost ground as he made a precautionary pit stop. Prost came through to take the race and the title, the first man to win successive championships since Jack Brabham in 1959-60.

Williams had been victims of their own success, with Piquet and Mansell scoring off each other all season and splitting valuable points. But take nothing away from Prost. He had won four races and was consistent throughout the year. His victorious campaign merely added to his reputation for being the most complete driver of his era.

The year also had its share of tragedy. Elio de Angelis was killed while testing his Brabham at Paul Ricard; a crash at the first corner at Brands Hatch ended Jacques Laffite's career; and off the track Frank Williams was involved in a car crash which confined him to a wheelchair.

Above: Drama on the first lap of the British Grand Prix, as Thierry Boutsen's Arrows smashes into the crash barrier.
Left: The steely eyes of reigning champion Alain Prost. The "Professor" focuses on winning the British Grand Prix, but is beaten on the day by the Williams duo Mansell and Piquet.
Previous page: Senna leads Mansell at Monaco, where the two great rivals finish 3rd and 4th respectively. It was McLaren's day, Prost crossing the line ahead of team-mate Rosberg.

Multiple pile-up on the first corner

Opposite above: Boutsen's car bounces back across the track, precipitating a multiple pile-up.
Opposite below: The main victim of the accident is Jacques Laffite, whose Formula 1 career is
ended by severe leg injuries. The race was eventually won by Nigel Mansell with Nelson Piquet
second. Mansell was the chief beneficiary of the carnage. A broken driveshaft would have ended
his chance of success, but the pile-up in which Mansell wasn't involved meant a restart. Mansell
was able to switch to a spare Williams, and he grabbed his second chance with both hands.
Above: Nigel Mansell takes a break from his preparation for the British Grand Prix. He qualified
second, behind his Williams team-mate Piquet.

Piquet on the fast track to success

Right: After two indifferent years with Brabham, Nelson Piquet moved to Williams in 1986. Piquet's scooter is suitably emblazoned, the former champion having just put himself at the front of the grid for the British Grand Prix. He acknowledges the feat at a rather more sedate speed than the 140.536 mph at which he lapped the Kent circuit in his Williams.

Below: Nelson Piquet is presented with champagne by the Daily Mail's Des Nicholls, after setting the fastest lap during practice at Brands Hatch. In the race he was beaten into second place by his Williams team-mate Nigel Mansell.

Williams' pair hand Prost the title

Left: The top drivers are ice cool, adept at keeping their emotions in check until a victory comes along. When success comes on home soil, the elation is even greater, as Nigel Mansell shows.

Below: Senna crossed the line just 0.014 seconds ahead of a disappointed Mansell in the Spanish Grand Prix, the closest finish for 15 years. Reigning champion Alain Prost was a distant third. Ultimately a win here would have won the championship for Mansell. Williams had been victims of their own success, with Piquet and Mansell scoring off each other all season and splitting valuable points. Prost was consistent throughout the year. His victorious campaign merely added to his reputation for being the most complete driver of his era.

1987
Piquet edges out Mansell

This season saw the introduction of two new awards, for drivers and constructors in the non-turbo category. This was an interim measure and an inducement in gearing up for 1989, when all Formula 1 engines would be 3.5-litre, normally-aspirated units. Tyrrell was quick off the mark in making ready for the big change, and dominated this category. The team won the Colin Chapman Cup, for constructors, and Tyrrell driver Jonathan Palmer took the drivers' award, the Jim Clark Cup.

If this was the sub-plot in 1987, the main drama had the same four chief characters as 1986: Prost, Senna, Piquet and Mansell. In fact, the season was very nearly a rerun of the year before in that these four shared the first 14 races, then Gerhard Berger stepped in with a victory in the penultimate round. Only in the final race did the script diverge.

Prost equals Stewart's record

The reigning champion got off to a good start, winning two of the first three races. This surprised everybody, for Prost had the uncertainty of an all-new car, while Piquet and Mansell were still aboard the tried and tested Williams-Honda. The Williams pair were quickest in practice for Brazil, but in conditions which were severe on tyres, Prost conserved his rubber very cleverly to win from Piquet. It was a Williams front row in Belgium, too. There was a huge shunt involving both Tyrrells early on, and in the restart Senna and Mansell had their latest spat. Their cars touched and both went off. Senna's race was over; Mansell retired some laps later. Piquet profited briefly, but he, too, failed to finish and Prost went on to win comfortably. It was the Frenchman's 27th win, equalling Jackie Stewart's record. That happy note was in stark contrast to Mansell's unseemly assault on Senna in the pit lane.

Japan's Nakajima and Honda join Lotus

Sandwiched between these Prost victories was a win for Mansell at Imola. In that race Prost's alternator failed, while Piquet didn't make it to the start, having been involved in a 200 mph crash in practice. Senna took pole and led early on, but Mansell soon took over and won easily.

Senna won the next two races, Monaco and Detroit. It was the 27-year-old's third year at Lotus and he saw it as a make-or-break season. The team had switched to Honda power, for Renault had withdrawn from Formula 1. Lotus clinched the Honda deal by taking on driver Satoru Nakajima as part of the package. Senna's new team-mate became Japan's first F1 driver. The other big change in the Lotus camp was the introduction of active suspension.

Senna's wins in Monte Carlo and the United States were not without some good fortune. At Monaco he inherited the lead from Mansell, who was looking comfortable in front before retiring on lap 29. Mansell then had pit-lane trouble while leading in Detroit, and Senna took advantage.

Mansell's heroics at Stowe

Mansell had scored just two points from three races, all of which he might have won. Things finally went for him in France. He was on pole again and this time made no mistakes, easing home 8 seconds ahead of team-mate Piquet. It was another one-two for Williams at Silverstone. Mansell won it, famously passing Piquet on the 63rd lap out of 65 at Stowe. It was the Briton's finest hour. He'd been almost half a minute down on Piquet, following an unscheduled pit stop for a wheel change.

Mansell took his 6th pole of the year at Hockenheim, but a seized engine ended his hopes. At that point the race looked to be heading Prost's way. The McLaren team had ironed out a technical problem that blighted the cars in the two previous races. The Frenchman appeared to be cruising to victory when his alternator failed 5 laps from home. Piquet, who had looked resigned to his 6th second place of the year, came through for his first win instead.

Senna was 3rd at Hockenheim, though a lap down. It was around this time that he finally decided that Lotus wasn't competitive enough, and set in train the negotiations which would take him to McLaren the following year.

Senna's departure was to bring Piquet to Lotus in 1988, and it was against the backdrop of these behind-the-scenes negotiations that the two fought for top spot in Hungary. Piquet won, having inherited the lead from the unlucky Mansell 6 laps from the line. Mansell had led for 70 laps, then lost a wheel nut with the race seemingly at its mercy. Senna was second, Prost third.

Mansell won by a distance from Piquet in Austria. In a race that was twice restarted only the Williams duo went the full distance. Both Senna and Prost all but conceded the title after Austria. Senna, on 43 points, was still 4 ahead of Mansell but couldn't see his Lotus reproducing the form of Monaco and Detroit in the final races. A forlorn Prost was back on 31. Piquet, somewhat disgruntled at the way he was being treated by Williams, led with 54 points.

Piquet extended his lead by winning at Monza. It was an excellent debut for Williams' own version of active suspension, which Piquet's car sported but Mansell's didn't. Senna may have been unhappy with his Lotus but drove a stunning race to finish second. He might have won, had he not gone into sand 7 laps out.

Derek Warwick's 160mph smash

Prost won for a record-breaking 28th time at Estoril, but more critical was Piquet's 3rd place. Senna and Mansell failed to score. Cynics doubted that Honda would want Mansell to win the title, given the moves already declared for 1988. But he won in Spain and Mexico to put himself right back in contention. He led all the way at Jerez, while in Mexico he came out on top on aggregate as the race was split into two halves. This was the result of Derek Warwick going into the tyre wall at 160 mph. Neither Prost nor Senna finished in Mexico and their title hopes were officially over.

The championship was decided in practice for the penultimate race at Suzuka. Mansell, desperate to take pole, went off at 120 mph and was ruled out of the race. He was bitterly disappointed that once again winning more races than his rivals wasn't going to bring him the coveted title.

Piquet's honour

The honour was now Piquet's, whatever happened in the last two rounds. In fact, he failed to score in either race, both of which were won by Gerhard Berger for Ferrari. Senna crossed the line second in each, but was disqualified at Adelaide over a brake irregularity. That cost him second place in the championship, but he still had 57 points to put him 3rd behind the Williams pair. What would he be capable of in 1988, at the wheel of the Honda-powered McLaren?

Above: Mansell spins off at Woodcote during practice for the British Grand Prix. His last chance to wrest pole position from Piquet had gone, but he had the final word in the race.
Previous page: Nigel Mansell salutes the crowd after his Silverstone victory, while Ayrton Senna, who finished 3rd, prepares for the traditional celebration.

Piquet's consistency brings success over Mansell's winning formula

Below: The strain of staying ahead of the field shows on the face of Nelson Piquet. A mammoth effort had put him on pole at Silverstone, breaking the stranglehold of his Williams team-mate Nigel Mansell, who had taken that honour in 5 of the first 6 rounds.

Opposite top: Nelson Piquet had three victories to Mansell's six in 1987. But consistency and reliability were the key factors in the Brazilian gaining his third world title.

Left: Piquet used all his guile and experience to get the better of Mansell in 1987. He claimed the title at Suzuka, after Mansell was forced to withdraw through injury.

One-two for Williams

Above: Prost leads the Williams duo Piquet and Mansell into the first bend at Silverstone. The "Professor" failed to finish, while Williams scored one of their four one-two successes of the season.

Plenty to shout about for victorious Mansell

Above: Mansell's Silverstone victory in 1986 was stupendous; this one was even better. Piquet (left) congratulates Mansell on his Silverstone success. Senna finished 3rd, a lap adrift of the winner.

Left: Ronnie Petersen's widow Barbro is found dead at her £600,000 home in Cookham, Berkshire, by the man who shared her life, John Watson.

Opposite: A focused Ayrton Senna gears up for Silverstone. Concerned about his Lotus's fuel consumption, he drove a percentage race to finish 3rd.

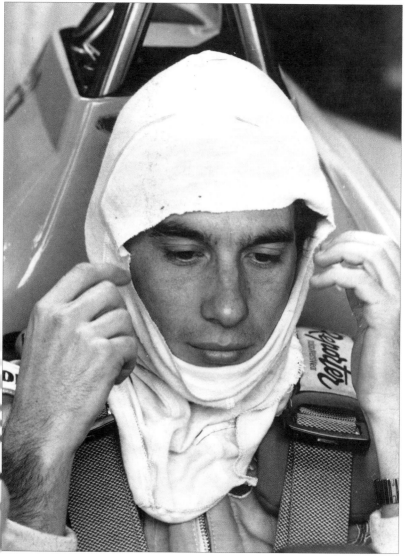

1988
Senna and McLaren dominate

The big news for 1988 was actually trailed the previous season. Senna was joining Prost at McLaren and both would be running under Honda power. It looked like a winning formula, and so it proved. While the championship turned into a two-horse race between the McLaren duo, the decline in Williams' fortunes was dramatic. After two highly successful years, the team turned to unproven Judd power to replace the superb Honda unit. Mansell and new team-mate Riccardo Patrese were now down among the also-rans.

The McLaren show got under way immediately in Brazil. Senna took pole. As they lined up for the start, he frantically gestured that he had a gear selection problem. He was forced to start from the pit lane, but by lap 20 he'd cut his way through the field to lie second behind Prost. It was to no avail, as he was disqualified for switching cars after the light had gone green. Technically, it wasn't a new race so Senna had contravened the rules by changing to a spare car.

Senna slip lets Prost in at Monaco

The Brazilian made no mistake at Imola. He won from Prost, with the rest of the field a lap off the pace. Senna sensed a problem with his car. Fortunately for him, it ground to a halt just over the finishing line. He got home 2.3 seconds ahead of Prost.

Senna left Monaco a very angry man. Having set a blistering 1m 23.998-second pole time, he led to lap 67. There he made an expensive mistake, hitting the Armco before the tunnel. He had been well clear of Prost at the time. The Frenchman needed no second invitation to cash in, with Ferrari's Berger and Alboreto following him home.

The resurgence of the Scuderia had a lot to do with the arrival of ace designer John Barnard, who had moved from McLaren the year before. The Ferraris continued to show their mettle in Mexico, Berger and Alboreto finishing 3rd and 4th. McLaren were dominant again, however. The pair occupied the front row and Prost led the whole way.

In Canada, Prost led from his team-mate until the 19th lap. Senna then made what proved to be the decisive manoeuvre. Approaching a left-right kink the Brazilian moved up and reached the right-hander on the racing line. He held the lead for the remaining 50 laps.

Detroit saw Senna take his 6th successive pole, equalling a record set by Moss and Lauda. The race was yet another McLaren procession, although there was a gap of some 40 seconds between Senna and second-placed Prost. Thierry Boutsen took 3rd, as he had done in Canada, but a lap down on this occasion.

Berger takes pole at Silverstone

Prost broke Senna's amazing run by taking pole at Paul Ricard. The Frenchman set the early pace, then lost the lead to Senna when he came into the pits with tyre trouble. Prost re-emerged some 3 seconds behind his team-mate, but chased him down and regained the lead at the three-quarter distamce

The next race, at Silverstone, was remarkable in that a slight chink in the McLaren armour revealed itself. Gerhard Berger took pole, with Alboreto's Ferrari beside him on the front row. Berger led for 13 laps. It was the halfway mark in the championship and it was the first time that anyone other than Prost or Senna had led at any stage at any race. Berger's novel experience of having a clear track ahead of him came to a halt when Senna passed him on lap 13. Senna held the lead to the end. Mansell finally had some success in the Williams-Judd by finishing second. Prost had retired with handling problems, declaring the rain-soaked track a threat to safety. Going into the second half of the season Prost led Senna by 54 points to 48.

Senna cuts Prost's lead

Prost was criticised in some quarters of the press for his withdrawal in France. Conditions were similar at Hockenheim and he went the distance this time, finishing second behind Senna, who had led all the way. Normal McLaren service had been resumed, while Prost's championship lead was cut to 3 points.

It was hot and sunny two weeks later at the Hungaroring. The result was just the same, although this was a much closer affair, the Brazilian edging out his team-mate by just half a second. The races were becoming a battle for third place, and on this occasion it was the Ford-powered Benetton of Boutsen that took the honour, ahead of Berger.

Senna had yet another start-to-finish win at Spa. It was his 4th victory in a row and 7th of the season. That equalled the record of Jim Clark (1963) and Prost himself (1984) and there were still five rounds to go. Just as importantly, this win in Belgium put the Brazilian ahead of Prost for the first time: 75-72.

Ferrari break McLaren's hold

The 12th race of the year finally broke McLaren's stranglehold. All looked well as Senna took a record-breaking 9th pole and led for 49 of the 51 laps. He then hit Jean-Louis Schlesser's Williams, and his race was over. Prost had already retired, and the way was left clear for a Ferrari one-two, Berger heading Alboreto home to the delight of the Italian fans.

Back came McLaren at Estoril, in a race that showed there was little love lost between the team-mates. Running level with each other as they vied to gain the upper hand on the first lap, Prost and Senna came perilously close to contact, the consequences of which could have been dire. Prost pressed on to take the advantage, and the race. He later criticised the recklessness of Senna, who trailed home 6th.

Prost won again in Spain. He and Senna were once again next to each other on the front row, and the Frenchman again got his nose in front and led all the way. Senna, who was getting a negative reading from his fuel gauge, eased his car home in 4th.

The best 11 finishes counted towards the title, a fact that favoured Senna. He had the chance to discard his 1 point from Estoril, while Prost only had a string of second places to drop. After Suzuka Prost had another six points, while Senna's win enabled him to swap 9 points for the 1 gained in Portugal. The title was now his. If any race showed what a worthy champion he was, this was it. He had been left at the start, and was 14th by the time his engine caught. Prost was then leading, with clear track in front of him. Senna's charge through the field was extraordinary and he took a decisive lead on lap 27.

Prost won the final, academic race in Australia, followed home by the new world champion. It was a fitting end to a season in which McLaren had carried all before them.

Above left: Speed merchant Niki Lauda established his own airline after walking away from Formula 1 in 1979.
Above right: McLaren made two key acquisitions in 1988: Honda engines for the MP4/4, and the mercurial Ayrton Senna.
Previous page: Ayrton Senna: champion in waiting.

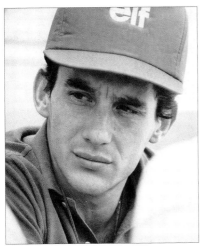

Senna's charge wins the title

Opposite and left: Off the track the enigmatic
Senna was intense and introspective.
Prost (below) and McLaren suffered at the
hands of Williams' domination in 1987. In
1988 the situation was reversed and the battle
for the driver's championship was only
between the McLaren pair. The decisive race
was at Suzuka. A win for Senna would give
him the title over Prost.
If any race showed what a worthy champion
Senna was, this was it. He had been left at the
start, and was 14th by the time his engine
caught. Prost was then leading, with clear
track in front of him. Senna's charge through
the field was extraordinary and he took a
decisive lead on lap 27.

1989
Third win for Prost

"Ayrton has a small problem. He thinks he can't kill himself because he believes in God, and I think that's very dangerous for the other drivers."

This was Prost's verdict on his team-mate in 1988. In 1989, the start of the new non-turbo era, simmering unrest turned to open hostility. Both stayed at McLaren, but it soon became clear that the two could not be accommodated within the same team. The question was: could they rub along reasonably amicably on the same side for one more season? The answer came in emphatic style at Suzuka as the championship reached its climax.

Senna was embroiled in controversy as early as the first race in Brazil. It was Gerhard Berger who was the aggrieved party on this occasion. He, Senna and Patrese approached the first corner abreast, and there certainly wasn't room for three cars. Senna would never cede ground in such situations, and his car and Berger's Ferrari touched. The Austrian later expressed his anger at the way Senna had cut across him.

Mansell - "Il Leone" - wins for Ferrari

The victor's laurels that day went to Mansell. After his hugely disappointing year with the Williams-Judd, Ferrari had made him an offer he couldn't refuse. Mansell was as desperate as ever to win the title, and Ferrari offered him the best chance for the current campaign. Victory first time out meant jubilation in the Ferrari camp and a new soubriquet for Mansell: "Il Leone", the Lion.

The race at Imola had to be restarted after Berger had a huge spill early on. He was lucky to escape with minor injuries. The latest Prost-Senna spat came when Senna jinked past Prost on the first corner and stayed in front all the way. Prost claimed a breach of their agreement that the leading McLaren at the first corner wouldn't be challenged by the other. Senna argued that his manoeuvre began before the corner was reached. McLaren boss Ron Dennis did his best to calm the situation. The fact that he had such a big headache after scoring a one-two success was not without a certain irony.

Senna also took pole and led all the way at Monaco. There was no argument here; the Brazilian was on scintillating form and finished nearly a minute ahead of Prost. In Mexico the Brazilian had his third start-to-finish win in a row. This round provided the latest landmark in his career: it gave him his 33rd pole, equalling Jim Clark's record.

The next race which was a first-time visit to Phoenix saw Senna break the record. He was out of luck in the race, though, retiring after leading for 10 laps. Prost took over and comfortably notched his first win of the year.

Boutsen wins in the Montreal rain

Stormy conditions followed by a drying track made tyre selection a headache in Montreal. Senna started in wets, came in for slicks as things improved, only for the rain to start falling again. Repeated pit stops all round meant that the lead changed hands several times. Senna made up all the time he'd lost and was ahead with three laps to go, when his engine failed. With Prost also out of the race, victory went to Boutsen, an acknowledged wet-weather specialist. Patrese made it a one-two for Williams. After the problems of 1988, Williams had struck a deal with Renault, an alliance that would eventually take the team back to the top.

Senna suffered retirements in both France and Britain. In the latter race he wrestled with gearbox trouble and finally spun off while leading. Sections of the crowd applauded the failure; Senna's icy single-mindedness didn't always endear him to neutral racing fans. Prost won both races, with Mansell second each time.

Mansell carves out another victory

At Hockenheim Prost lost top gear with three laps to go and Senna powered past to win. Mansell had his fourth podium finish that day, but the best was to come in Hungary. Having started 12th on the grid, he carved his way through the field, overtook Senna on lap 58 and was nearly half a minute clear at the flag.

Less than two seconds covered Senna, Prost and Mansell as they crossed the line in that order at Spa. Before Monza, Prost gave vent to his feelings of unequal treatment within the McLaren team. Dennis tried to paper over the cracks, but Prost revealed that he'd had enough and was off to Ferrari the following year. In the race Senna led for 44 laps, when his engine blew up. Prost stepped in to increase his lead in the championship. He paraded the trophy in front of the adoring Italian fans, wonderful PR with his future team in mind.

Race ban for ignoring black flag

The next round in the Senna-Mansell saga occurred at Estoril. Mansell overshot the pits and reversed, breaching regulations. Not only did he rejoin the race, ignoring the black flag, but he collided with Senna on the 48th lap. Mansell was fined $50,000 and given a one-race ban, but that was little consolation to Senna, who believed that a driver who oughtn't to have been on the track may have cost him the title. Senna won comfortably in Spain, ahead of Berger and Prost. He now needed to win at Suzuka and Adelaide to retain his title.

The Brazilian took his 12th pole of the year in Japan, but Prost got the better start. Senna made his move at the chicane on lap 47. Prost closed him off, the cars touched and both spun off. Prost headed back to the pits, while a frantic Senna rejoined the race with the help of a push start. He performed heroically to cross the line first, but disqualification was inevitable for the assistance he'd received. Alessandro Nannini thus scored his debut victory in his Benetton.

Prost saw no reason to risk competing on a very wet Adelaide circuit. Senna's season fizzled out with a shunt involving Martin Brundle, whose Brabham he was trying to lap. Senna limped home on three wheels, while Prost joined the exclusive club of drivers who had won three world titles.

Top left and right: Riccardo Patrese spectacularly crashes out of the British Grand Prix at Silverstone. 1989 was Riccardo Patrese's 13th year in Formula 1, and despite the crash at Silverstone, his best. Joining Williams the year before had revitalised a career that was threatening to go into decline.

Above: Ayrton Senna on his way to yet another pole position in 1989. Senna took pole in 13 of the 16 races, converting 6 of them into victories.

Previous page: Prost joined the exclusive club; the drivers who had won three world championships.

Champion Prost moves to Ferrari

Above: Senna's relationship with Prost turned to outright hostility during 1989. The feud reached boiling point at Suzuka, where Senna for once came off second best. Although the collision affected both drivers, Senna needed the points to catch Prost in the title race. Prost eventually won the championship from Senna by 16 points.

Right: Prost test drives the Ferrari 641. 5. He hadn't been champion for very long before he was offering advice to his new team, Ferrari (opposite page), and his new team-mate Nigel Mansell. Going into 1990, Prost and Mansell made very positive noises about each other and about their intention to unseat Senna and McLaren.

1990
Senna wins following Suzuka crash

There was a little brinkmanship to occupy the close season after Prost had won his third world title. It revolved, almost inevitably, around the controversial figure of Senna. He was told to retract allegations he had made concerning FISA's handling of the Suzuka incident. Senna maintained his innocence, but grudgingly accepted that the sport's governing body hadn't acted unduly. McLaren paid Senna's fine and the former champion was welcomed back into the fold for 1990 with the granting of his superlicence.

He immediately showed his intentions in the first race, Phoenix. He lost the lead to Jean Alesi's Tyrell, but retook it in fine style to win by 10 seconds. Even though he'd won, Senna complained of a lack of motivation after all the off-track goings-on. That was an ominous sign for his rivals: what would he do when his motivation returned?

Senna's desire

The desire was back with a vengeance in front of his home crowd. He didn't win - he collided with Nakajima while lapping him - but the fire was back. His car needed a new nose-cone and he finished 3rd, behind Prost's Ferrari and Senna's new McLaren team-mate, Gerhard Berger.

Senna was on pole at Imola, but his race was over after three laps, when a stone flew up and damaged his brakes. Riccardo Patrese, in his third season with the Williams team and his 14th overall in Formula 1, scored the 3rd win of his long career.

Senna won the next two races, at Monaco and Montreal. He led the whole way in the former, but owed his victory in Canada to a 60-second penalty given to Berger. The Austrian had jumped the start, an expensive mistake, for it relegated him to 4th. Piquet, now with Benetton after a couple of indifferent years at Lotus, finished second, with Mansell's Ferrari 3rd.

Senna led for 60 of the 69 laps in Mexico, then suffered a puncture. Prost was the man to profit, and with Mansell in second, it meant a good day's work for Ferrari. However, the result masked some simmering discontent which was to surface in dramatic fashion before the season was out.

The lead changed hands no fewer than six times at Paul Ricard. One of the leaders was Senna, but a 16-second pit stop for tyres spoiled his chances. Ivan Capelli, driving for the Leyton House team, held the lead for 44 laps, only to be passed by Prost just three laps from home. The Italian had to be content with 2nd, equalling his best ever performance.

Ferrari back on form

Prost scored his fourth win for the rejuvenated Ferrari team at Silverstone. Boutsen was a distant second, with Senna, who had had a spin, back in 3rd. The result was overshadowed by Mansell's reaction to his retirement from the race with gearbox trouble. In a theatrical gesture he tossed his gloves into the home crowd and subsequently announced his retirement. His complaint was that the team was favouring Prost at his expense. The Briton was still desperate to win the title; playing second fiddle to Prost wasn't going to help his chances.

Senna got back to winning ways at Hockenheim, then became embroiled in yet another controversy at the Hungaroring. Boutsen led for the entire race. Behind him there was a four-way dogfight involving Senna, Mansell, Berger and Nannini. When Senna attempted to pass Nannini's Benetton at a corner on lap 64, their cars touched. Senna appeared to infringe the rule which stated that a driver had to draw alongside a rival to claim a corner. If Nannini was the wronged man in the manoeuvre, there was little natural justice, for his car was pitched into the air, while Senna blithely carried on and finished 2nd behind Boutsen.

Arch-rivals fight it out

Senna won from arch-rival Prost in the next two outings, at Spa and Monza. The press conference after the Italian race saw the two reach a kind of accommodation: agreeing on their passion for the sport, if not on their versions of various past incidents involving the two of them. With Senna now on 72 points to Prost's 56 and just four races to go, the sport's top two would be fighting for the spoils for the third year running.

Senna increased his lead to 18 points at Estoril, where he came 2nd and Prost 3rd. Mansell did his team-mate no favours by cutting across him at the start, a manoeuvre which relegated Prost several places down the field.

Prost all but conceded the title before the Spanish Grand Prix, then proceeded to win the race. Even better from his point of view was the fact that a damaged radiator meant that Senna failed to finish.

Senna still led by 9 points, but if Prost could score well in the last two races he had a 5th and 4th place to discard. Senna, by contrast, had fared no worse than 3rd in the 11 finishes he had racked up thus far. There were many scenarios by which Prost could snatch the title; Senna could dash them all with a win in the penultimate round, Suzuka. He took pole, but Prost got the better start. Senna immediately attempted to wrest the lead from the Frenchman, and both ended up in the run-off area.

The collision gave Senna the title. Even a victory for Prost at Adelaide, with Senna failing to score, now wouldn't be enough. In the event, Prost came 3rd in Australia, behind Piquet and Mansell. Senna had gone off the track while holding a comfortable lead, but had the consolation of already having the championship in the bag.

Tactical crash

Prost suspected foul play in the critical round, Suzuka. Ferrari waded in, railing about the possibility of teams deploying "tactical crashes" to gain an advantage. FISA responded by setting up an inquiry into the circumstances in which Senna had won his second world crown. Only the man at the centre of the row could know for sure what his intentions were in Japan, and Senna did later admit that it had been a deliberate act on his part.

Top left: Ayrton Senna has Prost in his sights. The Brazilian reclaimed his world crown after yet another controversial clash with the Frenchman at Suzuka.

Top right: Prost completes a hat-trick of wins at Silverstone. There were two more victories for the Professor in 1990, but his chance of another title disappeared when Senna nudged him out of the Japanese Grand Prix at Suzuka.

Above left: A frustrating year with Ferrari meant that Nigel Mansell (seen here with Barry Sheene) was still chasing his dream at the end of 1990.

Above right: While many regard teaming up with Senna as a poisoned chalice, Gerhard Berger prefers to see it as the ultimate way of gauging his own level of performance.

Previous page: The Ferrari dream team: Prost and Mansell.

Ferrari put Mansell in a spin

Left: Nigel Mansell's engine blows and he crashes out of the US Grand Prix. Disappointment at Phoenix was followed by a string of other failures, prompting Mansell to announce his retirement.

Below: Senna beats Mansell to the first corner at Silverstone. Mansell was leading when his Ferrari ground to a halt 8 laps from home. His disappointment was compounded by the fact that Prost once again had a trouble-free ride and sailed past him to win the race.

Opposite left: Mansell acknowledges the fans as he makes the long walk back to the Silverstone pits.

Opposite right: Avid golfer Nigel Mansell gives a lift to his good friend the Great White Shark, Greg Norman. Champion golfer Norman sits in on a Ferrari working lunch at Silverstone (Opposite bottom).

Patrese off the pace - Berger third

Left and opposite bottom right:
Riccardo Patrese at the wheel of the
Williams FW13B. The season
produced a win each for Patrese and
team-mate Thierry Boutsen, but
McLaren and Ferrari were the
dominant teams. Patrese's third
season at Williams yielded 23 points
and 7th place in the championship.

Below and opposite below left:
Gerhard Berger's first season at
McLaren brought no victories, but
he accumulated enough points to
secure 3rd place in the
championship, equalling his best
ever performance.

Opposite above: After Prost's
departure from McLaren, Gerhard
Berger (right) becomes the latest
driver to attempt an amicable team
relationship with Ayrton Senna.

1991
McLaren's fourth title in a row

After three years of titanic and acrimonious struggles between Senna and Prost for the coveted title, the "Professor" took a back seat in 1991. He failed to register a single win in the season, something that hadn't happened since 1980. Minor placings would put him on 34 points, respectable by most standards, but for the three-times champion it was only good enough to earn him 5th place. Prost hadn't finished that low in the table since 1981. Few were surprised when it was announced even before the season was out that Ferrari and Prost were parting company.

Four straight wins for Senna

Prost's indifferent year didn't quite mean that Senna and McLaren had things all their own way. It looked like a foregone conclusion early on, however, as the Brazilian made a blistering start. With the new V-12 Honda unit powering the McLaren, Senna had four straight victories. Those four races constituted 282 laps of racing. Senna, starting on pole each time, led for 273 of them. Patrese ran him close at Interlagos, and Berger got to within a couple of seconds of the champion at Imola. The margins over Prost and Mansell, at Phoenix and Monaco respectively, were more comfortable. Senna's maximum haul for these efforts was 40 points, for a new points structure now meant 10 for a win. Also new for 1991 was that all 16 races were to count towards the championship.

Nelson Piquet ended Senna's run in Montreal. That honour should have gone to Mansell, who, having led all the way, suffered an agonising engine failure with victory in sight. Piquet nipped through to take the flag, while Mansell trailed in a disconsolate 6th.

Williams' success

Senna had retired with alternator trouble in Canada. In Mexico he suffered his first defeat in a race where he went the full distance. The two Williams cars came home first and second, with the Brazilian 3rd. It was an early omen for the opposition of the domination the Didcot team was to enjoy over the next few years. Patrick Head's superb FW14 wasn't quite the finished article; another year and a few more refinements and the Williams would be the car that everyone had to beat.

Mansell had finished behind his team-mate Patrese in Mexico. At the French Grand Prix, held for the first time at Magny-Cours, he went one better, the start of a fine mid-season run for the Briton. Mansell and Prost traded the lead several times in France, but Mansell was in front when it mattered.

A start-to-finish triumph at Silverstone was a far cry from the frustrating experience of the year before. Senna was the unfortunate man on this occasion, running out of fuel just before the finish. That dropped him down from second to fourth, his McLaren team-mate Berger and Prost's Ferrari slipping by him to finish 2nd and 3rd.

Three in a row for Mansell surge

Mansell made it three in a row at Hockenheim, with Patrese making it a second one-two of the year for Williams. Senna again ran out of fuel on the penultimate lap, which proved an expensive mistake. From the front row of the grid he finished just out of the points in 7th. The combination of Mansell's form and these mid-season blips for McLaren meant that Senna's lead was now cut to just 8 points.

The championship was becoming a McLaren-Williams battle, and the four protagonists came out on top in the next race, Hungary. It was here that Senna got back to winning ways. He had seen Williams occupying pole in the last five races, but the Brazilian was quickest in practice at the Hungaroring. He led all the way in the race, with Mansell crossing the line 5 seconds behind him. Patrese was 3rd, ahead of Berger.

The fastest lap in Hungary was set by Bertrand Gachot, driving the new Team 7-Up Jordan. It was the latest mini-triumph in a fine debut season for the team. Gachot and team-mate de Cesaris had both finished in the points in Canada and Germany, and one of the Jordans had finished in the top six in three other rounds.

In the next race, Spa, the new team might have had a dream first-season victory, but de Cesaris's engine overheated when he was running second. His fine effort was overshadowed by the man driving the other Jordan that day. It wasn't Gachot, for the Belgian had been jailed over an incident with a London taxi driver. De Cesaris's new and temporary team-mate was Mercedes sports car driver Michael Schumacher. Schumacher amazed everyone by qualifying 7th on an unfamiliar circuit. Although a clutch problem meant that he didn't even complete one lap of the race, the young German had done more than enough to make people sit up and take notice. In the race itself Senna and Berger enjoyed a McLaren one-two, and with Mansell failing to finish the gap at the top of the table was opening up again.

Enter Michael Schumacher

In the two weeks before the next race, Monza, Benetton swooped to sign Schumacher. He immediately outscored his new team-mate Nelson Piquet, finishing 5th, one place ahead of the three-times champion. Ahead of them, Mansell scored his fourth win to keep his hopes alive, but Senna took 2nd, so the Briton only pegged back 4 points.

Senna was 2nd again at Estoril, behind Patrese. It was a result that really must have hurt Mansell. He was disqualified after a pit lane fiasco in which a wheel was changed in an illegal area.

Senna clinches second title for McLaren

Mansell hit back with his 5th win of the season in Spain, while Senna managed just 2 points back in 5th. But there were now just two races to go and the Brazilian's lead was still 16 points.

Senna clinched the title at Suzuka. With Mansell out of the race he could even afford to sacrifice first place on the final lap, allowing Berger to come through for his 6th career win. Senna and Mansell finished first and second in the academic final round in Adelaide. It was McLaren's year, but that team's 4-year winning streak was about to come to an abrupt end.

Above left: Senna had eight poles and seven wins on the way to his third world crown.
Above right: Piquet finished 6th in the 1991 championship, his second year with Benetton. The arrival of Michael Schumacher made the former champion surplus to requirements at the end of the season and he retired from F1, after more than ten years at the top.
Previous page: The Williams crew leave nothing to chance or so they think. Mansell lost two wheel balance weights during the Silverstone race, and the FW14's gearbox gremlins reappeared. Mansell still managed an 18-second win over Gerhard Berger's McLaren, however.

Old stagers, young Turks...

Above: Wilson Fittipaldi, Derek Bell and Jackie Stewart
take a back seat behind their sons, Christian, Justin and
Paul. Damon Hill makes up the quartet of talented
young drivers.

Opposite top left: Nigel Mansell made inroads into
Senna's championship lead by winning at Silverstone.
Three more victories followed, but disastrous incidents
at Spa and Estoril ended Mansell's hopes of winning the
title.

Opposite top right: Four drivers crashed out of the
fiercely competitive British Grand Prix: De Cesaris,
Alesi, Suzuki and Patrese.

Opposite bottom: Ayrton Senna in action at Silverstone.
He was set to finish 2nd behind Mansell when he ran
out of fuel in the dying stages. Berger and Prost passed
the championship leader, who limped home 4th.

Right: In 1991 Patrese equalled his best performance by
finishing 3rd in the championship

Mansell's taxi service

Above: Mansell breaks off during his victory lap to give Senna a lift back to the pits. The
Brazilian was bemused and disappointed after running out of fuel on the final lap.
Opposite top: Nigel Mansell puts the new Williams through its paces.
Opposite bottom right: Nigel Mansell embraces a member of the Williams team after his win at
Silverstone.
Opposite bottom left: Nigel Mansell and wife Rosanne relax before the French Grand Prix, where
the Briton enjoyed the first of his five wins in 1991.

Michael Schumacher - a young man travelling fast

This page: 22-year-old Michael Schumacher's impact on Formula One has been nothing short of sensational. Following his defection from Jordan to Camel Ford Benetton after just one Grand Prix, he absorbed all the pressure and controversy to take fifth place in Italy.

Opposite: Mansell's second place in the 1991 championship meant that he had finished runner-up three times. He was hoping that he wouldn't emulate Stirling Moss, four times a runner-up but never a winner of the coveted title.

1992
Mansell breaks all the records

After more than a decade in the sport and 21 career wins to his name, it finally all came right for Nigel Mansell in 1992. He had the advantage of being in the right place at the right time, for the new Williams proved unstoppable. However, that couldn't detract from the fact that Mansell finally answered those critics who believed he was a gritty, determined driver, but not champion material.

The car in which Mansell stormed to the title was basically the same as the preceding year's model, but with active suspension. Williams had flirted with such ideas several years earlier, after Lotus had introduced the innovation. They abandoned it then, but got it right in 1992, with devastating effect.

Mansell wins the first five Grands Prix

Senna had blown the opposition away in the early rounds of 1991; Mansell was even more dominant as 1992 got under way. He won the first five races, starting on pole each time. In four of them - South Africa, Mexico, Spain and San Marino - he was never headed. This run constituted a record in itself, and there was even more good news for Williams as Patrese followed Mansell home in four of the races, making it an awesome display of early-season domination for the team. The man who prevented a total clean sweep of the first five rounds was the sport's new sensation, Michael Schumacher. He finished second to Mansell in Spain, although Patrese had fallen by the wayside after an early spin.

Fifth success at Monaco for Senna

The reigning champion had just two 3rd places to show for his efforts at this point. Even the introduction of the new MP4/7 didn't make much difference. Senna did end Mansell's run at Monaco, but he had to put in a superhuman effort to achieve his victory. He also needed Mansell to have an off day, and that manifested itself in a pit stop delay with a tyre problem. Even having lost time, Mansell finished the race breathing down Senna's neck, just 0.2 seconds behind the Brazilian. Senna was shattered at the end of the race. As well as his first win of the season, he was able to celebrate equalling Graham Hill's record of five Monaco wins.

Both Williams cars missed out in Canada. Gearbox trouble did for Patrese, while Mansell sustained the only blemish in an otherwise faultless season. He blamed Senna for the incident in which he spun out of the race, but as ever when these great rivals were concerned, the post-race accounts provided more heat than light. Gerhard Berger won the race, a welcome boost for McLaren and the new car.

200,000 hero's welcome for Mansell

It was yet another Williams one-two in France, a race that was restarted due to rain. Patrese was the early leader. Mansell passed him just after the restart. The Briton insisted that the manoeuvre was genuine and not the result of team orders. That took Mansell to Silverstone and a fervent, 200,000-strong home crowd. He was determined not to let them down, and he didn't. Victory that day brought another record: his 28th win, taking him past Jackie Stewart's all-time British record of 27.

Mansell's joy should have been unbounded, but in fact there were rumblings of discontent behind the scenes as Frank Williams was sounding him out on the prospect of Alain Prost joining the team for 1993. Mansell was horrified at the thought. His mind went back to 1990, when he felt undermined by Prost's presence at Ferrari. He wanted to block the move, but it later transpired that it was already a done deal.

Mansell champion by August

On the track, meanwhile, the Williams bandwagon rolled on. Mansell beat Senna into second place at Hockenheim, and even though there were six rounds still to go, a win or second place in the next race would give him an unassailable lead in the championship. The place was Hungary, the date: 16 August. There were no team orders, and Patrese was out of the blocks quickest. The Italian spun off at the halfway mark, and although he rejoined the race, he was out of contention. That left Mansell tracking Senna, knowing that he only needed to hold his place to take the greater prize. A moment of crisis came when a puncture forced him into the pits. That put him back to 6th. Schumacher spun out, and Mansell passed Hakkinen, Brundle and Berger to reclaim second. This time he held the position to the end, although as results worked out 3rd place would have been enough. Mansell was champion at last.

Controversy to the bitter end

Mansell scored one more win, at Estoril, giving him a record-breaking 9 victories for the season. One of the highlights was Michael Schumacher's debut win in Belgium. In his first seeason he had finished in 12 races, scoring points in all but one of them and stepping onto the podium 8 times.

The big news of the latter part of the season came off the track. Mansell had reluctantly agreed to team up with Prost for 1993. Then, in a dramatic gesture, Senna let it be known that he would drive for Williams on almost any terms. With Prost on board and Senna in the wings, Williams made Mansell a demeaning offer, which the new champion promptly refused. He decided that if Williams didn't want him and he couldn't defend his title in a competitive car, then he would walk away from the sport. Williams relented at the 11th hour and put the original deal back on the table. The damage was already done, however, and Mansell turned his back on Formula 1.

Left: The media scramble for a comment and a picture after Nigel Mansell secures his 8th pole of the season at Silverstone.
Above: Mansell started on pole and led from start to finish at Silverstone. His 28th Grand Prix victory put him out on his own as Britain's most successful F1 driver. Jackie Stewart with whom he had shared that honour correctly predicted that Mansell wouldn't be a member of the "27 Club" for very long.
Previous page: Nigel Mansell and Frank Williams share a quiet word.

Mansell out in front

Opposite top: Mansell's win in front of an ecstatic home crowd gave him a healthy 36-point lead in the championship. But with seven races still to go and vivid memories of 1986, Mansell wasn't among those who believed the title was in the bag.

Opposite middle: Jean Alesi in action in the Ferrari F92A. He accumulated 18 points during the season, finishing 7th in the championship

Opposite bottom: Riccardo Patrese was understandably overshadowed by Nigel Mansell in 1992. 2nd place in the championship behind his Williams team-mate proved to be the high point of the Italian's long career.

Above: Ayrton Senna and the McLaren camp look somewhat concerned during preparations for the British Grand Prix. After four successive championships - 3 of them with Senna at the helm- McLaren was struggling to match the performance of the Williams.

Mansell's record nine wins

Opposite top: Nigel Mansell relaxes with his family. From left to right: Chloe, Nigel, Leo, Rosanne and Greg.

Opposite bottom: Mansell sets a scorching pace at Silverstone on the way to his 7th win of the season. After responding to a first corner challenge from Patrese, Mansell's date with destiny was never in doubt. He won by a distance as he threw in a record-breaking 141mph lap of 1min 22.539. Mansell finished the season with a massive 108 point haul and a record-breaking 9 wins.

Above: Mansell celebrates becoming the most successful British driver in the history of Formula One.

Right: Playing for high stakes. Nigel Mansell who left Williams at the end of the year can still afford a flutter at the tables, even after turning his back on Williams and F1.

Make or break time for other Brits

Top left: Breakthrough year or another false dawn? Martin Brundle knows that it is time for him to deliver in F1. After a stuttering career over the last seven years, he recognises that a seat with Benetton in 1992 is the opportunity he has been waiting for. Brundle pounds his way through the countryside near his King's Lynn home (top right), part of a gruelling pre-season training programme. Brundle finished sixth in the championship with 38 points.

Above left and right: Damon Hill's input as Williams test driver played an important part in Nigel Mansell's championship-winning season. Alongside his test-driving duties at Williams, Damon Hill had his first taste of Formula One in 1992, in an uncompetitive Brabham. A year on, circumstances landed him a seat in the best car on the circuit.

Schumacher sensation

The man who prevented a total clean sweep of
the first five rounds by Williams was the
sport's new sensation, Michael Schumacher,
seen here moving at a slower pace on his
bicycle and with his girlfriend. He finished
second to Mansell in Spain, although Patrese
had fallen by the wayside after an early spin.
Schumacher finished the season with a
staggering 53 points, only three less than
Patrese.

Fabulous season ends badly for Mansell as Prost secures drive

Opposite: Nigel Mansell's golden year on the track earns him the BBC Sports Personality of the Year award. He is pictured with heavyweight boxing champion Riddick Bowe, each holding the other's trophy.

Left and above: The Professor's back. After his acrimonious exit from Ferrari and a year on the sidelines, Prost is signed by Williams and is quick to test his new car in December 92. The deal was marred by controversy when Ayrton Senna discussed the possibility of joining Williams. Prost had to defend himself against the charge of being the man responsible for ousting Mansell from the Williams team. Following a derisory offer, Mansell decided that if Williams didn't want him and he couldn't defend his title in a competitive car, then he would walk away from the sport. Williams relented at the 11th hour and put the original deal back on the table. The damage was already done, however, and Mansell turned his back on Formula 1.

1993
51 career wins for victorious Prost

Following his year's sabbatical, Alain Prost returned to racing in 1993. As Mansell walked away from Williams to try his hand at IndyCars, the three-times champion stepped into his shoes as the Didcot team's number one. Few believed that political forces hadn't played at least some part in bringing him on board. Renault and Elf were French concerns, and suddenly that country's top driver was on the team. Patrese wasn't retained, either. He moved to Benetton to line up with rising star Schumacher. Prost's team-mate came from within the Williams camp, Damon Hill being promoted from the role of test driver.

Prost won the opener in South Africa, with only second-placed Senna on the same lap when he crossed the line. Senna was still with McLaren. For 1993 he faced an additional handicap in taking on the mighty Williams cars: Honda had withdrawn from the sport, and the latest MP4 model was powered by an unspectacular Ford V-8 unit. The Brazilian followed up his second place at Kyalami with a win in Brazil, showing that he could be competitive in almost any set of wheels. Prost and Hill had occupied the front row at Interlagos. Prost spun off, and Senna picked off new leader Hill and held the advantage to the end.

Senna flying in the rain

Senna was mightily impressive again in the European Grand Prix at Donington Park. The Williams pair were again quickest in practice, but were well beaten by the wily Senna in wet conditions. The man who had been so desperate to get inside a Williams that he had reportedly offered to drive for nothing now had two wins and a second place in the McLaren-Ford. Senna was apprehensive, though, for he had only agreed a race-by-race deal with £1m per appearance the reported fee.

Senna was running second at Imola, when his hydraulics went. Hill led in the early stages, but Prost took over when his team-mate spun off. The Frenchman held the lead for the last 50 laps to win from Schumacher, with Martin Brundle's Ligier 3rd. Spain was almost a repeat performance. Prost took pole, but Hill was again quickest away and led for the first 10 laps. Hill's race ended with engine failure this time, and Prost again took over to win from Schumacher.

Senna took maximum points at Monaco, although he was helped by the fact that race leader Schumacher was forced out with hydraulics problems. Senna led the title race at this point, making light of the fact that he was driving a car without Honda power for the first time in six seasons. The bubble was about to burst, however. Prost asserted himself with four straight wins, in Canada, France, Britain and Germany. The only driver who headed the Frenchman in any of these races was team-mate Hill. The number two man was away first in all of them, but Prost hit the front and stayed there each time. Like Mansell before him, Prost was finding that critics tended to put stunning victories down to the car, while defeats were down to the driver. Prost had seven wins from 10 starts to answer his detractors.

Hill's run of bad luck

Hill had been unlucky during Prost's run. He was delayed in the pits at Magny-Cours, which proved expensive as he finished just a quarter of a second behind Prost; his engine then blew up at Silverstone; and, most cruelly of all, he suffered a puncture while leading at Hockenheim with just two laps to go.

Hill's luck now changed dramatically as he reeled off three successive wins of his own. He was on the front row of the grid behind Prost in Hungary, Belgium and Italy. At the Hungaroring he led all the way, Prost having been relegated to the back of the grid after stalling on the parade lap. Schumacher pushed him hard all the way to the line at Spa, a race in which Hill showed his mettle. At Monza it was Hill's turn to have a stroke of luck for he inherited the lead from Prost after the Frenchman's engine gave out five laps from home.

Schumacher's nine top-three finishes

Schumacher beat the Williams pair into the minor placings at Estoril. This was his best race in a season which would see him on the podium 9 times. His remarkable level of consistency would have received greater acknowledgment had he not been up against the dominant Williams.

Prost's second place behind Schumacher in Portugal was enough to secure his fourth world title. The "Professor" then announced that he was retiring from the sport, a decision at least in part influenced by the fact that Senna was joining Williams for 1994.

It was Senna who won both of the remaining races, in Japan and Australia, beating his arch-rival Prost into second in each race. In 3rd place behind these two giants of the sport at Suzuka was Mika Hakkinen. The Finn's gamble to leave Lotus and become a McLaren test driver had paid off. He made an immediate impact, having replaced the struggling Michael Andretti as McLaren's number two. Suzuka also provided off-track drama as Senna and Jordan driver Eddie Irvine came to blows. Senna took umbrage at the fact that the lapped Ulsterman had blocked his way.

Prost bowed out with a record 51 wins from his 199 Grands Prix, and, of course, those 4 championships which put him second only to Fangio in the all-time list.

Senna keeps McLaren guessing

Below left: AyrtonSenna keeps his own counsel in the early weeks of 1993, refusing to confirm whether he will drive for McLaren in the coming season. With Williams and Prost waiting, and a 4th world title at stake for both, it wasn't long before the Brazilian signed on the dotted line.

Below right: The less glamorous side of Formula One. Ayrton Senna pictured at a chilly Silverstone for early-season testing of the new McLaren. Senna turned 33 at the start of the 1993 season. The three-time champion's desire to win was as strong as ever.

Left: After the rigours of a first full season in F1, Damon Hill is happy to take a back seat behind Georgie and son Joshua.

Previous page: Senna shows off his latest love, Adriana Galiston, at the Grand Prix Drivers' Gala, held at Monte Carlo Sporting Club.

Best of British

Left: Cafe society. Martin Brundle (left) and Mark Blundell win over many antagonistic French motor racing fans with some fine performances for Ligier.

Below: The cream of British driving talent pose before doing battle in the European Grand Prix at Donington Park. From left to right: Johnny Herbert, Damon Hill, Derek Warwick, Mark Blundell and Martin Brundle.

Opposite top: Prost was widely regarded as the most complete driver of his era. In the 12 years in which he competed between 1981 and 1993 Prost was champion four times, runner-up on three occasions and never finished worse than 5th in the championship.

Opposite middle: The tiny logo towards the rear of Senna's McLaren shows the big change for 1993: Honda had withdrawn and the team's cars were now running under Ford power.

Opposite below: Alain Prost on his way to a 6th championship victory at Silverstone. The Professor capitalised after team-mate Hill hit engine trouble.

Senna
wins at Monte Carlo

Right: Senna wins in Monte Carlo, beating Hill into second place for the third time. The presentation ceremony is hosted by Prince Albert of Monaco. McLaren win the constructors' cup.

Bottom: Damon Hill during practice at Silverstone. After qualifying second, he led for 41 laps, only to be robbed of a maiden victory when his engine blew.

Fourth title for Prost

Top left: "You have to be as hard as nails in this game. If you start cracking up after things like this, you're never going to get to the top." Damon Hill puts on a brave face after the disappointment of Silverstone, where team-mate Alain Prost scored his 6th win of the year.

Above: Damon Hill takes the applause at Monte Carlo after finishing second to Ayrton Senna. It was the third time that the Brazilian had stood between Hill and a maiden victory.

Left: Alain Prost was 38 when he came back for a glorious swansong year with Williams. Seven wins on the way to his 4th title made a career total of 51 victories from 199 starts.

1994
Mercurial Senna killed at Imola

Mansell had blown away the opposition in 1992; Prost had been dominant in 1993; now it was the great Senna's turn at the wheel of the Williams. That was the prevailing thought at the start of 1994. There were a few niggling problems with the latest Williams, the FW16, in the early part of the year. The car performed well in practice, but struggled in the opening two races.

Williams slow off the mark

Senna took pole in Brazil, with Schumacher beside him on the front row. Senna led in the early stages, but Schumacher's Benetton took over after the first pit stop. Senna, desperately trying to stay on the pace, spun out on lap 55. Schumacher went on to win, with Damon Hill in the other Williams second but a lap down.

The second round took the circus to Japan for the first of two visits during the season. This extra round, held on the narrow T I circuit, was included at the expense of the South African round and was dubbed the Pacific Grand Prix. Senna was again on pole, ahead of Schumacher, but a nudge from Hakkinen's McLaren ended his interest in the race on the first lap. Schumacher led all the way. Only Berger's Ferrari finished on the same lap, and he was over a minute behind.

Horror at Imola

Next was Imola, where Senna had won three times. The whole weekend of 29 April - 1 May is etched in the memory of motor racing fans as one of the blackest in the sport's history. Rubens Barrichello had a lucky escape after a major spill during Friday's practice session. Prompt action from Formula 1's renowned doctor Sid Watkins prevented the Jordan driver from swallowing his tongue. The following day Roland Ratzenberger wasn't so fortunate when his Simtek crashed into a wall.

Senna was on pole yet again and got away first, with Schumacher breathing down his neck. After five laps Senna's Williams went into a concrete wall at Tamburello Corner. It was a huge impact, but one that Senna might have survived had a part of the suspension not become dislodged and struck his head. He was pronounced dead later at Bologna Hospital. The cause of the accident has never been fully explained.

Schumacher won the shortened, restarted race, and made it four out of four with a victory at Monaco two weeks later. With pole position, fastest lap and a start-to-finish win and Senna so tragically lost to the sport Schumacher was suddenly looking unstoppable. Damon Hill did win in Spain, but he profited from the fact that Schumacher had gearbox problems. The German still finished second, less than half a minute behind Hill, a fine performance in the circumstances.

The combination of the rapidly maturing Schumacher, the new Benetton 194 and the V-8 Ford engine was again irresistible at Montreal. Hill was a distant second that day. The man who now found himself as Williams' number one was thus a further 4 points behind Schumacher. To have any chance he needed to score heavily, with Schumacher out of the points. That didn't look very likely after six races, but events would conspire to make the 1994 championship a dramatically close-run thing.

David Coulthard promoted at Williams

David Coulthard had been promoted from within to take the number two spot at Williams. He was in the points second time out, in Montreal, where he came 5th. For the next race, however, the team brought back its big gun Nigel Mansell. The former champion had had a successful stint in IndyCars, but there was to be no dream return to Formula 1. Magny-Cours was the venue for Mansell's return to the Grand Prix stage. Transmission problems ended his race after 45 laps, when he was running 3rd. Schumacher won, making it six wins and a second from the first seven rounds. Hill followed him home for the second successive race.

The season reached the halfway mark at Silverstone. For Hill this was a glorious home triumph, in a race that father Graham had never won. There was a bonus for Hill, too, as Schumacher, who crossed the line second, was dramatically disqualified. The German had broken ranks on the parade lap, and then ignored the black flag that was subsequently shown. Not only did he forfeit the six points, but he also received a 2-race suspension.

Neither of the top two scored at Hockenheim. Schumacher retired with engine trouble, while Hill finished out of the points. A first-lap accident had taken 10 cars out of the race, which was won by Berger. This gave Ferrari their first win for four years.

Schumacher won from Hill in Hungary, the fourth time the two had finished in that order. 3rd that day was Schumacher's Benetton team-mate Jos Verstappen. He had been lucky to be competing at all, having had a miraculous escape in Germany. The Dutch driver had been engulfed in a fireball during a refuelling stop at Hockenheim.

Schumacher crossed the line ahead of Hill again at Spa, but a new controversy saw him disqualified for the second time. Illegal skidblock wear was the infringement on this occasion. Hill thus inherited first place in Belgium, and turned up the heat by winning in Italy and Portugal, the two races for which Schumacher was suspended. It was very nearly a Williams one-two in both of these rounds. Coulthard was second at Estoril, and held the same position when he ran out of fuel close to home at Monza.

Schumacher by one point from Hill

Hill's 30-point haul, with Schumacher failing to register, put him just one point behind the German. They each took a first and second from the next two races, so Schumacher carried his slender advantage into the final race at Adelaide. Schumacher led until lap 35, when he hit a wall and rebounded into Hill's path. With both contenders out of the race, it left the way open for Mansell to notch his 31st win.

In the post-race deliberations some blamed Schumacher for a deliberate ploy to take out his rival; others thought Hill could have taken evasive action. It was certainly an unsatisfactory ending to the championship, but the record books showed that Schumacher had become the first German to hold the coveted title.

Above left: Damon Hill in action at Silverstone. Victory on home soil was something his illustrious father never achieved.
Above right: Hill is totally focused as he assumes the mantle of number one at Williams following Senna's death at Imola. His performances and Schumacher's suspension so nearly brought him the title.
Previous page: Williams' drivers Damon Hill and Ayrton Senna, planning the season.

Schumacher's title by one point

Below: Damon Hill on his way to securing pole at Silverstone. After Senna's death the new Williams number one was left to carry the fight to Benetton and Schumacher.

Left: Michael Schumacher carried his slender advantage over Hill into the final race at Adelaide. Schumacher led until lap 35, when he hit a wall and rebounded into Hill's path. It was certainly an unsatisfactory ending to the championship, but the record books showed that Schumacher had become the first German to hold the coveted title.

Consolation for Hill

Left: There's some consolation for Damon Hill's narrow defeat in the championship as he is voted the BBC Sports Personality of the Year.

Bottom left: Wondering whether denim is in, that's Damon Hill as he attends the London Fashion Show with Georgie.

Below: Gerhard Berger arrives at an awards ceremony accompanied by a glamorous girlfriend. The Austrian ace, now back at Ferrari, added a win at Hockenheim to his list of credits, but finished the year a distant 3rd behind Schumacher and Hill.

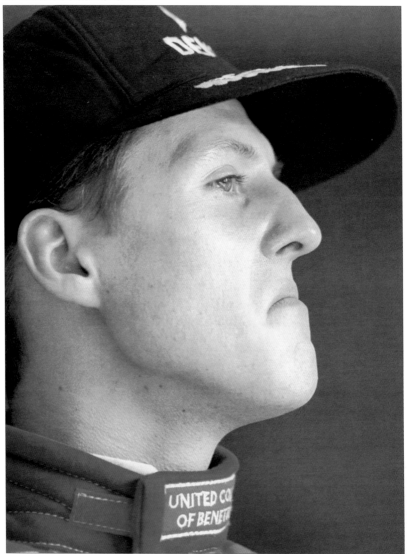

1995
Schumacher by a distance

Michael Schumacher's fourth full season at Benetton was to be his last, but before moving on to pastures new he was to have his most impressive year to date. Schumacher dominated the series in much the same way that Mansell had in 1992. Both men recorded nine victories, and both finished the year a country mile ahead of their nearest rival.

The German set the pace immediately with a win at Interlagos. Damon Hill, who was again to pose the biggest threat, could count himself unlucky. He took pole in Brazil and was leading on lap 30 when his suspension failed.

Hill then scored back-to-back wins in Argentina and San Marino, with Alesi bringing his Ferrari home second in both races. An unusually lacklustre Schumacher trailed home third in Buenos Aires, and crashed out in the early stages at Imola.

Mansell finally bows out

The San Marino Grand Prix was also notable for Nigel Mansell's first outing in the McLaren Mercedes. The well-documented debacle of the undersized cockpit, into which Mansell was unable to squeeze himself, had caused him to miss the first two rounds. The former champion now discovered that McLaren had revamped the cockpit but it was the same unimpressive car underneath. Mansell was scathing about the McLaren's poor handling and performance. He finished 10th at Imola, retired in the next race, in Spain, then told Ron Dennis that he had had enough.

Schumacher was back on form in the Spanish Grand Prix, and Johnny Herbert made it a one-two for Benetton. For 1995 the team had switched from Ford engines to the same Renault unit that powered the Williams cars. It was to prove critical. With evenly matched hardware Schumacher was simply too good.

Damon Hill was on pole at Monaco, but again lost out to Schumacher as Williams opted to run a two-stop race to Benetton's one. Schumacher and Hill occupied the front row again at Montreal, but it was to be a good day for some of the lesser lights. With Hill out of the race, Schumacher led for the first 57 laps and looked set for yet another win. But an unscheduled pit stop allowed Alesi, Barrichello, Irvine and Panis to come through. For Alesi it was a maiden victory, in his 8th year in F1. It wouldn't be enough to prevent him leaving Ferrari at the end of the year, however. After five years with the team, he finally fell out of favour with Maranello boss Jean Todt.

Magny-Cours was a repeat of Monaco in that Hill got the better of Schumacher in practice, with the roles reversed when it mattered. Benetton were too canny for Williams when it came to pit stop strategy, and with just half a minute separating the two at the finish, that played a crucial part.

Coulthard penalised

The big two departed the Silverstone scene after clashing at Priory Corner on the 46th lap. The race still centred on Benetton and Williams, though, as the respective number two drivers vied for victory. Johnny Herbert came out on top for Benetton, after Coulthard who had taken the lead 10 laps from home was penalised for speeding in the pit lane. The Scot may have represented the future, but he was still learning his trade and prone to the odd error. It all made Mansell rather embittered, since Williams had opted for Coulthard over him. Mansell was by now on the sidelines, looking covetously at the Williams FW17, which he felt should have run Schumacher and Benetton a good deal closer.

Hill took his third successive pole at Hockenheim, but crashed out again, this time on the first lap and with no help from anyone. Schumacher crossed the line 6 seconds ahead of Coulthard, extending his championship lead over Hill to 23 points.

Schumacher's stunning victory

Williams enjoyed their only one-two success of the season in Hungary. Hill and Coulthard were first and second on the grid, and finished the race in that order, Hill having led the whole way. A fuel pump problem ended Schumacher's chances of getting in the points.

Incredibly, Schumacher qualified only 16th at Spa, yet drove one of the races of his life to win from Hill. Coulthard was the unlucky man on the day, suffering gearbox trouble while leading on lap 13. There was an element of déjà-vu for the Scot at Monza, when he was again blighted while leading, also on the 13th lap. This time it was a wheel bearing that did for his chances. Hill and Schumacher had their latest spat, colliding on lap 23. Johnny Herbert came through to win his second race of the year, ahead of Hakkinen and Frentzen.

After two very unlucky races, it all came right for Coulthard at Estoril. The Scot dominated; he took pole position, set the fastest lap, and led for 66 of the 71 laps. Schumacher held off Hill for 2nd place.

10th pole for Williams

It was back to Germany and the Nürburgring for this year's European Grand Prix. Coulthard was again on pole, the 10th time that a Williams had taken that honour yet it was Schumacher who again produced the goods in the race. The German had to work hard for his victory on home soil. He passed Alesi who had dominated the race three laps from home, and crossed the line less than three seconds ahead of the Frenchman.

The fact that Damon Hill crashed out in Germany for the fourth time in seven races meant that he now trailed Schumacher by 29 points with just three races to go. The hopes of those who clung to Hill's mathematical chances were dashed by Schumacher's win at the

TI circuit. Yet again the Williams duo occupied the front row, yet again Schumacher came out on top. He eased past Coulthard on the 50th lap and finished the race some 15 seconds ahead of the Scot.

Schumacher out on his own

With the title in the bag, Schumacher scored his 9th win of the year at Suzuka. Damon Hill won by two laps in the final race of the year at Adelaide. A string of retirements took out all of the big names, and only eight cars were running when Hill crossed the line. Even with that belated success Hill finished the season 33 points behind Schumacher. The implication was clear: Schumacher could win albeit narrowly with a run-of-the-mill Ford engine. With the advantage of the Renault unit there was a veritable gulf between him and his nearest contenders.

Above left: Some of F1's top stars unwind with a jam session after the British Grand Prix. After Johnny Herbert's popular win, there's only one song to kick off Jordan's paddock party: Johnny B. Goode. Damon Hill takes the lead...but only on guitar and vocals. A collision with Schumacher ended his interest in the main event.

Above right: David Coulthard and girlfriend Andrea Murray arrive back at Heathrow, following the season's opening race at Interlagos. The Scot finished second to Schumacher in the race, but both had disqualification hanging over them for using illegal fuel. Following an appeal, the drivers kept their points, but the teams were penalised. Coulthard has Schumacher and team-mate Damon Hill firmly in his sights in his first full season in Formula One. The Scot's maiden victory came at Estoril, and he was unlucky not to win three other races.

Previous page: Michael Schumacher's public persona suggests he is cold and aloof. Those who know him tell of a much warmer personality.

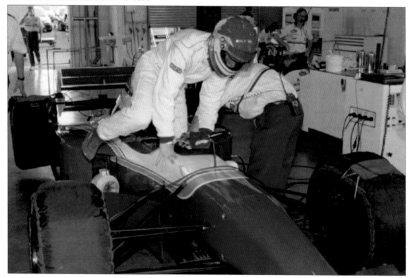

IndyCar star Villeneuve tests for Williams

Above: Jacques Villeneuve takes time out from dominating the IndyCar series to test for Williams at Silverstone, with a view to joining the Didcot team in 1996. 24-year-old Villeneuve adjusted to the F1 car brilliantly on the circuit where his father made his Grand Prix debut 18 years earlier.

Left: Champion forever. The hand-written legend penned by an adoring fan says it all. A year on from the fateful day at Imola, Tamburello is turned into a shrine to Ayrton Senna.

Schumacher's record-equalling nine victories brings another crown

For Michael Schumacher an air of satisfaction and superiority wouldn't have been out of place in 1995: the German ace scored a record-equalling nine victories as he comfortably retained his title. The implication was clear: Schumacher could win with a run-of-the-mill Ford engine. With the advantage of the Renault unit there was a veritable gulf between him and his nearest contenders.

Below: An isolated moment of despair for Schumacher, after his Ferrari failed him in Hungary in the previous year.

1996
Hill seizes his golden chance

Instead of being red-hot favourite to make it a hat-trick of titles with Benetton, Michael Schumacher was lured to Ferrari for 1996. If he wanted a fresh challenge, he certainly chose well, for the sleeping Maranello giant hadn't won the championship since 1979, when Scheckter and Villeneuve finished first and second.

Hill wins first three races

Having played second fiddle to Benetton for the past two years, Williams now emerged as the team to beat. Hill made the best possible start to a season which he must have regarded as his golden chance to emulate his father and capture the coveted crown. He won the first three races, at Melbourne, Interlagos and Buenos Aires. Even Schumacher couldn't work overnight miracles at Ferrari, and after those three rounds he had registered just one 3rd place, in Brazil, and two retirements. But while the reigning champion and Ferrari were finding their feet, Hill found that his main rival was his new Williams team-mate Jacques Villeneuve. The year before, Frank Williams had brought Villeneuve over from America, where he had enjoyed great success in IndyCars. Testing had gone extremely well and Villeneuve was duly signed up for 1996, replacing David Coulthard, who moved to McLaren.

Brundle's spectacular crash

Villeneuve took pole in his very first outing, in Australia. In the race which was being staged at Melbourne for the the first time Villeneuve had to settle for second behind Hill. The Canadian clipped a kerb on lap 33, damaging an oil-line in the process. He eased off to ensure a finish and took a creditable six points on his debut. For Hill it was a milestone: his 14th win equalled the career tally of his father. But Melbourne 1996 was perhaps most memorable for one of the most spectacular spills in the sport's history. In the first-lap shake-up Martin Brundle's Jordan barrel-rolled through the air, landing on Johnny Herbert's Sauber before coming to rest in the sand. Amazingly, Brundle dusted himself off, obtained the necessary clearance from the medical team and climbed into his spare car for the restart.

Villeneuve spun off in Brazil, and was second to Hill again in Argentina. The Canadian's maiden victory came in only his fourth race, the European Grand Prix, held at the new Nürburgring. From second on the grid, behind Hill, he led all the way, crossing the line less than a second ahead of Schumacher. With Coulthard and Hill half a minute back, followed by Barrichello, Brundle, Herbert, Hakkinen and Berger, Villeneuve had outgunned all the big names very early on in his F1 career.

Only four finish in Monaco

Having lost out by a whisker in Germany, Schumacher took pole at Imola. He hadn't taken long to squeeze the best out of the Ferrari 310. Damon Hill edged him into 2nd place in the race, however. Gerhard Berger who had moved in the opposite direction from Schumacher in the close season brought his Benetton home in 3rd.

A spate of accidents decimated the field at Monaco. Just four cars were still running at the end of the race, which was won by Olivier Panis. The Frenchman was in his third season in F1, each of them spent with Ligier.

Ferrari on the march

The seventh race of the year saw Michael Schumacher put Ferrari back on top of the podium. He gave a virtuoso performance in atrocious conditions. Hill retired, but Schumacher relegated Alesi and Villeneuve to the minor placings. The German had thus got the better of a Benetton and a Williams, the marques that had dominated the sport in recent years. Ferrari were on the march now that they had Schumacher on board, but their time was still some way off.

Schumacher's car didn't allow him to build on this success. The Ferrari failed him in each of the next three races, all of them won by Williams. Villeneuve followed Hill home at Montreal and Magny-Cours. Having lost out to Hill on home soil, Villeneuve returned the favour by coming out on top at Silverstone. Hill's race ended on the 27th lap, when a loose wheel nut caused him to spin off. With six races to go Hill's championship lead was now down to 15 points. The margin went back up to 21 after Hockenheim, where Hill won and Villeneuve finished 3rd. It was a fortunate win for Hill; he inherited the lead a couple of laps from home when Berger's car suffered a blown engine. His Benetton team-mate Jean Alesi split the Williams duo in 2nd place.

Williams pair battle it out

The championship was now a two-horse race. Villeneuve clawed four points back by crossing the line a whisker ahead of Hill at the Hungaroring. At least one issue was now settled: Williams claimed a record-equalling 8th Constructors' Championship.

The next two races Spa and Monza belonged to Schumacher. The latter victory, predictably, was greeted with wild scenes of joy as the Ferrari faithful celebrated their first home success since 1988. Villeneuve was second to Schumacher at Spa, while Hill could finish only 5th. Neither of the title contenders scored in Italy, so with two races to go Hill led Villeneuve by 13 points. Estoril was the scene of the penultimate round. Hill was still a hot favourite, but the pressure was on. And the heat was turned up even further when it was announced that Heinz-Harald Frentzen would be replacing Hill the following year.

Villeneuve's sublime move

The Williams pair slugged it out in fine style in Portugal. Hill had made a bad mistake at Monza. He did nothing wrong this time out, but Villeneuve gained a vital edge after the third of their pit stops and pressed home his advantage to win by 20 seconds. Few will forget his stunning passing move on the outside of the mighty Schumacher on the very last corner.

Hill clinches title at Suzuka

It was an anti-climax for Hill, but a 9-point advantage going into Suzuka meant that just one point from that final race would be enough. Villeneuve took pole, but Hill got away first. He led for the entire race, although the championship was assured even before he took the flag, Villeneuve having lost a wheel and crashed out on the 37th lap.

Above: Villeneuve sweeps round a tight corner at Silverstone. With every race the reigning IndyCar champion was becoming more used to the demands of Formula One.
Left: Villeneuve gives a raised arm salute after his Silverstone triumph.
Previous page: Galvanised into action by the suggestion that Schumacher is the fittest driver on the circuit, Damon Hill undertakes a gruelling fitness programme.

Hill kept waiting

Opposite above: After you, Damon. Villeneuve waves Hill through at Estoril, but this is only practice. The Canadian wasn't quite so charitable in the race. He swept past his team-mate to win, taking the championship to a nailbiting climax in Japan.

Opposite below: The expressions say it all. Victory at Estoril would have confirmed Hill as champion. The title was finally clinched in the following round at Suzuka where Hill got away first and led for the entire race.

Above: Jacques Villeneuve leads into the first corner at Silverstone.

Right: Tony Blair and his wife Cherie visit the Williams motor racing team pit at Silverstone.

1997
Villeneuve wins crown for Canada

The biggest news going into the 1997 season was on the commercial front. The longest and most succesful sponsorship deal in the history of F1 finally came to an end when Marlboro and McLaren parted company after 23 years. Philip Morris now put its name and considerable resources behind the resurgent Ferrari team. The new car, the 310B, was unveiled early in January, with the red team bus forming the backdrop. Large white lettering on the side of the bus proclaimed the newly-formed association: Scuderia Ferrari Marlboro.

Schumacher and Irvine were still there, charged with the task of supplanting Williams as the top team and bringing the title back to Italy for the first time in 18 years. Villeneuve, having lost out to Hill the year before, had ambitions to go one better. His new Williams team-mate, Heinz-Harald Frentzen, was under pressure to perform, having displaced the reigning champion.

A dramatic season got off to a dramatic start at Melbourne, where Irvine took out Villeneuve and Herbert as he tried to overtake at the first corner. Frentzen and Coulthard traded the lead several times during the course of the race. The German suffered a brake disc failure three laps from home, leaving Coulthard and McLaren to take the opening honours.

Villeneuve put the disappointment behind him by winning in Brazil and Argentina. At Interlagos he crossed the line less than five seconds ahead of the veteran Gerhard Berger's Benetton. Villeneuve's win in Buenos Aires was a tighter affair where he staved off a Ferrari challenge by less than a second.

Stewart team make the podium

After a disappointing opening three races, Frentzen claimed his first win for Williams at Imola. He emerged from the final pit stop fractionally ahead of Michael Schumacher, and they finished in that order. Irvine's 3rd place meant that he now had 10 points from 4 races, having scored just 11 all season in 1996.

A wet Monaco saw the race curtailed under the 2-hour rule. Schumacher dominated both the conditions and the field to win by nearly a minute from Barrichello. The Brazilian's fine showing meant a podium finish for the Stewart team at only the fourth time of asking.

After failing to finish at Imola and Monte Carlo, Villeneuve hit back to win in Spain. He led for 62 of the 64 laps and took the flag ahead of Prost's Olivier Panis, who drove superbly after qualifying only 12th on the grid. Schumacher then spoiled Villeneuve's party by winning in his rival's own back yard. The Montreal race was stopped after an accident involving Panis, who broke both his legs when his Prost went into the crash barriers. Schumacher was declared the winner, although Coulthard could count himself desperately unlucky. A pit stop delay relegated the Scot who had been leading to 7th place when the race was halted.

Berger's final victory

With his Ferrari sporting the new 046/2 engine, Schumacher came out on top again at Magny-Cours. The Maranello team regarded this an important staging post, for it was a victory which hadn't relied on the mistakes or misfortunes of others.

Back came Villeneuve with a win at Silverstone, although a lengthy pit stop thanks to a jammed wheel nut nearly proved expensive. Schumacher capitalised and built up a sizeable lead, only for a rear wheel bearing failure to end his chances.

Gerhard Berger had missed the last three races with a sinus problem. He returned on top form at Hockenheim, putting his Benetton on pole and winning the race from Schumacher and Hakkinen. It would be the 10th and final win of the Austrian's long career, as he would call it a day at the end of the season.

Schumacher looked like increasing his 10-point championship lead in Hungary. He took pole and led for the opening 10 laps, but had to pit as the team had opted for the wrong tyres. Damon Hill took up the running, and had victory in sight when clutch problems slowed him right down. Villeneuve passed him on the last lap, and Arrows were denied their maiden success.

The heavens opened just before the race at Spa. The safety car was deployed until the start of lap 4, from which point Schumacher dominated the race. With most of his rivals on wets, Schumacher opted for intermediates and stormed to victory ahead of Fisichella.

There was great pressure on Schumacher to follow his Belgian success with a win at Monza, as he had done the year before. The fervent Italian fans were to be disappointed, however. Their man qualified only 9th on the grid his worst position of the year although his time was just 0.6 seconds behind Alesi on pole. Schumacher crossed the line 6th, but Ferrari were consoled by the fact that Villeneuve finished only one place ahead of him. Coulthard scored his and McLaren's second win of the season, with Alesi and Frentzen occupying the minor placings.

10-second penalty setback for Schumacher

Austria proved disastrous for Schumacher. The German was lying 3rd behind Villeneuve and Frentzen, when Irvine and Alesi were involved in an accident that brought out the yellow flag. Schumacher didn't see it, overtook Frentzen and incurred a mandatory 10-second penalty. It put him back to 9th, and the best he could manage was to fight his way back up to 6th place and one point at the end of the race. Villeneuve won, cutting Schumacher's championship lead to just one point.

Next came the Luxembourg Grand Prix, staged at the Nürburgring. Michael Schumacher's interest in the race ended early on, after he was given a mighty thump by brother Ralf at the first corner. It looked like being a good day for McLaren, as Hakkinen and Coulthard were running first and second. Schumacher and the Ferrari camp must have been crestfallen as they saw both McLarens hit trouble, leaving the way clear for a Villeneuve victory.

Schumacher stripped of all points

Following victory at Suzuka, where Villeneuve was disqualified for a yellow flag infringement during practice, Schumacher led Villeneuve by one point going into the decider, the European Grand Prix at Jerez. The two occupied the front row, with Villeneuve on pole. By lap 48 the German held the advantage, with Villeneuve breathing down his neck. The crucial moment came when Villeneuve dived through on the inside. Schumacher, momentarily caught off guard, tried to shut him out but only succeeded in clipping the side pod of the Williams and putting himself in the gravel and out of the race. Villeneuve managed to nurse his car over the remaining 21 laps. Both McLarens passed him, but 3rd place was enough for Villeneuve to take the crown by 3 points.

The FIA held an inquiry into the race's controversial and decisive moment. The governing body's decision was to strip Schumacher of all the championship points he had gained over the season.

Above: Damon Hill in the wet during a morning practice session. The world champion's season in his Arrows car yielded just seven points.
Previous page: Jacques Villeneuve.

Opposite top: Jacques Villeneuve, having lost out to Hill the year before, had ambitions to go one better.

Opposite bottom: Champion Damon Hill takes the chequered flag for only the second time this season and collects his first championship points for sixth place.

Above: 1997 was an extraordinary year for Michael Schumacher and for the history of the sport. The crucial moment came in the final round of the championship when Villeneuve dived through on the inside. Schumacher, momentarily caught off guard, tried to shut him out but only succeeded in clipping the Williams and putting himself in the gravel and out of the race. Villeneuve managed to nurse his car over the remaining 21 laps. Both McLarens passed him, but 3rd place was enough for Villeneuve to take the crown by 3 points.

The FIA held an inquiry into the race's controversial and decisive moment. The governing body's decision was to strip Schumacher of all the championship points he had gained over the season.

1998
Hakkinen wins battle royal

1998 saw the introduction of new tyre regulations, the departure of Renault and a battle royal between Schumacher and Hakkinen for the title.

The narrower, grooved tyres were brought in to reduce speed and increase safety. Michael Schumacher thought that the governing body would have been better advised to do something about increasing overtaking possibilities. Even some of F1's greatest enthusiasts had remarked that too many races turned into a procession, with place changes all too often dictated by pit stops and retirements, rather than sheer racing prowess. Interestingly, in order to address that very issue, Schumacher regularly returned to his karting roots in the close season, much to the consternation of the Ferrari team bosses.

New engine deal for Williams

Reigning champion Jacques Villeneuve was also unconvinced by the new regulations, but for rather different reasons. He felt that speed and danger were key elements in the sport, and was wary of any action which might sanitise the spectacle. The Canadian's more immediate concern was trying to keep Williams on top now that Renault had departed the scene. A deal with BMW had been done, but that wouldn't come into effect until 2000; for the two interim seasons Williams would be supplied by Renault's engine development company, Mecachrome.

Just as surely as Williams were bound to struggle, so the McLaren-Mercedes looked to be the car to beat in 1998. That seemed even more likely after the opening race in Melbourne. The McLarens dominated, Coulthard leading from Hakkinen, with no one else in sight. The Scot stuck to the pre-race agreement and allowed his team-mate through to win. It was to set the tone for Coulthard's season; 1998 would see him confined to a supporting role as McLaren strove to take their first title since 1991.

Another one-two for McLaren followed in Brazil, Hakkinen again crossing the line first. It was already looking ominous for the other teams, but Schumacher who was 3rd that day could never be written off. He had proved time and again that he could compete well beyond the potential of the hardware he was given. He got the better of the MP4/13s in the very next race, Argentina. Irvine finished 3rd, making it a good day's work for Ferrari. Hakkinen's second place meant that he had 26 points from three races as the circus headed for Europe.

At Imola, with Hakkinen out of the race, Coulthard was able to concentrate fully on his own performance, and he held off Schumacher to take what would be his only win of the year. Hakkinen was back on song at Barcelona, where he notched his fourth win of the year.

Coulthard and Schumacher took the minor placings.

Monaco was even better for the Finn. Not only did he win there, too, but his closest rivals failed to score. Schumacher clashed with one of Benetton's new young drivers, Alexander Wurz, and was classified 10th.

Schumacher scored his second win of the year in a restarted race at Montreal. He did enjoy the advantage of having no McLaren to push him, however. Hakkinen's car failed him on the grid, while Coulthard suffered his second successive retirement after holding the lead. Fisichella took six points again. Benetton's Flavio Briatore must have felt that the contractual wrangle with Fisichella's former team, Jordan which had been settled in court had been well worth it.

Schumacher hat-trick

Schumacher made it a hat-trick of wins by taking maximum points at Magny-Cours and Silverstone. The French Grand Prix also had to be restarted. Schumacher and Irvine managed to get the Ferraris ahead, then stave off the challenges. The appearance of the safety car at a waterlogged Silverstone held up Hakkinen. That ate into his sizeable lead, and a spin allowed Schumacher to come through for victory.

Hakkinen and Coulthard hit back with successive one-two finishes in Austria and Germany. Schumacher was in the points in both races - finishing 3rd and 5th - but it obviously meant that he lost considerable ground to the hot favourite from McLaren.

3rd place at Hockenheim went to the reigning champion, whose name had been notable by its absence from the top three in the first 9 rounds. Villeneuve was giving it his best shot in the FW20, and often put the car further up the field than it had any right to be. But the unhappy truth for Williams was that success this year was limited to scrambling for points, with the odd podium being a bonus.

Schumacher was on top form in Hungary, where the team ran a three-stop race that worked to perfection. Hakkinen took just one point away from the Hungaroring, so with four races to go the Finn was looking over his shoulder and seeing the intimidating figure of Schumacher just behind him. Hakkinen 77 points, Schumacher 70.

That position was unaltered after a dramatic race in the wet at Spa, where neither driver finished. Damon Hill seized the opportunity and brought his Jordan through to give the team a famous first victory. It was Hill's 22nd win, and must have been particularly satisfying. No one could level the criticism that this success was down to the superiority of the car, something that he had lived with during his time at Williams.

After Monza, Schumacher and Hakkinen were tied on 80 points. A jubilant tifosi witnessed their man win after Coulthard, who had been leading, retired, and Hakkinen dropped back to 4th place with brake problems. Hakkinen's win over Schumacher in the Luxembourg Grand Prix again staged at the Nürburgring was probably his best performance of the year. It gave him a 4-point advantage going into the final round at Suzuka.

Hakkinen worthy winner

Unfortunately, the mathematical permutations had little chance to come into play in Japan. Schumacher stalled on the grid, and in accordance with regulations had to start from the back of the field. A brilliant drive took him up to 3rd, when some track debris punctured a tyre and with it his remaining championship hopes.

Hakkinen went on to score his 8th win of the year, giving him a round 100 points for the season. Schumacher had excelled himself to even be in the hunt in the final race, but the quiet, introspective Hakkinen was a worthy champion. Of the 16 races he had completed 13, scoring in every one of them. There were 9 poles and 6 fastest laps; and there were 11 podium finishes, including those 8 victories. For a long time Hakkinen had had to put up with being dubbed the natural successor to Keke Rosberg. After a gap of 16 years, F1 now had a new 'Flying Finn'.

Left: Hakkinen's victory in the final race of the season gave Finland its first champion since Keke Rosberg in 1982. *Above:*David Coulthard played a support role for team-mate Hakkinen and finished third in the championship. At Silverstone he spun off on the wet circuit on the 38th lap. *Previous page:* Schumacher was left with plenty to think about at the end of 1988. There were six more wins, but a mistake in Japan cost him dearly in his pursuit of a third championship.

1999

'Flying Finn' makes it two in a row

The 1999 season was all set up as another head-to-head between Hakkinen and Schumacher. It certainly turned out to be a battle royal between McLaren and Ferrari, but it was Eddie Irvine who carried the fight for the Maranello team, after Schumacher's season was drastically curtailed by injury.

The McLarens dominated practice for the season's opener in Australia, and when Hakkinen and Coulthard disappeared into the distance at the start of the race, it looked like turning into a procession. Both McLarens were out by the halfway mark, however. Coulthard had gearbox trouble, while Hakkinen had a throttle problem. Irvine inherited the lead from the McLarens and held it to the end. After six years and 82 starts the Ulsterman had his first Grand Prix victory.

Heinz-Harald Frentzen pushed Irvine hard all the way to the line, finishing just a second behind. It was Frentzen's first outing for Jordan. Eddie Jordan had swooped to sign the German following his disappointing year with Williams in 1998.

Barrichello off to a flyer

Rubens Barichello was away first at Interlagos, much to the delight of the home crowd. A first win for the Stewart team looked a possibility, but Schumacher senior took up the running after the Brazilian pitted. Hakkinen then passed his great rival and held the lead to the line.

Hakkinen held a comfortable lead in the early stages at Imola, when he crashed out of the race. Coulthard, who had been in the front row alongside his team-mate in all three races, took over in front. After successive retirements the Scot looked good to seal his first win in over a year. But after a pit stop he emerged in traffic and lost vital time. Schumacher was the man to benefit, finishing 5 seconds ahead of the McLaren.

Schumacher split the two McLarens at the front row of the grid for the Monaco Grand Prix, and went on to dominate the race. A mistake by Hakkinen allowed Irvine to come through for a glorious Ferrari one-two. The world champion had to settle for 3rd place, while Coulthard again failed to finish.

The McLarens hit back by taking first and second in Barcelona. This was the first race where the team's superiority in practice was translated to the race itself. Hakkinen and Coulthard were followed home by the two Ferraris; already the season was shaping up into a see-saw battle between the two giants.

Montreal saw Schumacher break Hakkinen's run of five successive poles, the Finn relegated to second on the grid. Schumacher's race ended after he made a mistake on lap 29 and crashed into a wall. That was just one in a spate of accidents which precipitated the appearance of the safety car no less than four times. Hakkinen scored his third win of the year and with it edged ahead of Schumacher by 4 points in the championship.

Schumacher breaks leg at Silverstone

Difficult qualifying conditions made for a strange-looking grid at Magny-Cours. Barrichello took pole, while Hakkinen and Irvine were back in 14th and 17th places. Hakkinen stormed through to lead with 7 laps to go, but a pit stop pushed him down to second, where he finished. Frentzen ran a one-stop race and scored his and Jordan's second Grand Prix victory. This was a remarkable result, for the German was nursing a fractured leg sustained at Montreal.

Silverstone was both the halfway point and the turning point of the season. Schumacher's first-lap crash at Stowe resulted in a broken leg and an enforced lay-off that lasted for six races. In a race which changed hands several times, David Coulthard came out on top, his first success since Imola the year before.

Irvine is Ferrari's new No.1

Irvine rose to the challenge of now being Ferrari's number one by winning in Austria, beating the McLarens of Coulthard and Hakkinen into the minor placings. Coulthard was the early leader, having nudged his team-mate into a spin on the opening lap. Irvine took over when the Scot pitted, and the Ulsterman built up enough of a lead to hold first place when he in turn made his stop. Irvine crossed the line less than 0.1 seconds before the Scot, the closest finish since Spain 1986.

Irvine was a narrow winner again at Hockenheim, this time over his stand-in Ferrari team-mate Mika Salo. Hakkinen was on pole for the 8th time but lost his lead thanks to a lengthy refuelling stop. A tyre then blew to put him out completely. It might have been a memorable win for Salo, but team orders prevailed and the Finn waved Irvine through.

Irvine now led the championship by 8 points, but McLaren responded with a one-two in Hungary. The result looked as if it would mirror the grid positions Hakkinen, Irvine, then Coulthard. A mistake by Irvine in the latter stages allowed Coulthard to swap places with him.

Under no pressure Hakkinen spun out while leading at Monza. The Finn was inconsolable after his error, and was lucky that Coulthard and Irvine could finish only 5th and 6th respectively. Frentzen's second win of the season put him on 50 points, just 10 behind joint-leaders Hakkinen and Irvine. The German could easily have hit the 60 mark himself as he led the European Grand Prix at the Nürburgring. An electrical problem put him out of the race at the halfway mark. Coulthard spun out a few laps later and Johnny Herbert came through to give the Stewart team its first success. Hakkinen crossed the line back in 5th, with Irvine finishing 7th. It meant that the Finn took a 2-point advantage into the penultimate round.

Schumacher, complete with a metal plate in his leg, returned for the Malaysian Grand Prix. He took pole, but his role was now to provide support for Irvine. He did so perfectly, lying second and acting as a buffer between Irvine ahead of him and Hakkinen behind. The jubilation of a Ferrari one-two nearly turned to despair when the cars initially failed the post-race inspection and were disqualified. But the barge boards the subject of the dispute were later found to be within the regulations and the original result was upheld.

Irvine held a 4-point lead going into the final race at Suzuka. Hakkinen was on peerless form, however. He won the race comfortably, with Schumacher in second place not able to make any impression and do his team-mate a favour. Irvine himself was a distant 3rd to finish 2 points behind Hakkinen in the final table. Hakkinen had become the 7th man in the history of the event to win back-to-back titles.

Above left: David Coulthard celebrates victory in the British Grand Prix. The Silverstone race was the turning point of the season. Schumacher's first-lap crash at Stowe resulted in a broken leg and an enforced lay-off that lasted for six races. In a race which changed hands several times, David Coulthard came out on top, his first success since Imola the year before.
Above right: Prince Harry sits in the Stewart Ford car while Jackie Stewart explains the finer points of Formula One.
Previous page: Mika Hakkinen with Sophie Dahl at a charity auction.

2000
Ferrari end 21-year wait

The big two once again engaged in a long, attritional battle for supremacy in 2000, with fortunes fluctuating as the season progressed. The statistics reveal the extent of McLaren and Ferrari's domination. Of the 442 points up for grabs in the 17-race series, the two teams scored 332 between them.

There was one change in personnel at the top table for the new campaign. Barrichello moved from Stewart-Ford to Ferrari, replacing Eddie Irvine.

First blood went to Ferrari. The McLarens had the edge in qualifying but the Ferraris as Schumacher had confidently predicted came out on top in the race.

The McLarens ran with one heavy load at Interlagos, while Ferrari opted for speed and an extra stop. Starting from the second row, both Schumacher and Barrichello passed their McLaren rivals. Barrichello's engine blew, but Schumacher built up a sizeable lead. However, the happiest man of all was Jensen Button. After crossing the line in 7th place in the Williams-BMW, he now had his first championship point.

Hakkinen and Coulthard finally got off the mark at Imola, but with Schumacher relegating the McLarens to the minor placings, the Ferrari juggernaut rolled on.

Coulthard had an excellent win at Silverstone, despite gearbox problems that looked so bad on telemetry that the engineers didn't tell him about them for 20 laps.

The balance altered markedly at Barcelona. A flawless performance by Hakkinen saw him take the flag 16 seconds ahead of Coulthard.

At the Nürburgring Schumacher showed why he was called the 'Rainmaster'. He won convincingly, only Hakkinen finishing on the same lap. Coulthard was the best of the rest, but well off the pace. Schumacher looked a cast-iron certainty for his 5th win of the year at Monaco until a cracked exhaust caused the rear suspension to overheat and fail. Coulthard profited from his exit, with Barrichello and Fisichella following him home. Celebrating in 4th place was Eddie Irvine, who gave Jaguar their first points.

Schumacher's 5th win was delayed just one race when Coulthard, the only serious challenger, received a 10-second stop-go penalty for an infringement at the start of the parade lap, and the race was effectively over.

Coulthard again showed himself to be Schumacher's greatest threat by winning at Magny-Cours. His victory came in spite of Schumacher's blatant attempts to block him, a tactic that prompted the Scot to gesticulate angrily at his Ferrari rival. Coulthard finally managed to get by, and Hakkinen came through to make it a McLaren one-two after Schumacher's car failed to finish.

Barrichello's tears of joy as long wait ends

Schumacher was pitched out of the Austrian Grand Prix at the first corner by BAR-Honda driver Ricardo Zonta. His exit turned the race into a stroll for McLaren, Hakkinen winning imperiously, with Coulthard second. Barrichello shed tears of joy after winning at Hockenheim. His maiden success came after seven years and 123 races; no other winner of a Grand Prix had waited so long.

After three races in which he had failed to finish, Schumacher was back in the points in Hungary. He started on pole, ahead of Coulthard and Hakkinen, but had to settle for splitting the McLaren duo and taking 6 points. Hakkinen scored his 3rd win of the season, and followed it up with a victory at Spa. Despite his blistering start to the year, Schumacher now found himself 6 points adrift of top spot, with Coulthard still in contention on 61.

After a worrying mid-season stall, Schumacher fired brilliantly in the last four rounds. Victory over Hakkinen at Monza put him to within 2 points of the Finn. The pendulum swung back towards Ferrari at Indianapolis where Schumacher cruised to victory. It was the German's 42nd win, putting him ahead of Senna, whose record he had equalled at Monza. Schumacher's 8-point lead became an unassailable 12 after the Japanese Grand Prix. The big two again slugged it out in front. Not for the first time Ferrari's technical director Ross Brawn astutely judged the pit stop strategy to give his man a critical advantage. Schumacher did the rest and delivered the prize the team had sought for 21 years. A 9th victory for Schumacher followed in the final race at Kuala Lumpur, a win which also sealed the constructors' title for Ferrari. This glorious double meant that the Scuderia could finally emerge from the shadow of 1979.

Right: The "voice of Formula One", Murray Walker, announces that he will retire from commentating at the end of the 2001 season. Walker, 77, has been commentating on the sport for the last 51 years.

Sir Stirling Moss

Above: The former motor racing driver Sir Stirling Moss with wife Susie (right), daughter Allison, 33, and son Elliot, 19, after he received his knighthood from the Prince of Wales at an investiture at Buckingham Palace in London in March.

2001
Schumacher
rewrites the record books

Several drivers enjoyed their moment in the sun in 2001. Hakkinen proved he wasn't a spent force, while Coulthard and Ralf Schumacher also tasted victory. In his maiden season Juan Pablo Montoya enjoyed one notable success in a campaign bedevilled by ill fortune. But these were bit-part players next to the star of the show, Michael Schumacher.

In the Melbourne curtain-raiser Schumacher took up where he left off at the end of the previous season, and never looked to be in trouble. Coulthard took up the McLaren challenge after Hakkinen suffered suspension trouble while running second. The Scot did well to split the Ferraris. The race was marred by the death of an official, who was struck by a wheel after Villeneuve's BAR-Honda clashed with Ralf Schumacher's Williams.

Monsoon conditions prevailed at Kuala Lumpur, causing the safety car to be deployed for seven laps early on. Ross Brawn made the inspired decision to send the Ferraris out on intermediates on a drying track, and Schumacher ripped through the field to win.

Coulthard took third place in Malaysia, and made it three podiums in a row by beating Schumacher into second place at Interlagos. The Scot picked up six more points at of the San Marino Grand Prix, and as Schumacher failed to finish for once, the two were level on points in the championship. Coulthard couldn't entirely shake off the Schumacher family though. Ralf was in blistering form in his BMW-Williams and claimed his first victory at Imola.

Hakkinen came within a whisker of making it four successive wins in Barcelona, but his car gave out on the last lap. Michael Schumacher, who had trailed the Finn by 40 seconds, was the beneficiary. Things evened themselves up in Austria, where Coulthard profited from a clash between Montoya and Schumacher to gain an unlikely victory.

Fifth Monaco for Schumacher

Schumacher recorded his fifth Monaco success, while his closest rival, Coulthard, stalled on the grid after taking pole. Barrichello finished second, and Eddie Irvine made it a red-letter day for Jaguar, giving the team their first podium finish at the 24th attempt.

Ralf Schumacher took the honours in Canada, his second career victory. He had started on the front row, brother Michael taking pole. Those positions were reversed at the end of the race, but with Coulthard failing to finish, it still represented a good day's work for the reigning champion.

Brotherly love was in short supply at the European Grand Prix, where Michael

Schumacher cut across Ralf at the start and nearly put him into a wall. Ralf was left fuming, and added to his woes by incurring a 10-second penalty for crossing the safety line on exiting the pits. Montoya took up the cudgels for Williams, but never seriously threatened Schumacher's lead.

Schumacher notched his 50th victory at Magny-Cours, putting him one short of Prost's all-time record. He started second on the grid behind Ralf, but took over at the first pit stop and was untroubled thereafter. Two-time champion Mika Hakkinen looked back to his best at Silverstone. He put the disappointment of Spain behind him to record his first win in almost a year. Hakkinen, on a two-stop strategy, chased Schumacher down after just five laps and disappeared into the distance. He established such a huge lead over the chasing pack that the team advised him to rein in the MacLaren. Schumacher took second place.

For 25 laps at Hockenheim Montoya again established his credentials as a champion in waiting. With the race at his mercy, Montoya's Williams succumbed to the scorching pace. Schumacher also limped out of the race, leaving brother Ralf to take the flag.

Ten years on

Schumacher was back to his unbeatable best in Hungary. He led all the way in broiling heat to match Prost's record. The victory also sealed his 4th Drivers' Championship. He now had four chances before the end of the year to hit the magic mark of 52 race victories. He needed only one. It came at Spa, the circuit where he had made his F1 debut 10 years earlier. Football-mad Schumacher had just watched his national team suffer a 5-1 thrashing at the hands of England. He promptly took his revenge in a race that was littered with accidents and mechanical failures.

It all finally came right for Montoya at Monza. In terms of natural talent and ferocious competitiveness, the 25-year-old had been hailed as the pretender to Schumacher's crown, though few thought his first victory would come so soon.

Indianapolis was all about farewells. Hakkinen announced his decision to take a sabbatical from F1 at the end of the season. He bowed out with a victory, although he was helped by the fact that Montoya's temperamental Williams failed again when the Colombian was looking favourite to notch back-to-back victories. F1 also bade farewell to Murray Walker. The voice of motor sport gave his last television commentary after more than half a century in the business.

The season ended as it began, with a Michael Schumacher victory. Suzuka provided Schumacher with his 9th win of the season, equalling Nigel Mansell's record. It also gave him 801 points, overhauling the previous mark set by Prost. Schumacher finished on 123 points, 58 more than his closest rival, David Coulthard. Even as the end-of-season party got under way, the finishing touches were being applied to Ferrari's 2002 car, already heralded as an awesome machine. With the world's best driver hungry for even more success, the question was clear: who could stop Ferrari?

Top: Michael Schumacher, focused and ready to go. Schumacher finished the season with 123 points, 58 more than his nearest rival, Coulthard.
Bottom: David Coulthard (right) and Jenson Button enjoy a relaxed moment at the British Grand Prix at Silverstone.

2002
Ferrari domination continues

The best driver found himself in an even better car in 2002. While purists pointed to the history books and the cyclical nature of success, others began to worry that the sport was turning into a predictable procession.

The season got off to a dramatic start at Melbourne. Rubens Barrichello was the catalyst in an eight car pile-up at the first corner. Some team bosses were angry that with the field so depleted a restart wasn't ordered. As it was, only eight finished the race. Eddie Irvine and debutant Mark Webber weren't complaining; they avoided the carnage to finish 4th and 5th respectively. David Coulthard was the early leader, but after his McLaren gave out, Michael Schumacher streaked home ahead of Juan Pablo Montoya.

In Malaysia, Schumacher and Montoya clashed as they dived for the first corner. The Colombian was unhappy to be adjudged the guilty party, for which he was given a drive-through penalty. Amazingly, both he and Schumacher clawed their way through the field to claim second and third place respectively, behind the Colombian's Williams' team-mate, Ralf Schumacher.

Montoya was equally unhappy at Interlagos. He took pole, but Schumacher got by at the first corner and promptly shut the door, a manoeuvre Montoya thought deserved to be penalized. Michael finished half a second ahead of Ralf, with David Coulthard on the podium after actually finishing a race at last.

Schumacher won at a canter at Imola, and Barcelona proved to be yet another day at the office for the champion, who led from start to finish. The master had time to soak up the applause from the crowd at the Circuit de Catalunya. It was a different story at Zeltweg. The result was the same, but the cynical way in which race leader Rubens Barrichello allowed his team-mate through to take the chequered flag won Ferrari - or the sport in general - few friends. The world's best driver surely didn't need such a helping hand.

Coulthard holds off Schumacher at Monaco

Coulthard took the honours at Monaco in front of his adopted home fans. He held off Schumacher superbly for most of the race, after the champion only qualified third. The fact that it was a terrific battle and one not dominated by Ferrari provided a much needed fillip for the sport.

As if incensed with only scoring six points, Schumacher roared back in Montreal, his fifth victory at the circuit. It was billed as a showdown between Schumacher and Montoya, who took pole, but the Colombian's engine blew up 13 laps from home. Barrichello was the unluckiest driver. He got the better of both Schumacher and Montoya at the start, but when Jacques

Villeneuve crashed out after 10 laps, the safety car came out, allowing the field to close up.

With Ferrari still facing a carpeting over the shenanigans in Austria, the team allowed Barrichello his moment of glory at the European Grand Prix. However, with the German 46 points ahead in the championship, it was hardly a victory for sportsmanship over pragmatism. Montoya made it a hat-trick of poles at the Nurburgring, but again he failed to add to his points tally. Coulthard was furious after the Colombian rammed him on lap 27 when the two were contesting 4th place.

Schumacher notched his 60th victory at Silverstone. The combination of the master driver, the Ferrari, wet conditions and Bridgestone tyres made the the aura of invincibility even more emphatic. Schumacher lapped everyone except second and third placed Barrichello and Montoya, and they trailed home 15 seconds behind.

Magny-Cours saw Schumacher equal Fangio's record of five championships. He had to wait three agonizing hours to have his victory - and championship - confirmed. He had slipped past race leader Kimi Raikkonen five laps from home after the latter hit an oil patch. McLaren were quick to alert stewards that the overtaking manoeuvre had occurred under a yellow flag, but the authorities allowed the result to stand.

Schumacher led from start to finish at Hockenheim, an attritional race in which only nine cars survived. It underlined the inescapable fact that the premier driver also had the fastest and most reliable car.

The Ferraris lapped the Hungaroring with metronomic precision, Schumacher allowing Barrichello his second moment in the spotlight atop the rostrum. The champion reasserted himself at Spa, and strolled to yet another record. He had shared a season's best haul with Nigel Mansell, nine victories apiece. By claiming his tenth win in Belgium, Schumacher was now out on his own.

The season continued to be a monotonous race for third place, and the unlikely occupier of that position at Monza was Eddie Irvine. After a miserable year, the Jaguar finally looked the part. It was Irvine's first podium finish for 16 months, and a long way from the days of being a title contender himself at Ferrari.

A stage-managed blanket Ferrari finish at Indianapolis went slightly awry as Barrichello inadvertently inched ahead to cross the line 0.011 seconds ahead of Schumacher, the closest finish in F1 history. 10 points guaranteed the Brazilian second place in the championship.

At Suzuka the Scuderia claimed their 15th one-two of the campaign, yet another record. Congratulations on a stunning year of success should have been the order of the day. But F1's movers and shakers were worried that the corollary of such dominance was a potential loss of appeal, and ultimately, revenue. The demise of the Prost team, with the fate of Arrows and Minardi hanging in the balance, polarized the issue still further. As the curtain rang down on the season, the FIA began to consider a range of rule changes aimed at reinvigorating F1 as a top-drawer sporting spectacle.

Top: Coulthard makes one of four pit stops during the British Grand Prix at Silverstone.
Bottom: Michael Schumacher with Ferrari's technical director, Ross Brawn, in the background.
Ferrari again dominated the season, as in 2001.